# MORE WILDLIFE
## On Your Land

### A Guide For Private Landowners

**Neil F. Payne** College of Natural Resources, University of Wisconsin-Stevens Point

Photography by Mark F. J. Payne, Bay Beach Wildlife Sanctuary, Green Bay, WI

**First Edition**

ISBN Number: 0-9711634-0-5
Library of Congress Number: 2001117759

Published by: **Barberie Publications**
P.O. Box 212
Plover, WI 54467
npayne@uwsp.edu

Designed and Proofread by:

**Graphic Liaisons LLC**
Amherst and Waupaca, WI
graphicliaisons@excite.com

# TABLE OF CONTENTS

## OTHER BOOKS BY NEIL F. PAYNE

**Environmental Impacts of Harvesting Wood for Energy**
(1987, Council of Great Lakes Governors) with James E. Johnson
and others

**Techniques for Wildlife Management of Wetlands**
(1992, McGraw-Hill), reprinted as
**Wildlife Habitat Management of Wetlands** (1998, Krieger)

**Techniques for Wildlife Management of Uplands**
(1994, McGraw-Hill) with Fred C. Bryant, reprinted as
**Wildlife Habitat Management of Forestlands, Rangelands,
and Farmlands** (1998, Krieger)

**Wildlife and Human Cultures in North America**
(2002, Krieger) with Richard D. Taber

*To Jan,*
*of "the mutual admiration society"*
*since 1961,*
*my dear friend and wife.*

White-tailed deer

# Preface

For many years I taught a course in wildlife habitat management at the University of Wisconsin-Stevens Point. No textbook strictly on wildlife habitat management was available. After finally getting sick and tired of sending my wildlife students over to the university library to read various articles published all over the place on habitat management, a few years ago I decided to write my own textbooks on the subject—one on wetlands and one on uplands. But they were technical books written for aspiring and professional wildlifers, especially those managing large tracts of public land.

This volume is written in everyday language for the layperson—mainly the landowner who owns a few or many acres in the United States and Canada. I reviewed more than 2,200 literature references, and selected for inclusion what I considered to be the best and most practical techniques. Techniques for managing large areas of public land, such as land owned by the U.S. Forest Service, U.S. Bureau of Land Management, U.S. Fish and Wildlife Service, state forestry and wildlife agencies, and Canadian crown (public) lands, are not included, although the principles and some of the techniques recommended for private land would apply to public land too.

In *A Sand County Almanac with Other Essays on Conservation from Round River,* Aldo Leopold mentioned that one of the penalties of acquiring an ecological education is that such a person tends to live alone in a world filled with ecological wounds, many of them quite invisible to the layman. As a professional wildlifer, I have suffered such penalties, from the grand, such as extinction and endangered species, to the local, such as my neighbors' spreading asphalt over a 2-lane driveway and replacing wildflowers with Kentucky bluegrass and then using a riding lawn mower. **The layperson in most cases just doesn't know, rather than just doesn't care.**

A healthy ecosystem is the basic life-support system of a healthy society, no matter where people live. Now our population growth and technology have seriously compromised that connection. Much of society just does not get it. That's the fault of our elementary and high schools mostly, universities for not training those teachers to teach environmental education, and state and provincial legislatures for not requiring it.

There are 2 ways to manipulate wildlife populations: population management (for game species—season length, harvest quota, and harvest methods) and habitat management. But without habitat, nothing else matters.

This is a how-to book. I strove for a self-contained book, but sometimes the detail (or danger, as with prescribed burns) needs the advice of a professional field wildlifer on site, and I so indicated. If a technique does not apply directly to a local situation, perhaps it can be modified to do so, or stimulate an idea for local application.

I thank those professional wildlifers who reviewed sections of material used in this book. I thank my son, Mark, for his photographic contribution, and my daughter, Erin, for her professional skill in promotion. For other suggestions I also thank Mark and Erin, my son Adam, and my stepdaughters, Patty Lyman, Gail Lyman, and Shari Murphy. I thank Cheryl Felckowski of the College of Natural Resources, University of Wisconsin-Stevens Point, for her kindness, dedication, and time and skill at the computer with my revisions. Especially I thank my dear wife, Jan, for her love, tolerance, support, and help during this project.

Moose

# CHAPTER 1

# YOUR LAND'S ECOLOGY

## (What Have You Got And How Does It Fit?)

You love to watch wildlife. You get up in the morning, maybe fix yourself some coffee, and look out the window. You see a couple of does in your field, right next to your woods. You hear the mournful cooing of a mourning dove, and the rat-tat-tat of a woodpecker hammering on a dead tree. You feel relaxed. Each morning is different and interesting.

You wonder if there isn't something you could do to make your place better for wildlife. Could you attract more variety, and larger numbers of them? It makes sense that you could, if you knew what was needed by the various species of wildlife you would like to attract. Well, that can be very complicated, but it does not have to be if you consider the basic requirements of the wildlife species you prefer. They need food, water, cover, and space. Take deer for example. They need brushy woods and openings such as a field. Woodpeckers need some dead trees, a few large enough to house their chicks in a den. Diversity in habitat produces diversity in wildlife.

So, what kind of habitat have you got on your land, and how does it fit together with your neighbors' land? Figure 1.1 shows an example of "The Big Picture" on a farmer's land, but "The Big Picture" should also include the adjacent land. If you can tie in your land management or wildlife land improvements with your neighbors' lands, your wildlife gains will be higher than otherwise.

Wildlife needs space. Your land might be large enough to include the home ranges of squirrels, rabbits, grouse, and songbirds, but it might not be large enough for deer, turkeys, and foxes. Thus, your wildlife plan should complement the neighboring landscape if good wildlife habitat exists there, so that you can attract wider-roaming species to use your land too. Draw yourself a map of your land and land use, and then get an air photo from the courthouse, showing your land use relative to the land use on your neighbors' lands (see Chapters 2 and 7). That is a good way to start.

So, what is a habitat type? Well, you might own an oak woodlot, a grassy field, an alder thicket, an aspen stand, a spruce grove, a cattail marsh, a pond, a rock pile. Each of these is a habitat type, and each supports specific types of wildlife. Even a ravine, cave, sand flat, gravel bar, abandoned building, and your own

# MORE WILDLIFE ON YOUR LAND

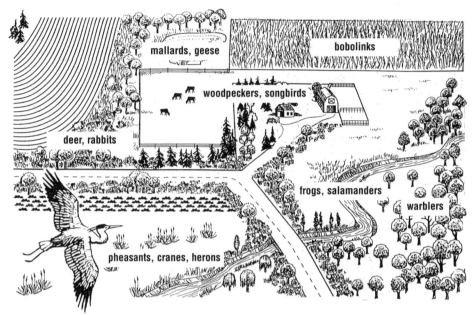

**Figure 1.1** *"The big picture" of farmland showing habitat diversity and travel lanes connecting 2 different habitat types, such as woodland and wetland or farm field and wetland. (Judd et al. 1998)*

backyard are habitat types. But most wildlife species use more than one type of habitat. They like areas of adjoining habitats, or **ecotones**. That is known as **edge effect**.

Most wildlife species, although by no means all, like locations that include 2 or more habitat types. That results from **fragmentation**, that is, the landscape is fragmented naturally or it is fragmented unnaturally from human encroachment. For example, deer are known to have highest densities along the edge where a woodland joins a field. That way the deer can have the best of both worlds: food in the field and escape cover in the woods. In fact, most game species of wildlife are edge species. So are many non-game species, for example, robins. A **covert** is a location where at least 3 habitat types come together, such as field, woods, and pond; or oak woods, aspen woods, and field; or mature woods, sapling woods, and wetland. Coverts are extremely valuable wildlife habitat. Keep an eye out for them, so that existing coverts can be protected and new ones developed.

Edge is not all good. It's just that edge is what you will likely have on your property. Interior habitats of grassy fields or forests require more unfragmented habitat than you are likely to have to support those interior wildlife species that do not like edge. That results in a combination and variety of edge and interior habitat types and wildlife species producing much biodiversity. But you cannot really manage for interior wildlife unless you own at least 250 acres of unfragmented forest or 250 acres of unfragmented grassland.

Edges have higher densities of wildlife, but edges also have higher predation rates because they attract higher densities of predators too. Edges also have more nest parasitism from cowbirds, which do not build nests but lay their eggs in the nests of other birds, thus reducing the survival rate of the host chicks.

You also should understand a little something about **succession**. That is the orderly replacement of one plant community with another until the last stage of succession, the climax stage, is achieved. For example, where enough precipitation exists (over 20 inches/year), if a grassland is left alone, shrubs eventually will invade, and then trees eventually. Each of these stages of succession, or plant community, will have a specific associated wildlife community (Fig. 1.2). As the plant community changes through growth or species composition of the plants, the wildlife community will change too. Some species of wildlife will become more abundant, some less abundant, and others will disappear altogether. For example, forest succession generally has 6 successional stages (stand conditions) through which the forest community passes to become old growth after a disturbance from something like cutting or fire: grass/forb, shrub, open sapling/pole, closed sapling/pole sawtimber, large sawtimber, old growth. All of your vegetation can be classified into 2 major categories of 6 life forms that combine to form a certain stage in succession: herbaceous plants (grasses, grass-like plants such as sedge, and forbs such as violets and all other broad-leafed herbaceous plants often called wildflowers) and woody plants (shrubs, vines, and trees). If you live in an area with 10 to 20 inches of precipitation per year, you will have a grassland; you will not get a woods. Less than 10 inches per year and your climax stage will be a desert.

And then there is **structure**. Mostly, we are talking about woodlots, which have a third dimension—height—that most other habitat types, such as fields, do not. (Aquatic environments also have that third dimension.) Various species of wildlife associate with the various layers within the structure of a woodlot (Fig. 1.3). Too many cows and too many deer can destroy the lower layers and associated wildlife.

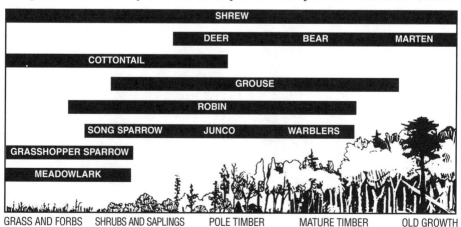

**Figure 1.2** *Forest succession and examples of associated wildlife. (Judd et al. 1998)*

For maximum **biodiversity** of wildlife, as many habitat types as possible should be represented on your land. Things such as fire, grazing, tree cutting, flooding, plowing, and other disturbances will set back succession to an earlier stage, with an associated change in wildlife composition, too. Sometimes that is good strategy, as we shall see.

Just as your pasture will support a limited number of grazing cattle, so too does your land have a limit as to the number of each wildlife species it can support. That is called **carrying capacity**. Habitat alteration will alter your carrying capacity, increasing some species of wildlife, decreasing others. But the social carrying capacity often is different from the biological carrying capacity, i.e., landowner tolerance is lower than the biological carrying capacity, resulting in "nuisance" wildlife, and management must be geared to it (see Chapter 10).

Some folks really get into birding. They not only use plantings, bird feeders, birdhouses, and birdbaths to attract birds to the yard, they also buy a good pair of binoculars (7 x 35), a good field guidebook, and tapes of bird songs, and they actively pursue bird-watching throughout the country as they add to their life list of birds in this interesting, challenging, and fastest growing outdoor hobby in North America. (Birds add splashes of color to the green plant community that mammals and most other animals cannot, and are more readily seen, except for nocturnal birds and those in challenging habitats.) Other folks get into wildlife photography or art. Some folks enjoy hunting, and some will lease their land to private individuals or hunting clubs to earn some income from their wildlife production. Other folks are fascinated by gaining knowledge about the interesting biology of various wildlife species. In any case, you love to watch wildlife, as do more and more people in society, and you can do something about it on your own land.

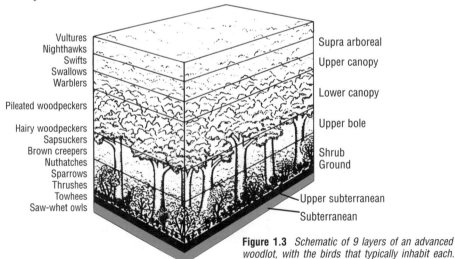

**Figure 1.3** *Schematic of 9 layers of an advanced woodlot, with the birds that typically inhabit each. Some layers might be lost as a result of fire or practices such as grazing. Rock or soil type might reduce the potential soil layers. (Giles 1978)*

# CHAPTER 2

# HOW TO IMPROVE YOUR WOODS

About 75 percent of people say enjoyment of wildlife is their main reason to own woodland! About 70 percent say scenic enjoyment is another reason, according to that same recent study in Wisconsin. About 35 percent listed the prevention of development as another reason. About 45 percent listed farm and domestic use, and about 30 percent listed timber production. So by far, wildlife and scenic beauty are the most important reasons people own woodlands.

Of all commercial forestlands in the United States, 58 percent are woodlots of less than 250 acres, and 90 percent of those are in the East. Two-thirds of those are in hardwoods. So the chances are that your woodlot is mainly deciduous, that is, it consists mostly of hardwoods, which tend to be more valuable for wildlife than conifers (softwoods) are. Still, some woodlots are mainly coniferous, especially if developed from a plantation. There are things you can do to improve any woodlot for wildlife, whether the woodlot is deciduous, coniferous, or a mixture of both.

Two of the main problems with woodlots are building a house in them and high-grading them, which means cutting out the biggest and best trees and leaving the less desirable ones. Such practices will reduce your wildlife numbers and variety as well as your future wood production. And oh yes, one more main problem: if you have cows, keep them out of the woods. They will screw things up for you royally by eliminating the entire shrub and ground layers and associated wildlife, trampling vegetation, compressing the porosity of the soil, and rubbing against trees. Sure, they add manure, but that does not offset the damage they do. You will get what is known as a **browse line**. From the road it looks like someone had stretched a string 6 feet high through your woods and removed all green vegetation below it with a hedge clippers—so straight and obvious it appears. It is an embarrassment of mismanaging the woods. (Too many deer can cause a browse line too.) All wildlife, including songbirds, and plants associated with the shrub and ground layers, will suffer too. Your woods and wildlife will take years to recover. There is not that much forage in the woods for your cattle in the first place. So fence them out!

5

Also, have you got a messy, disorganized woodlot? Perfect! Wildlife loves it. It cannot be beat for food and cover. What about timber production, you say? That's different. But we are talking wildlife first and timber second in this book. Your woodlot's size and location are important, for that will influence the type of wildlife you can support there. If your woodlot happens to be next to a large

| Table 2.1. Average home range of selected animals* | | | | | |
|---|---|---|---|---|---|
| Species | Acres | Species | Acres | Species | Acres |
| Deer mouse | .01 | Mink | 130 | Fisher | 3,970 |
| Muskrat | 1.5 | Beaver | 130 | Black bear | 4,350 |
| Cottontail | 6 | Red fox | 150 | Coyote | 4,500 |
| Gray squirrel | 5 | Striped skunk | 250 | Wild turkey | 5,000 |
| Snowshoe hare | 6 | Raccoon | 300 | Otter | 7,430 |
| Short-tail weasel | 13 | White-tailed deer | 320 | Lynx | 14,000 |
| Opossum | 28 | Marten | 530 | Bobcat | 20,000 |
| Ruffed grouse | 40 | Mule deer | 1,030 | Cougar | 123,000 |
| Bobwhite | 70 | Moose | 1,850 | Wolf pack | 378,000 |
| Porcupine | 86 | Elk | 2,330 | Grizzly bear | 930,000 |

*Home ranges tend to be oval in shape. Size varies with season and habitat quality—the better the habitat, the smaller the home range. Home ranges overlap. Most animals use only a small part of their home range most of the time. (adapted from Harris 1984)

forested area owned, say, by the government, you could attract into your woods the wide-ranging wildlife that you normally would not have (Table 2.1). You really have 2 options then: (1) manage your woods similar to the adjacent forestland by creating less edge effect if that is how the adjacent land is being managed, or (2) manage your woods similar to the adjacent forestland by creating more edge effect if that is how the adjacent land is being managed. Option 2 would be similar to managing your woodlot as though it were an isolated island of habitat surrounded by ag land, which it very likely is.

The largest species of wildlife you can expect to attract to your woodlot would be deer. Like so many wildlife species (but certainly not all), deer are creatures of the edge, and woodlots tend to be edge habitats because the edge effect extends throughout them, unlike large unfragmented forests.

What you want is variety in your woodlot. That means you want a lot of vertical structure. That means you need at least 3 **layers of vegetation**: canopy, shrub layer, and ground layer (see Fig. 1.3). If your canopy is closed because your woodlot is well stocked with big trees, you will have tree squirrels, canopy-dwelling songbirds, and perhaps turkeys that feed on the acorns if oaks are present. But no sunlight will penetrate the canopy to develop the ground and shrub layers. So you will have few deer, ruffed grouse, rabbits, songbirds, or other wildlife associated with the ground and shrub layers. Such animals obtain both food and cover there.

## Inventory and Planning

But first things first. First, take a critical look at your woods and see what you have. Keep in mind that you want wildlife, and that wood production for logs, pulp, or firewood is incidental and a means to an end in your woodlot. That is, you will cut your trees in a fashion to improve the lot of wildlife a lot in the lot. So take inventory. For comparison, here is what you need, mainly:

Trees of various sizes

Live den trees

Snags, especially big ones

Logs of various sizes

Mast trees

Wolf trees

Fruit shrubs

Openings, perhaps

Shrub layer in areas, especially fruit and nut shrubs like raspberry and hazelnut

Brush piles and rock piles

Water

If I were doing the inventory of the woods, I would map the thing, with notes on the map and in the margins (see Restoration in Chapter 7). The map will be crude, but that is OK. Just so it is informative. What surrounds the woodlot is almost as important as what is in it. If it is isolated by being surrounded by fields and pasture, maybe there is some way to connect it with a corridor of woody plantings to another woody area on your property, or even to another woody area on the property next to yours. I would note where the big trees are, what kind they are, where the openings (open areas) are in the woods, their approximate size and shape, how many snags (standing dead trees) and logs occur per acre (I would count 2 or 3 acres of them to get the number per acre, and multiply that by the whole acreage of the woodlot to get my estimate), where the patches of raspberries, other shrubs, and grape tangles are and how big the patches are, where any clumps of conifers are, where any rock outcrops, kettles, dens, and other unique habitat features are, and where any water or potential for water development is, such as springs or seeps. I would note the ground and shrub layers (sparse, medium, thick) and the percent canopy closure. Some of that can be eyeballed in the summer. If you can see a long way through the woods, the shrub layer is sparse and needs to be improved. Stand in the woods to do this, not outside the woods where the border of the woods is always well developed. On a sunny day, the amount of sunshine on the ground in the woods gives some notion of canopy closure. But just by walking through the woods and looking up, you will be able to estimate canopy closure by the amount of sky or clouds visible between trees. Make sure you draw a north-pointing arrow and an approximate distance scale on your field map. Estimate the acreage of the various stands of trees occurring in the woodlot, for example, conifers, oak, oak/hickory, aspen, mixed hardwoods. Sketch on your map the approximate location of these stands, and the approximate ages, for example, shrubby stage, sapling stage, mature stage. If your land is hilly, record how steep the slope is and its exposure (north-facing, south-facing, etc.).

You will also want a wildlife inventory. What have you got to begin with, and how much? Animals are hard to count. They move and hide on you, especially at night. So note the animal sign, as well as the animals themselves. Have some fun with it. See how good you are. Look for signs such as:

Trees cut by beaver

Deer trails

Buck scrapes (soil patch scraped bare in fall, with hoof print of buck)

Buck rubs (young trees with some bark rubbed off in fall by antlers of bucks)

Furry pellets containing mouse skeletons regurgitated by an owl

A large stick nest built high in a tree by a red-tailed hawk

A leaf nest built by a gray squirrel

A woodpecker hole in a dead tree

A worn cavity in a live tree, used by a nesting wood duck or a raccoon or a squirrel

Tunnels made through a field of grass by field mice (which feed foxes, hawks and owls, skunks, weasels, snakes, and other predators)

Hickory nuts or acorns nibbled by deer mice (which support similar predators)

Shrubs browsed by rabbits (angular cut) or deer (rough cut—no upper incisors on deer)

Piles of cuttings from cones of pine and spruce by red squirrels

Tracks of deer and other wildlife in mud and snow

Dens and burrows

Porcupine droppings at the base of a tree

Pellet groups of deer

Rabbit droppings in raspberry patches

Grouse and turkey droppings

Last year's bird nests

Scattered feathers or fur from a predator's meal

Muskrat houses and their feeding platforms

Beaver lodges and dams

Otter rubs where otter slide into the water

If you like to cross-country ski, snowshoe, or walk in the snow, that is an excellent way to get an idea of what is around. It is really fun and even exciting to see animal tracks in the snow, knowing they had been recently moving or standing right where you are. A day or two after a snowfall will even give you some notion of how many such tracksters you have using your land.

But first, jot down what you know to be present, from what you have both seen and heard. Then take a walk around as a reminder, with pencil and notebook in hand. Always record the time, date, and weather (temperature, approximate wind speed and direction, precipitation, fog), for they will influence animal activity. And listen up. Can you hear any spring peepers, sandhill cranes, squirrels, cardinals, deer snorts? Those "observations" are just as good as actually seeing the animals. Take your walks periodically during different times of day and season. Each time will be different and interesting, and an altogether pleasant way to exercise too. But remember, most animals are crepuscular, i.e., most active around sunrise and sunset. An early morning probably will be the most productive and enjoyable. The more you walk your land, the better you will get to know its plant and animal inhabitants.

And it is not that tough to learn the plants. Get yourself a good field guide for plants (for animal tracks and birds too) (see Chapter 12) and you'll be in business. Getting to know the wildflowers and other plants can become an enjoyable hobby. If you know someone who knows some of the plants (and birds), invite that person to walk your land with you. That is a nice way for some folks to spend some time and get some exercise. Be patient with yourself, and before you know it, you will be able to name most of the plants on your property. Most of your land will be covered by the same species of plants, so you will see them over and over. With such repetition and reinforcement, learning the plants is not as formidable as it seems at first glance. Also, such an inventory should include identification and location of rare and uncommon plants, which should be protected from disturbances.

Go over to the county courthouse and get yourself a soils map and an aerial photo of your property, and then a topographic map from a local sport shop or engineering office. Study them to get some idea about the potential for various species of wildlife relative to soils, topography, climate, and vegetation present and possible. Studying maps, especially of your own area, can be interesting and fun. (See Maps in Chapter 12.)

Your completed plan should include (1) your objectives; (2) your inventory of the plants in and around your woodlot, arrangement of plant communities, and inventory of wildlife; (3) the list of plants needed for planting to improve the wildlife habitat, and procedures for planting and maintenance; (4) the timber harvest methods you will use to improve your woodlot for wildlife; and (5) a program to protect the woodlot from livestock grazing, fire, disease, and insects. Your plan should focus on native plants, should increase wildlife productivity on a sustained basis, and should be biologically and economically feasible. Items (3) and (4) are tall orders initially, but we'll get into them.

To manage your woodlot, you should view it as part of the area surrounding it, for as I said, that area can influence what species of wildlife use your woodlot. Your wildlife plan should complement the neighboring landscape and enhance it when possible or practical. The woodlot's surroundings will be important as a source of wildlife, a barrier to wildlife movement, or a vital habitat component missing in the woodlot. Does your neighbor's land contain mature forests, young shrubby woodlands, old fields, or cropland nearby? Estimate their size and sketch their location on your map. Maybe the neighboring land has habitat components you cannot provide. Also, wide fields might be a barrier for wildlife movement to and from your woodlot. Maybe your neighbors would be interested in forming a cooperative habitat management plan, so that more acreage is involved, especially for trophy deer management. One large unfragmented woodlot is better than several small woodlots. If you have several woodlots on your property, they would serve wildlife best if they could somehow be connected with wooded corridors to each other and to any woods on your neighbor's land, especially with riparian zones along streams. The **riparian zone** is the strip of woody and herbaceous vegetation along the shoreline of bodies of water (see Chapter 6). In other words, if a stream connects 2 woodlots, by all means protect the strip of vegetation running along it between the 2 woodlots! If you have an isolated water hole on your property, connect it with a wooded corridor to the woodlot. This might involve planting.

Unusually dense and variable wildlife populations can be produced by joining 3 or more desirable habitat types, called a covert. The best coverts combine water, food, and cover. It is not hard to develop coverts in woodlots, because the woodlot usually is surrounded by another habitat type already, often a field of some sort, which can provide some food. Thus, you have 2 habitat types together already (field and woods). A proper cutting arrangement would join 2 age classes of the same forest type with the field, thus producing a covert. Two different adjacent forest types next to the field also would produce a covert. A wetland, pond, or stream next to some combination of field, forest types, or forest stand conditions (stands of different age or size) also would produce a covert. Examine your woodlot to identify existing and potential coverts. Coverts are most efficiently designed when woods and fields are shaped in hexagons, the smaller the better. But small units can produce too much edge, which can result in nuisance numbers of wildlife. Also, small units can be uneconomical for commercial purposes, e.g., less than about 40 acres for timber and about 5 acres for fuel wood.

Like harvesting for pulpwood or timber, harvesting for fuel wood also produces some conflict of interest with wildlife production. For example, firewood cutting, especially of dead trees, caused the redheaded woodpecker and hairy woodpecker to be placed on the Audubon Society's "early warning list" of bird species declining in numbers. The best advice is to cut the tree species least valuable to wildlife (see Appendix I), and those species that are the most abundant.

### What Do You Want?

If you are interested in observing songbirds, or observing or hunting game species in your woodlot, then you must have a shrub layer and a ground layer in your woods, along with a more open canopy, because most songbirds are more readily viewed in those vegetation layers, and most game species are associated with shrubby conditions, and with edge effect; a woodlot tends to have edge effect throughout. But edge effect can be improved. If you are interested in songbirds and other non-game wildlife, you still need fairly well developed shrub and ground layers, along with the canopy, for you are dealing with a woodlot, not an extensive forest. Thus, wildlife habitat management for most woodlots is somewhat standard, whether you are interested in game species or non-game species. What you want is variety with the woodlot.

Gaps in the canopy allow sunlight to penetrate, which causes the shrub and ground layers to develop. These two layers support, for example, ruffed grouse, deer, cottontail rabbits, chipmunks, songbirds, and various associated predators.

A canopy of large seed-producing trees, especially oaks, will support a variety of wildlife species that eat the nuts and buds or live in the cavities and branches. We are talking deer, turkey, ruffed grouse, raccoon, gray squirrel, fox squirrel, songbirds, owls, hawks, wood ducks, etc. Large dead trees, called snags, also support an array of wildlife species, from nuthatches and woodpeckers to raccoons.

But let's get down to brass tacks. How do you get what you want?

## How Do You Get It?

### Old Growth

You do not get it, if you do not already have it. And chances are you do not. These are the big old trees, virtually all of which (in the East) were cut down a long time ago. So what you will have in your woodlot is second growth, which is nowhere near the size of the old-growth virgin trees once there. But maybe you are one of the lucky few who has some old growth or second growth approaching old growth in size. Be careful about the term "overmature." That's your old growth! "Overmature" sounds like it should have been cut long ago. Most of it was. Valuable as they might be for fiber, old-growth trees are even more valuable for wildlife and the ecosystem in general, for they are absolutely irreplaceable and should be considered a nonrenewable resource (like oil) because it takes so long to develop. In western Oregon, for example, 118 terrestrial vertebrate species use old growth as primary habitat, and another 35 species use it as secondary habitat. If you have any old growth, i.e., what loggers and some foresters call overmature timber, do not cut it. Old growth has a character different from any other stage of forest development, and thus different wildlife species use it. Old growth has larger trees more widely spaced, with more dead snags and open canopy, and better-developed shrub and ground layers. How old is old growth? That depends on the tree species; some grow faster and some live longer. The year of age at which old growth begins can vary widely, for example: red pine (180), white pine (180), jack pine (70-90), balsam fir (60), white spruce (150), aspen (60-70), oak (150), birch (100-110). For groups of tree species associated with certain habitat conditions such as northern hardwoods, lowland hardwoods, and swamp conifers, for example, old growth generally begins at 150 years. Many western species of trees begin their old-growth stage at age 250 years. The cutting strategy is, you don't. Protection, protection, protection.

### Cutting Strategy

One of the best ways to attract wildlife to a woodlot is to leave it alone. Woodlots are relatively small; as such, the edge effect from climate extends throughout the woodlot, producing some shrub layer and ground layer near the edge, even if large trees cause a closed canopy. Since large mature trees of old growth are essentially irreplaceable, they should not be cut. Thus, no improvement in wildlife habitat is needed, unless lack of water is a limiting factor.

If your woods is too thick, you might want to thin it out to improve it for wildlife. That is called **wildlife stand improvement**. It will allow the remaining trees to grow bigger faster, and help develop the ground and shrub layers by reducing competition and allowing sunlight to penetrate the canopy. Start your stand improvement on the east and south sides with the lowest gradient, for they are the most protected and support the widest ecotones with the greatest area and variety of plants. Thin to a basal area of 60 to 70 square feet per acre (see Mast Trees for basal area). Girdle some or all of the cull trees so that they become snags (see Dead Wood). A good guideline for wildlife is to select the tree to be saved, and remove all other trees in a circle around it, the diameter of the circle in feet to be the equivalent of 2 times the dbh (diameter breast height) of the preserved tree in inches 4.5 feet above ground level. For example, a tree 15 inches dbh would need a 30-foot diameter circle of cleared trees around it.

After stand improvement has allowed remaining trees to grow large enough, often a woodlot can be improved for wildlife in conjunction with a timber sale in it. In fact, that usually is the best way to accomplish habitat improvement for wildlife. You will have to enter into a contractual agreement with the logger. Before you sign on the dotted line, flag at least 15 specific trees per acre to be left uncut. These so-called **leave trees** should include large old trees, wolf trees, snags, live den trees, best mast (acorn) trees, unusual trees, and clumps of conifers. Also flag vigorous clumps of most shrubs such as raspberry, Juneberry, and hazelnut so that they will be avoided and undamaged by any logging activity. You also should preserve 1 to 5 acres of the woodlot near sensitive areas such as spring seeps, riparian zones (along streams or ponds), steep ravines, or along edges of coniferous stands. Such patches should comprise 1 to 3 percent of your woodlot.

Bear in mind that lower branches of trees are leafier at the edge of the woodlot where sunlight can hit them. Leave some of these edge trees. You might want to remove some of them on the south and maybe the west sides to allow sunlight to penetrate further into the woodlot so that the ground and shrub layers there will develop better. But on the side of your woodlot that faces prevailing winds, usually the west and northwest sides, lower branches, especially on conifers, reduce wind-chill inside the woods as snow collects on them. You should leave such an edge uncut about 45 feet wide.

The timber sales contract that you negotiate with a timber contractor should include location and description of the property; description and arrangement of the trees to be cut (i.e., species, size, groupings to create openings, etc.); price of timber, financial arrangements and guaranteed title to products; termination date; special features such as location of logging roads, log-loading sites, bridges, and culverts; erosion prevention; seeding of logging roads and loading sites, if desirable; and provision to settle disputes. Two examples of timber sale contracts can be found in Appendix II and III. Local wildlife managers can assist you with the specifics of a timber sales contract for wildlife habitat improvement. Your goal should be to maintain or increase the mix of species and sizes of trees and shrubs so that the vertical diversity of the ground, shrub, and canopy layers is improved on your property, and to have most stand conditions present.

Generally, because most woodlots are small, we are talking about **uneven-aged (all aged) management** rather than **even-aged management**. In other words, **seed tree cuts**, **shelterwood cuts**, and **clearcuts** generally are not used, with some exception discussed later. **Selection cuts** are used. Use **single-tree selection cuts** in sections of the woods that have a good mix of species, sizes, and shapes of trees, so that the most desirable trees for wildlife can be preserved (Fig. 2.1). That is a technique whereby individual trees are marked ahead of time for cutting, usually with spray paint, and only those marked trees are cut. Use **group selection cuts** where the woods is of somewhat similar shape, size, and species mix throughout. With group selection cuts, usually every tree within the group is cut. Group selection cuts (1) create small openings, which causes the ground and shrub layers in the opening to develop for wildlife, and (2) prevent high-grading, i.e., the undesirable removal of only the most profitable trees, which means the biggest and straightest of preferred species. The width of such cuts should be about twice the average height of the trees, with at least an equal area left uncut between the group selection cuts. The more irregular the edges of such cuts are, the more edge will be created along the border of the cut and the more valuable the cut will be to most wildlife in the woods. To remove excessive slash, see Dead Wood in this chapter.

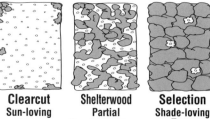

| Clearcut | Shelterwood | Selection |
|---|---|---|
| Sun-loving Trees | Partial Sun-loving Trees | Shade-loving Trees |
| Aspen | Oak | Ash |
| Birch | White cedar | Basswood |
| Tamarack | White spruce | Maple |
| Jack pine | Hickory | Balsam fir |
| Red pine | | |
| Black spruce | | |

**Figure 2.1** *Timber management practices of clearcut, shelterwood cut, and selection cut, with examples of tree species responding to each practice. (Judd et al. 1998)*

Cutting in winter disturbs the woods and wildlife the least because (1) in the North the ground is frozen and ruts and erosion from heavy equipment and trucks are reduced, (2) birds are not nesting then (except for some owls starting in February), and (3) stump sprouting of oaks is enhanced then. Cut so that stumps are over 18 inches high. This increases heart rot and eventual use by wildlife such as raccoon and fox which seek such cavities for dens.

Fig. 2.2 has an 80-year rotation with a 10-year cutting cycle, i.e., part of the woods is cut every 10 years so that eventually, in 80 years, the entire

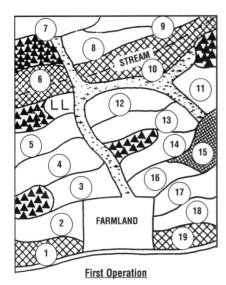

**First Operation**

▨ Selectively cut 1, 6, 10 and 19

▨ Clearcut 15

▲ Clearcut and plant conifers

⠿ "Daylight" log roads and seed roadbed to legumes

LL Clearcut log landing and seed to legumes after sale

**TEN YEARS LATER**
Selectively cut 1, 6, 10 and 19
Clearcut 4 and 9

**EACH TEN YEARS THEREAFTER**
Selectively cut 1, 6, 10 and 19
Clearcut two units not adjoining units cleared 10 or 20 years before.
Thin pine plantations.

**Figure 2.2** *Example of a timber cutting plan designed to produce wildlife on a typical 80-acre woodlot in northeastern hardwood country and similar places. (Shaw 1977)*

woods has been cut and you start over again. Well, your kids start over again. After the second or third harvest (in 20 or 30 years), (1) hardwoods will comprise 85 percent, conifers 15 percent, and even-aged stands 70 percent of the wooded area; (2) selectively cut stands will comprise 25 percent, and permanent openings from logging roads and landings will comprise 5 percent of the area; and (3) the age-class distribution will approach 50 percent in sawtimber over 10 inches dbh (diameter at breast height), 25 percent in pole timber 6 to 10 inches dbh, and 25 percent in the seedling/sapling stage up to 6 inches dbh. In the clearcut units, cut all woody stems over 2 inches dbh. You also should leave at least 10 percent sawtimber uncut in a contiguous patch to develop into old growth. If your woodlot contains mostly hardwoods, about 10 percent of the clearcut area should be in conifer patches for cover. If you divide the 80-acre woodlot into 4 compartments of 20 acres each, after the second cut each compartment would contain a new clearcut, at least 1 conifer plantation, a selectively cut stand, and some logging roads maintained in low plants (e.g., clover).

This example provides the ingredients of productive woodlot habitat: balanced age classes (sizes) of trees, good diversity, good cover and food, and good interspersion of it.

## Evergreen Cover

If you have clumps of conifers or even individual conifers in your hardwood woodlot, you have even better wildlife habitat than otherwise. Such conifer clumps provide especially good winter cover for winter resident songbirds, raptors, ruffed grouse, deer, and other wildlife. You want these conifers to develop vigorous crowns for a closed canopy that impedes snowfall, so that deer can move better beneath them. An individual conifer provides more cover than an individual hardwood tree (although hardwoods provide more food), especially if the conifer has developed into a wolf tree (see Wolf Trees). Best habitat consists of conifers in clumps of 1/4 to 1 acre to occupy about 2 to 5 percent of your woodlot. Do not allow logging roads, log landings, or other openings near your conifers, though, because raptors, i.e., birds of prey (hawks and owls), perch in the conifers for concealment, which is desirable, but they will prey easily on wildlife attracted to the openings, such as ruffed grouse. Still, grouse find good winter cover in a clump of conifers. Just do not put roads or other openings in or next to such clumps.

If the canopy of your woods is relatively closed, i.e., little sunlight penetrates to the ground, you can plant shade-tolerant conifers beneath. Trees such as spruce probably will work best; plant them in clumps of about 5 trees, each tree about 6 feet apart.

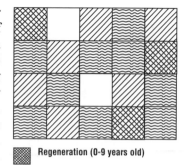

Regeneration (0-9 years old)

Base Cover (10-30 years old)
(where hares spend the day)

Travel Cover (30-60 years old)
(where hares move to food)

Herbaceous Openings

**Figure 2.3** *A timber-harvesting plan to produce wildlife on a 20-acre area of conifers that is managed on a 60-year rotation with 10-year cutting cycles. (Royar 1995)*

If you have pretty much a solid coniferous woodlot, you should use patchcuts (small clearcuts) to improve it for wildlife, especially snowshoe hare and its predators (if you live in the north or mountains) and deer (Fig. 2.3).

## Wolf Trees

Wolf trees tend to be undesirable for forestry because they tend to be crooked with many large spreading branches that suppress development of nearby trees. They are desirable for wildlife because they provide an unusually large amount of food and cover for denning, nesting, perching, etc. Preserve your wolf trees.

## Mast Trees

Mast can be hard (nuts, seeds) or soft (fruit), and is produced by some trees and shrubs. Mast trees and shrubs provide important food for a variety of your wildlife in late summer, fall, and winter. If you have a conifer plantation, you should preserve the hardwood mast trees and shrubs that tend to grow in it. In your mostly hardwood woodlot, 25 to 50 percent of the trees should be mast producers. In most cases we are talking oaks; their mast crop is acorns.

The most important mast trees are oak, hickory, walnut, butternut, beech, ash, cherry, and conifers. Other trees and shrubs, such as birch, hazelnut, alder, and aspen produce male catkins, buds, and in some cases nuts or other seeds eaten by wildlife. But oak is the single most important tree due to its broad distribution, variety, abundance, and use by so many wildlife species. About 80 species of oak occur in the United States and Canada. Oaks in the black (red) oak group produce acorns every 2 years because their acorns need 2 seasons to develop. Such oaks include northern red oak, southern red (Spanish or cherrybark) oak, pin oak, scarlet oak, black oak, jack oak, blackjack oak, nuttal oak, shumard oak, turkey oak, scrub oak, shingle oak, laurel oak, willow oak, sand oak, sandjack oak, water oak, and darlington oak. Oaks in the white oak group produce acorns every year, which wildlife prefers because the acorns have less tannin. Such oaks include white oak, overcup oak, post oak, bur (mossycup) oak, swamp oak, chestnut oak, basket (cow or swamp chestnut) oak, chinquapin oak, dwarf oak, and live oak. Production of acorns varies with species of oak. As a general rule, large trees produce more mast than small trees do. Tree crowns fully exposed to the sun produce more mast than shaded trees or shaded portions of trees do. To provide optimum habitat diversity for wildlife with vertical structure of vegetation in the woods and maximum sustained yield of acorns, your woods should contain a variety of ages and species of oak. But because oaks are such commercially valuable trees, the temptation must be resisted to cut all or even most of the big oaks. A compromise is needed.

How many oaks do you need? Well, individuals of various game and non-game wildlife species need an estimated 100 pounds of acorns per acre annually. The average oak of 14 inches dbh produces about 4 pounds of acorns annually. So, about 25 14-inch oaks per acre are needed for maximum wildlife support—if they produce every year, which they do not. So, more or larger trees are needed.

If you want a high population of gray squirrels and various other wildlife, you should have a basal area of at least 60 square feet per acre of sawtimber-sized oaks (see Cutting Strategy). The county forester could advise you on how to measure your woods for basal area, but essentially you measure the dbh of a tree 4.5 feet above ground level, using a diameter tape, then multiply the diameter in inches by itself ($d^2$), then multiply that by 0.005454 to get the square feet of basal area for that tree. So, you measure a few sawtimber oaks to get an average basal area per oak, count or estimate the number of such oaks per acre, and multiply the average basal area times the number of sawtimber oaks per acre to see how close it comes to 60 square feet per acre. If you can borrow a simple device called an angle gauge, you will expedite estimating the basal area in your woods. (See Oak/Hickory in Chapter 3.)

## Apple Trees

If you have any old apple trees on your property, save them! Wild or neglected apple trees are excellent wildlife trees for the fruit, browse, cavities, and nesting cover produced. (In some states, apples are used to bait deer for hunting or photography.) If the trees are not bearing well, you can rejuvenate them with proper pruning. Do your pruning in late winter or early spring.

If more than 1 main stem exists, save the most vigorous stem by cutting off the others close to the ground. Remove all other shrubs and trees, including overtopping trees, back to the drip line, i.e., the end of the outer branches. Be certain to prune the apple tree before cutting competing trees and shrubs, to avoid infecting the apple tree with potential diseases and insects from other trees. Remove all diseased and insect-infested branches, and burn them. Between cuttings, spray or soak your cutting tools (saw and pruning shears) with bleach to avoid infecting healthy branches and trees. Remove about 1/3 of the remaining growth on the tree, especially vertical branches that shade the others. Remove the branches in the center of the tree, those that hang across or below others, and those with a narrow crotch. Trim back all drooping branches. The best branches to retain are those at a 45- to 90-degree angle, as well as the short spur branches that produce fruit on the side of the larger branches.

If you do not have any apple trees, plant some. That is good strategy if you want to improve your property for wildlife. Plant them in the sun near the woods, which thus can be used for handy escape cover. The edge corner of a field or pasture is good, or an odd area such as a steep hill. Use planting stock 60 to 70 inches high, protected by expandable plastic strips of 1/4-inch mesh hardware cloth buried 6 inches deep. You also can buy commercial plastic tree shelters.

To expedite growth (and wildlife results), in the spring you should fertilize the new apple trees you plant, as well as your old ones, with calcium nitrate or a complete fertilizer such as 10-10-10 at a rate of 5 pounds for a large tree, 3 pounds for a small tree, and 1 pound for a sapling. Scatter it evenly from the drip line to within 1 yard of the trunk. You also can use a crowbar to poke 10 to 15 holes each a foot deep, all spaced evenly with the drip line, and then pour fertilizer into the holes. Fertilizer lasts about 3 years.

### Woodlot Borders and Other Brushy Areas

Brushy cover and food consists of (1) young trees in the brushy stage of development and (2) shrubs and vines. Newly developing trees in the brushy stage provide cover and much food for about 5 to 10 years after the original trees are harvested. Almost any species of tree in the brushy stage provides good cover, although conifers are best. As for shrubs and vines, you cannot beat the raspberries, cherries, hawthorns (thornapples), Juneberries, hazelnuts, blueberries, dogwoods, and grapes for food. They also provide cover, although mostly in summer. Raspberry and its relatives probably are the most used woody plant by wildlife in North America for their mast (berries), browse, and cover.

You can establish a brushy border along a woodlot edge, logging road, skid trail, log landing, and other opening if you cut all trees taller than 3 yards or larger than 3 inches dbh in a border 6 to 9 yards wide, especially on the west, south, and east sides which receive the most sunlight. But on the sides that face the prevailing winds, usually the west and northwest sides, you must strike a compromise. On the west side, if you have trees with abundant lower branches, especially the conifers, do not cut them for about 15 yards into the woods. Such lower branches on west and northwest sides improve thermal cover in winter by reducing wind-chill as snow gets hung up on the branches and retards wind speed.

Brushy areas will develop in areas exposed by group selection cuts. If individual tree selection cuts are used, you might want to identify areas where groups of trees will be removed to create small brushy openings. You should maintain some of these brushy openings every 5 or 6 years by cutting them with a brush-hog to invigorate them and to keep trees from developing there. If it is a border that needs mowing, mow about half of it each time you mow, leaving the other half as brushy habitat for fall and winter. Mow in late summer when most nesting is completed.

Size up the grapevines in your woods. The female grapevines produce grapes, the males do not. So, retain female grapevines in about 2 non-commercial trees per acre. Grapevine thickets on the ground hold snow and provide pockets of shelter. By cutting adjacent trees, you can improve the vigor of the grapevines for food and cover because more sunlight will strike them.

You can always plant a border of shrubs and trees along the edge of the woodlot, but that is expensive. If you do it, make the edge 9 to 15 yards wide and plant the stuff in 1 to 4 rows (Fig. 2.4). Plant conifers in row 1 next to the woods, and when they are 5.5 to 6 yards tall, cut off the leaders to retard additional height and create bushiness. Plant tall shrubs in rows 2 and 3. Plant short shrubs in row 4. Plant species that flower and fruit at different times of the year (Appendix IV ) (See Field Borders in Chapter 4).

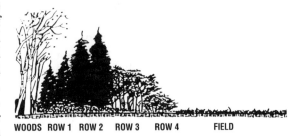

WOODS  ROW 1  ROW 2  ROW 3  ROW 4        FIELD

**Figure 2.4** *Cross section of a typical field and woodlot border planted for wildlife. (Connors undated)*

## Brush Piles

Well, first off, brush piles are generally beneficial. But avoid building them where you are concentrating on building the ruffed grouse population. Brush piles are absolutely excellent for rabbits and various other wildlife including some songbirds that perch in them for cover. But they also provide concealment for predators of grouse. Nevertheless, grouse will survive where you have brush piles, although in lower numbers. But more about grouse management later.

As I said, in general, brush piles enhance wildlife habitat. You will get rabbits, woodchucks, chipmunks, mice, weasels, skunks, foxes, cardinals, towhees, thrashers, catbirds, chipping sparrows, juncos, garter snakes, salamanders, and more, using them. So take the slash (branches) remaining from your tree harvest, and build about 1 to 4 brush piles per acre, spaced 30 to 60 yards apart. Place the big stuff on the bottom and the little stuff on top, crisscrossed, so the animals can crawl in the openings underneath (Fig. 2.5). The brush piles should be about 4 to 10 yards across and 1.5 to 2.5 yards high. Actually, logs, old fence posts, stumps, and rock piles make good bases for brush piles. But do not put the brush pile close to your garden or house, or you might have a skunk too close or rabbits chewing in your garden. It is not a good idea to place the brush pile under a snag because you will be setting the table for hawks and owls using the snag as a perch or nesting site, and you will defeat your purpose of trying to build up populations of rabbits and other such critters.

You can attract scaled quail and bobwhite quail by placing an old grill or grate, about 2.5 x 2.5 yards square, on cinder blocks and piling it with brush. You can attract California quail and Gambel's quail with a raised platform roost topped with brush (Fig. 2.6). For javelina, brush platforms should be 3 feet tall and 10 x 10 feet square.

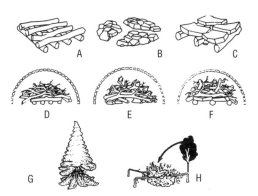

**Figure 2.5** *Construction of brushpile shelters with base construction of logs (A), boulders (B), log and boulder combination (C), dead brush over each base (D-F), and living brush piles built with conifers (G) or hardwoods (H). (Gutiérrez et al. 1979)*

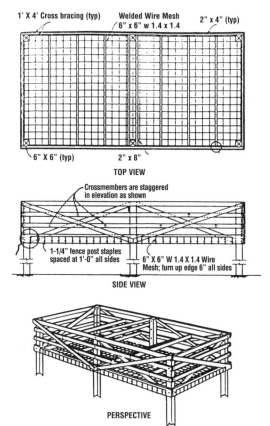

**Figure 2.6** *Plan of roost for California quail and Gambel's quail. (U.S. Army Corps of Engineers 1979, Kosciuk and Peloquin 1986)*

You also can build tepee shelters with 10 to 20 6-foot logs, or fence posts, or railroad ties, shaped like a tepee and wired together at the top. Bobwhites, for one, seem to prefer them. Old Christmas trees also can be stacked like a tepee preferably, or just piled together on the ground.

## Rock Piles

Maybe you live in a glaciated or other area that has lots of rock. Make a few rock piles; lots of animals use them for dens and other cover, from woodchucks to reptiles. If large enough, rock piles provide an attractive interior with a fairly stable temperature and humidity. Use rock over 20 inches in diameter for the bottom layer, so a maze of spaces occurs, with the rock on top at least 8 to 12 inches in diameter. Use a dump truck and/or a front-end loader. Your rock piles should occupy an area of about 10 square yards, and be about 1 to 2 yards tall and 3 to 4 yards across. To provide adjoining microhabitats for small mammals, reptiles, and amphibians, place 3 such rock piles just 2 yards apart.

For best results, you need about 1 to 2 rock piles per acre located near habitat such as other cover, feeding areas, or water. Place them preferably along valley bottoms, in draws, on protected hillsides, and in other protected areas. Some raptors will use rock piles for perching and nesting if they are located on the leeward side of prevailing winds on hills near the top.

## Living Brush Piles

Yes, *living* brush piles. Find a group of 4 or more saplings about 6 to 10 feet tall or at least 4 inches dbh. About 6 to 10 inches above the ground, cut them partially through from the outside, and bend them inward toward the center of the group (see Fig. 2.5). Make sure that a hinge of wood and bark is left intact so that the trees continue to live for several years. These are called *half-cuts*. Make the cuts in the spring after the sap is running and the leaves have matured. Select deciduous trees which are not so brittle that they break off cleanly when bent over after the cut (Table 2.2). Saplings with fruit-producing vines in them also provide extra food. In time, these half-cuts will die. Then you can either cut them off and add more brush, or leave them as is and add more brush, whichever way provides the most cover.

Wildlife species such as deer, rabbits, ruffed grouse, and turkey will feed on the buds, twigs, and leaves of broadleaf living brush piles. Songbirds such as towhees, catbirds, and brown thrashers will eat the insects that live in a living brush pile.

You can make another type of living brush pile with conifers, by slicing partway through the top of each limb

Table 2.2. Some trees for living brush piles (half-cuts).
(Steele and Martin 1986)

| West | Midwest and East | South |
|------|------------------|-------|
| Willow | Willow | Willow |
| Aspen | Aspen | Post oak |
| Maple | Maple | Blackjack oak |
| California live oak | Post oak | Live oak |
| Choke cherry | Blackjack oak | Ash |
| Buckthorn | Ash | Hackberry |
| Toyon | Hackberry | Elm |
|  | Basswood | Mesquite |
|  | Elm |  |
|  | Hawthorn |  |
|  | Birch |  |
|  | Soapberry |  |
|  | Yaupon |  |

in the bottom 2 or 3 whorls of branches, and bending them down to form a "tepee" (see Fig. 2.5). You can do that with large branches of broadleaf trees too.

### Snake Hibernacula

Snakes tend to go after insects, mice, other small mammals, amphibians, and other reptiles. They are fascinating critters. For one thing, they can move without appendages, and are fun to watch in addition to being helpful against harmful rodents.

A snake hibernaculum is for hibernating snakes. It is essentially an underground brush pile (Fig. 2.7). Build the thing preferably on south-facing slopes for the sunlight, and along woods roads, log landings, and other forest openings where slash and stumps are plentiful.

Dig a trench about 8 feet deep and 9 feet across. Place a layer of logs on the bottom, then fill in with stumps and branches covered with soil to ground level. Across the top of it place logs 10 feet long side-by-side. Put more soil on these logs, and then more branches and soil on top of that. When done, you should have a mound about 10 feet high.

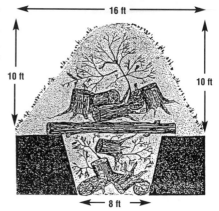

**Figure 2.7** *Cross-section of a snake hibernaculum. (Henderson 1987)*

### Dead Wood

A clean woods? Don't do it! Take the state of Washington as an example: there, more than 1/3 (36 percent) of the wildlife species depends on dead wood! That is a good indication of how things are everywhere. In other words, about 1/3 of your wildlife species depends on dead wood! Just some of the things wildlife uses dead wood (snags, logs, stumps, and brush piles) for include cavity nest sites, nesting platforms, sources of feeding substrate, plucking posts, singing or drumming sites, food cache or granary, courtship locations, overwintering sites, roosting, lookout posts, hunting and hawking perches, fledging sites, dwellings or dens, nesting under bark, communal nesting or nursery colonies, escape cover, and thermal cover (Fig. 2.8). Insectivorous birds that use snags extensively can reduce insect infestations of spruce budworm, etc., if enough snags exist.

So, watch the firewood cutting. Remember that you are managing the woods for wildlife.

There are 2 very general types of snags: hard and soft. Hard snags have a solid exterior usually with a few limbs still attached, and rotten centers. They make the best den trees. In time their limbs drop off and they become soft snags with pulpy wood fibers. Soft snags are used for foraging by insect-

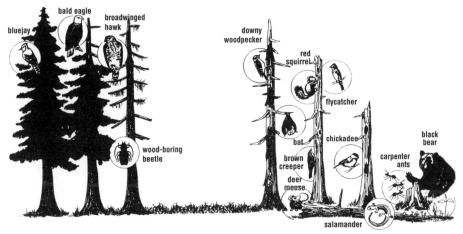

**Figure 2.8** *"Life cycle of a dying tree. The decline of a tree begins when heart rot fungi invade the tree through a wound to the tree's bark. Slowly the tree's core begins to rot—barren branches appear, perhaps a good site for an eagle nest or perch for broadwing hawks and flycatchers. Insects and beetles feast. Bark loosens. Woodpeckers soon follow, in search of food and potential home sites. Using their specialized bills, these birds chip away at the softened wood to create a cavity large enough for nesting. They raise their young, feed on the insects harbored within the decaying wood, and move on. The empty cavity then becomes home to another creature—perhaps an owl, squirrel, bluebird, or bat. Eventually the battered ghost of a tree topples, or remains as a soft stump, maybe half its original height. Carpenter ants invade, a healthy lunch for a passing bear or coon. Salamanders, snakes, and mice move in...while a nearby hawk, perched high upon a neighboring snag, takes note. The tree decays further until new plants and mushrooms sprout in the remaining organic matter. Life goes on..." (Judd et al. 1998)*

eating birds and for nesting woodpeckers and songbirds such as black-capped chickadees.

Primary cavity users tend to be woodpeckers, which make the cavity. Other cavity users, such as chickadees, owls, squirrels, and raccoons, are secondary cavity users.

Good cavity trees are hard trees such as sugar maple, oak, hickory, butternut, beech, and others. Softer trees grow fast, have short life spans, and rot quickly, like aspen and birch. They make great soft snags because they form cavities quicker than hardwoods, and also provide good habitat for insects, which feed many songbirds. Coniferous snags do not last as long as hardwoods. But snags of all species of tree have some value as wildlife habitat.

So how many snags should you have in your woods? About 2 to 4 per acre, and the bigger the better. Small snags cannot accommodate the larger woodpeckers and other wildlife, although some of them will use live den trees, if big enough. Take pileated woodpeckers, for example. They are the size of crows. Whereas crows make stick nests in the branches of trees, pileateds drill a hole in a tree for their nest. And they lay about 4 eggs. And the fledglings are adults when they leave the cavity! Calls for a big tree! At least 18 inches dbh.

And another thing. In time these snags will drop over and become logs (Fig. 2.9). So, leave some replacement trees to become snags ultimately.

Speaking of logs, you need some in your woods. In fact, you should have at least 2 to 4 logs for every 5 acres. And again, the bigger the better. At least 12 to 18 inches wide at the large end, and preferably 20 feet long or more. But any log is better than no log. Logs should come from all the species of trees in your

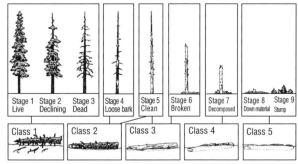

**Figure 2.9** *Upon falling, snags and trees enter log decomposition class 1, 2, 3, or 4. (Masser et al. 1979)*

woods. Logs, of course, will vary in decomposition status. Various species of wildlife, from salamanders to raccoons, use logs in various stages of decomposition, so all stages should be represented in your woods.

Incidentally, if you have a stream running through the woods and a tree drops over into it, or some branches fall in, leave them. Great fish habitat. Good cover for them, and foraging habitat too, because the aquatic invertebrates, on which fish feed, will attach to the wood. And the turtles like to haul out on the logs for their needed dose of vitamin D from the sun. The entire food chain benefits from that fallen tree.

The slash (branches mostly) from tree harvesting should be placed loosely in 2 to 4 piles per acre, or better yet, placed over logs or rocks to form regular brush piles (see Brush Piles). But too much slash from tree harvesting will provide too much fuel for a potential forest fire. Remove excessive slash by piling and burning or by chipping with a wood chipper and spread less than 1 inch deep. Look at the amount of dead wood on the floor of an unharvested woodlot for an idea of how much is natural and how much would be excessive.

## Openings

Most game species and many non-game species of wildlife use forest openings heavily, i.e., an open area in the forest or woods where no trees occur. Deer, grouse, turkey, quail, and rabbits love them because of the food produced and they are near cover. If your woods is large enough, you could cut it as indicated in Fig. 2.10 to maintain an opening.

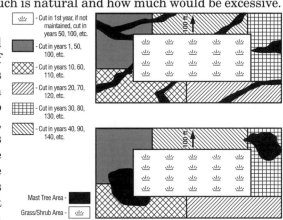

**Figure 2.10** *Cutting schedule in a woodlot to maintain an opening for wildlife. (Connecticut Department of Environmental Protection 1989)*

Normally, you do not have to make or maintain openings in your woodlot. The surrounding fields are openings, group selection cuts cause openings, clearcuts of shade-intolerant trees like aspen cause openings, log landings cause openings, logging roads cause linear openings, even an electric line right-of-way causes an opening. Canopy gaps from snags or blowdowns also cause openings.

Openings tend to fragment forests, which tend to be highly fragmented from human encroachment already. But maybe your woodlot is large and fragmented naturally. If so, one or more openings will improve your woods for edge species of wildlife.

Openings can be herbaceous or brushy. Both are valuable for wildlife. If your woods are surrounded by fields and pasture, which is likely, then a brushy opening in the woods is preferred for diversity. Openings should be 1 to 3 acres on a 40-acre tract of woods. An opening should be 3 to 6 times longer than it is wide, with the width at least 1.5 times the height of the adjacent trees. It should be S- or J-shaped if you have the room, and in an east-west direction or shaped something as in Fig. 2.11. Do not put it next to a stand of conifers because the raptors that use the conifers for perching and concealment will prey on the grouse and other birds attracted to the opening. (Ruffed grouse hens bring their chicks into openings to feed on the abundant insects the fast-growing chicks need for their high-protein diet.)

Build brush piles with the branches and smaller limbs lying around after a cut. You will have to maintain your opening, so completely remove all stumps and large rocks that would interfere with a tractor and disk, if you want a herbaceous opening. Openings require a lot of work. After you get rid of the junk, disk the site, lime and fertilize it if needed,

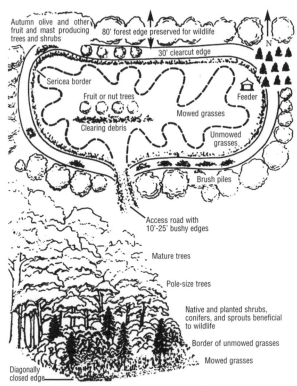

**Figure 2.11** *Features recommended for the design and edge management of forest wildlife clearings. (Giles 1978)*

and disk again. Then plant native grass seed, such as big bluestem, little bluestem, Indian grass, and switch grass. Otherwise, agricultural varieties will do, such as white clover, rye grass, millet, sorghum, buckwheat, alsike clover, and bluegrass. Then to keep brush from invading, you will need to mow the opening every 3 to 5 years, after mid-July to reduce harm to nesting birds, and before September to allow grasses to recover enough to provide residual cover for nesting birds that nest the following spring before new plant growth develops for cover.

If you want a brushy opening, mow or cut your opening every 5 to 10 years, but do not mow all of it the same year. Divide it into 3 or 4 parts and mow 1 part at a time to achieve a patchy opening best for wildlife. Do not locate the openings so that streams, caves, and ledges are exposed, for these are unique habitat types that require protection.

### Logging Roads and Trails

Make sure any roads that enter your woods do not follow the stream if you have one, because it will screw up your most valuable habitat type—your riparian strip (see Chapter 6). Also keep the roads as narrow as possible and away from wetlands, meadows, key winter range, wildlife travel lanes, feeding sites, reproductive areas, and key habitats for threatened, endangered, or unique wildlife. That means you will have to know something about your wildlife and where it does its thing, or where it is likely to do its thing after you improve your woodlot and attract more wildlife to it. Also keep the roads out of particularly vigorous patches of shrubs.

Keep to a bare minimum the amount of roads and trails in your woods. Remember that your woods is already a fragment of what once occurred on the land there. In other words, it has had more than its share of human disturbance and fragmentation, so do not add more than necessary to improve it for wildlife. Also, straight stretches of road should not be longer than 1,300 feet and should not pass through the woods if avoidable (Fig. 2.12).

All roads should be built to minimize erosion and stream siltation. If the road has to cross your stream, build a small bridge over it rather than driving right through it. And keep the stream crossing at a right angle to reduce disturbance to the riparian vegetation.

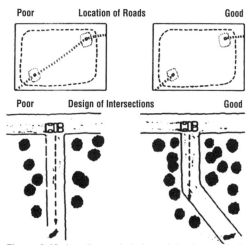

**Figure 2.12** *Location and design of logging roads to minimize impact on wildlife. (Armleder et al. 1986)*

You should use a grass/legume mixture to seed the woods roads and log landing sites. For roads averaging 5 yards wide, you should apply about 10 pounds of 10-20-20 fertilizer and about 100 pounds of lime for every 30 yards of road. Check soil conditions with your county agent for more specific advice. Check with the local wildlife manager for information on the grass/legume mixture.

A system of trails in your woods allows access for viewing and photographing wildlife, wildflowers, and fall colors; hunting; gathering nuts, berries, and mushrooms; and hiking, snowshoeing, and cross-country skiing. Trails provide excellent sources of food for wildlife; many mammals, e.g., deer and foxes, use the trails for travel.

To develop a trail, you must clear, seed, and maintain it. You could clear it as described in "Daylighting." Then rototill, disk, and seed it. You can use a mixture of 10 pounds white clover, 5 pounds perennial rye, 10 pounds annual rye, and 15 pounds creeping red fescue for each acre of trail, or whatever works for your area. A 9-foot-wide trail 1 mile long is about 1 acre. If the trail winds through a wet site, use alsike clover instead of white clover. Check with your local wildlife manager and county agent to find out what is most appropriate for your area.

Anyway, you will have to mow the trail every 1 to 3 years to stimulate growth of the herbaceous stuff and discourage invasion of the woody stuff. A good stand of clover provides excellent habitat for a variety of insects, which growing birds and insectivorous birds need. Therefore, if you run the trail through a stand of conifers, avoid seeding that stretch to clover because the raptors using the conifers for cover will feed on birds such as ruffed grouse using the insects and clover on the trail.

## Daylighting

Daylighting has to do with roads and trails. Maybe you want to open up their sides more to allow more sunlight to hit the ground and stimulate more profuse plant growth. That's daylighting. You might not need to, though, if you have a small woodlot, a large woodlot with plenty of roads, log landings, canopy gaps, grassy areas, wet areas, or other openings, or a large woodlot that is long and narrow (with much edge effect from adjacent fields). In those cases, you should make sure to leave a strip of shrubby vegetation at least 10 yards wide as security cover along each side of the road.

Anyway, let's say you want to daylight your woods roads. If so, cut out all woody stuff within 3 yards of each side of the road or trail. Clear out all stumps and rocks within 1.5 yards of each side so that you can plant and maintain a mixture of grasses and forbs, which will need mowing about every 3 to 5 years so that brush does not invade. You also should create a transition zone from herbaceous vegetation to woods. This is done by removing half the trees within 8 to 10 yards of each side of the road or trail.

# HOW TO IMPROVE YOUR WOODS

## Dusting Areas

Ruffed grouse, turkeys, pheasants, quail, and even some songbirds love to roll in dust periodically, and kick it under their feathers to rid themselves of external parasites. If there is no dusting area in your woods, you can provide some to improve the quality and attractiveness of your woods to such species of wildlife. Just choose several widely spaced areas of fine, loose soil, and spade up a spot 1.5 x 2 feet in a sunny location in a herbaceous opening, not a brushy one, and away from human disturbance such as hiking. (You could do this in a remote spot of your backyard.)

## Water

Now **water** can have a real impact on the quality of your woodlot. Most wildlife species need free water for drinking, reproducing (like frogs, salamanders, some insects), or living (like turtles, fish, muskrats, aquatic invertebrates, ducks). What use are insects and other aquatic invertebrates? Think your way through the food chain. Frogs and turtles eat them. Fish eat them. Ducklings eat them. Songbirds eat them. Etcetera. If you have a stream or pond in your woods, you are really lucky. And many woodlots have them. Maybe all you have in your woodlot is a depression and seasonal water standing in it, like during spring from snow melt (vernal pool) or rain runoff (ephemeral pool). That's still good. Or maybe you have some kind of a spring of free-flowing water or a seep that keeps soil moist to form a wet spot. That seep is still good. The only management you might need to do here is to preserve and protect these valuable wildlife areas and their surrounding buffer areas. Often you can do more.

Any springs or seeps you have in your woods (or elsewhere on your property) should be protected from cattle and logging. I have already said that you should fence your cattle (and other livestock) completely **out** of your woods. You could develop your spring or seep more for wildlife by leaving all food-producing shrubs and small trees uncut, removing all other trees and slash within a 20-yard radius, and locating any logging haul roads at least 50 yards away. (Also see Watering Devices in Chapter 9.)

Because many wetland wildlife species use grassy areas for cover, you should maintain at least 2 to 4 acres of nearby unmowed grassy cover for every acre of pond you have, as a rule of thumb. The best place to do this is where the pond joins woods and field. It is easier there if the field is a hayfield. If it is not, making some of it grassy would produce a highly attractive covert of woods, pond, grassy area, and cornfield or whatever. If it is a stream, stick some rocks in it in such a fashion that you build a small waterfall. Wildlife is really attracted to the sound of dripping or flowing water rather than still water. And keep in mind that wildlife is really attracted to the riparian areas associated with water. What's a riparian area? See Chapter 6.

## Corridors

Most woodlots by definition are isolated islands of forested lands surrounded by fields or something. You might own several of these. You can improve their quality by connecting them with a corridor. Corridors provide habitat for corridor dwellers, i.e., animals that live in them, and corridor travelers that move from 1 woodlot to another. That means you might have to do some planting. But you might not have to, if you have a stream on your property that meanders between the 2 woodlots. Just make sure you do not cultivate your fields too close to the stream. Protect at least 30 yards of shoreline on each side of the stream, if you can. Let the woody shrubs and trees develop there as a riparian zone. That might mean fencing your cows out. They should not be messing up the stream and streambanks in the first place, or you will end up with one of those streams you have seen in fields where cows can have access to it at any point, and the streambanks are eroded, there is no vegetation for cover, the stream is wide, shallow, slow, and dirty, and there are no fish either. That is a sure sign of poor land management. Your cows can still have access to the stream for drinking if they must. Just fence the stream such that the cows can drink only at one part of it (see Fig. 8.1).

But suppose you do not have a stream on your property, or it does not run between your woodlots. Then design a corridor connecting them, and plant some trees. The shrubs will come in on their own; probably from seeds in their droppings as the birds sit in the trees. How wide should the corridor be? Anywhere from 10 to 100 yards wide, depending on how much land you can devote to it. The wider the better. Maybe you do not have more than 1 woodlot, but your neighbor is a federal, state, or county forest. Then connect your woodlot to it with a corridor. If your corridor will be relatively narrow, a mixture of conifers, to include spruce, would be best to provide cover to corridor travelers. Ideally, you should not be able to see through the corridor. A relatively wide corridor should have a mixture of conifers, and various deciduous trees, especially mast producers such as cherries and oak, except oak grows so slowly. Popple (aspen) grows fast, and will give you a corridor in a hurry. It is also a valuable wildlife tree (see Aspen/Birch in Chapter 3).

But corridors are not all good, especially for corridor dwellers, for example, nesting birds. Corridors make nice travel lanes for predators which can efficiently search the narrow corridor for prey, causing abnormally high mortality.

White-tailed deer

# CHAPTER 3

# SONGBIRDS AND DEER AND GROUSE AND QUAIL AND TURKEYS AND RABBITS AND SQUIRRELS AND TYPES OF WOODLOTS AND FORESTS

Wildlife management is a compromise. The saying goes, if you manage for one kind of wildlife, you manage against another kind. You absolutely cannot manage for all species of wildlife at the same time at the same place. They simply have different requirements. It is a compromise all right. The question is, what is the **best** compromise for the desirable species and/or the most variety on **your** land? Let's take a look at some of the most common and widespread types of woodlot and forest and the best compromise management for wildlife.

Without wanting to get too provincial in wildlife management strategy, I will say that many folks like to have deer, grouse, quail, rabbits, squirrels, and turkeys around—for viewing and for hunting. These species have broad distributions in North America. Managing for them also will produce a variety of songbirds and other non-game species of wildlife associated with such habitats.

Of 36 species of deer worldwide in the deer family (Cervidae), we have 5 species in North America: white-tailed deer, mule deer, elk, moose, and caribou. Caribou and reindeer are the same species. European red deer and our elk are the same species. The key deer is a small race of the white-tailed deer, of which some 30 races (sub-species) exist; the black-tailed deer are 2 small races of mule deer, of which 7 races exist.

We have 10 species of grouse (Tetraonidae) in North America: ruffed grouse, spruce grouse, sharp-tailed grouse, greater prairie chicken, lesser prairie chicken, sage grouse, blue grouse, willow ptarmigan, rock ptarmigan, and white-tailed ptarmigan. We have 6 species of quail (Phesianidae) in North America: bobwhite, scaled, mountain, California (valley), Montezuma (harlequin or Mearns'), and Gambel's. All except the bobwhite are western species of quail, although the bobwhite has been introduced there in some areas. (Also in the family Phesianidae, the ring-necked pheasant, Hungarian [gray] partridge, and chukar partridge are not native to North America, but have been successfully introduced from Eurasia.) The wild turkey is in a family all to itself (Meleagridae). (Notice all the family names end in <u>ae</u>.) It is so uniquely North American that in the 1700s, Ben Franklin wanted it to be the national symbol instead of the bald eagle which he thought had nasty eating habits.

Discussing rabbits is a bit more complicated because the group is large. In the first place, the family (Leporidae) includes both rabbits and hares. Unlike hares, rabbits are born naked and blind, and tend to be smaller with proportionally shorter ears and hind legs. Jackrabbits are hares. Eight species of hare occur in North America: snowshoe hare, arctic hare, Alaskan hare, European hare (introduced), black-tailed jackrabbit, white-tailed jackrabbit, white-sided jackrabbit, and antelope jackrabbit. The snowshoe hare is the most widely distributed hare, ranging across the continent from Newfoundland to Alaska, into the northern part of the lower U.S., and in the mountains. Eight species of rabbit occur in North America: eastern cottontail, desert cottontail, mountain cottontail, New England cottontail, brush rabbit, swamp rabbit, marsh rabbit, and pygmy rabbit. The eastern cottontail is the most widely distributed rabbit, overlapping with 6 species of rabbit and 6 species of hare. It is the principle game species in the U.S. Of the rabbits and hares, most recommendations in this chapter apply to eastern cottontails, snowshoe hares, and associated wildlife.

Squirrels. Now that is a bit complicated too. The family name is Sciuridae, but that includes 43 species of ground squirrels (like chipmunks and woodchucks) and 10 species of tree squirrels in North America. And tree squirrels include the hunted species and the non-hunted ones (northern flying squirrel, southern flying squirrel, red squirrel, chickaree, tassel-eared [Abert or Kaibab] squirrel, Arizona gray squirrel, Apache fox squirrel). The eastern fox squirrel, eastern gray squirrel, and western gray squirrel are heavily hunted.

If you are curious, you can look up the distribution maps of all these animals in your field guides.

All of these species have fairly high reproductive rates, especially rabbits and squirrels. They are a renewable natural resource, and can tolerate fairly high harvest rates.

The focus of this chapter is on compromise management for wildlife in the most common and widespread types of woodlots and forests. That often includes the species of deer, grouse, quail, turkey, rabbit, and squirrel with the broadest distribution: white-tailed deer, ruffed grouse, bobwhite quail, wild turkey, eastern cottontail, fox squirrel, and gray squirrel. But some of the recommendations apply to all species of deer, grouse, quail, rabbit, hare, and squirrel associated with woodlands. The recommendations certainly apply to all species of associated wildlife—game or non-game—and a variety of these species will be produced too.

The key to good production of deer, grouse, quail, rabbits, and to some extent turkey and squirrels in wooded areas is a good understory, i.e., brushy conditions beneath the overstory (see Woodlot Borders and Other Brushy Areas, and especially for rabbits, Brush Piles and Living Brush Piles, in Chapter 2). One "word" of caution about deer. Too high a population can cause starvation conditions for them because they can create a **browse line** which also affects associated wildlife and plants (see introduction to Chapter 2). Your woods and wildlife will take years to recover from this effect. Heavy hunting is usually the best answer to control the deer population.

## Aspen/Birch

Quaking (trembling) aspen, often called popple, is a shade-intolerant, fast-growing, short-lived tree that has the broadest distribution of any tree species in North America. It is heavily used by white-tailed deer and ruffed grouse, among other wildlife species including various songbirds, snowshoe hare, beaver, moose, woodcock, and associated predators. Even black bears feed on the catkins.

Habitat management for white-tailed deer and ruffed grouse often involves aspen management, partly because it is so widespread, is high in protein, and responds so readily to management, i.e., it grows so fast and thus can impact a wildlife population quickly. (It usually grows 2 to 6 feet the first year.) Aspen often is associated with white birch, another shade-intolerant tree.

Even-aged management, specifically, clearcutting, is generally recommended for ruffed grouse as well as deer, but in large enough blocks to provide grouse some "interior" cover where predators have to search harder and less successfully to find them. Even-aged management provides the best variety of wildlife when all stand conditions are represented: grass/forb, shrub, open sapling/pole, closed sapling/pole sawtimber, large sawtimber, old growth. But we are talking large forests here; on small woodlots, all 6 of the stand conditions would be impossible to have.

Aspen also grows in clones of interconnecting root systems, and the trees in the clone are either all male or all female. Aspen flower buds are particularly important to grouse as winter food, used out of proportion to their availability relative to other foods. In other words, grouse select them. And not just any buds, but the buds of male trees are sought. Flower buds of female aspen trees are much smaller, nutrient-poor, and seldom used by ruffed grouse, although female as well as male catkins are eaten during the short time available. In 15 minutes of feeding, a grouse can obtain enough nutrients and energy from the male buds to last 24 hours, thus reducing exposure to predators and wind chill. A crop full of aspen flower buds can weigh 100 grams; a crop full of clover or strawberry leaves weighs 30 to 40 grams and a crop full of thornapples or mountain ash berries weighs 40 to

60 grams. Reduced exposure to predators is important because most grouse mortality is due to avian predation, especially from the goshawk, and some mammalian predation. Yet these predators are part of the ecosystem, and evolved with the predator-prey system involving grouse. These predators are thus important in the system, but good food and cover for grouse are essential. Aspen can provide both.

Many species of wildlife benefit from aspen. It is the preferred winter food of beaver. Deer, moose, and snowshoe hares will use recent cutovers at night to feed on the tops of cut trees, and continue to use the area when herbaceous and woody plants produce new growth in response to the increased sunlight. Woodcock sometimes use the new clearings as singing grounds, although they usually wait 1 to 2 years until some cover has developed around the edge. Woodcock will use sites too compacted for fast plant regeneration, such as log landings or skid trails. Woodcock and grouse begin using a new cutover as brood habitat about the same time. Cutovers will be used by various songbirds almost as soon as they are created. Killdeer, robins, and nighthawks are among the earliest to respond because they use the open terrain and bare ground. Later, the developing sapling stand will be used by various warblers, thrushes, vireos, and other insectivorous songbirds. Upon emergence from dens in April, black bears eat aspen catkins, for they are nutritious when little else is available for bears at that time.

Ruffed grouse need young forests. Habitat manipulation of older forests for grouse will not show immediate results. It could be several years before your grouse respond with increased numbers as your habitat quality improves. Deer and snowshoe hares will respond almost immediately. Wrens and sparrows will use the slash and logging debris, but many other songbirds will wait until sprouts and suckers begin branching to provide nesting sites. Raptors and mammalian predators will respond as the prey species become plentiful.

Aspen needs some form of disturbance to regenerate profusely, because it regenerates mainly from suckers from the root system. These suckers will not develop if your aspen die of old age. Then the stand will be replaced by something else, often balsam fir. As a short-lived shade-intolerant species, aspen evolved with fire as a disturbance factor, and clearcutting simulates fire to some degree.

Recommendations for aspen management will be specific to grouse, because deer and certain other wildlife will benefit too, while the reverse is less true. Even the best habitat will not entirely eliminate the periodic 9- to 11-year cycle typical of ruffed grouse in northern forests. But after a cyclic loss, the loss is less severe and recovery faster from a grouse population declining from a density of 1 pair per 10 acres of excellent habitat vs. 1 pair per 50 acres of poor habitat. In other words, habitat improvement modifies the so-called 10-year cycle that ruffed grouse undergo.

Male grouse are territorial, needing about 7 acres, and one male will not tolerate another within about 150 yards. Good grouse habitat will support one breeding male per 20 acres. Anything less than 1 breeding male per 50 acres is poor habitat. Because few extensive forest tracts are prime habitat, a density of 1 drumming male per 10 to 12 acres in the spring, the time to census them, seems to be an achievable goal that will produce 1 grouse per 2.5 acres in the fall.

The needs of ruffed grouse can be satisfied when aspen constitutes no more than 12 to 14 percent of the forest composition. Ideal habitat for ruffed grouse consists of abundant aspens, including saplings, pole-sized trees, and mature trees, all within the annual foraging range of grouse. Ideally, forests containing aspen should have properly spaced **clearcuts** per 10-acre area, with 1 of the 2.5-acre units consisting of male aspen at least 30 years old, which grouse will use for food. For optimum growth and survival of suckers, you will need a complete clearcut; as little as 10 to 15 square feet of residual basal area will retard sprout growth by 35 to 40 percent. A good scheme is to divide your aspen into 40-acre tracts, if you have enough land, with each tract subdivided into 16 2.5-acre cutting units (Fig. 3.1). Every 10 years, 4 of the 2.5-acre units should be clearcut on a 40-year rotation. Keep the edges straight to reduce edge effect and predation so lethal to ruffed grouse. If that is commercially unacceptable, or if aspen regeneration is inhibited by inadequate sunlight or air circulation in 2.5-acre cuts, you could use the same strategy of cutting except each clearcut unit would be 10 acres instead of 2.5 acres, if enough aspen exists. You should clearcut the southern units in Fig 3.1 first so that some improvement in cover will occur along the southern edges of the 2 northern units long before they are cut. Cut the birch too, but do not clearcut other hardwoods or conifers mixed in with the aspen and birch. Leave them for later selection cuts for sawlogs, or leave them to develop into old-growth trees. Clumps of conifers will provide good winter cover for many wildlife species, from winter resident songbirds to deer.

Initial cutting

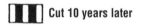 Cut 10 years later

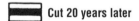 Cut 20 years later

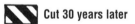 Cut 30 years later

**Figure 3.1** *Cutting schedule for 40-acre tract of aspen. (Schulz 1984)*

Where your aspen persists only as widely scattered individual trees or small clumps, a group selection cut (i.e., a clonal clearcut) should be made to stimulate root sucker growth. Cut all the aspen in the group, and all trees within a 1-chain (66-foot) radius around the outermost aspens in the group. In addition, the clearcut should be extended at least 100 feet to the south, southeast, and southwest, to allow sunlight to reach the ground over all the area likely to contain aspen roots. Leave at least 1 clump of 30 to 50 male aspen trees per 10 acres to provide a food source. The male aspen trees most used for food are over 30 years old.

All cutting should occur during the dormant season for maximum sucker development. If possible, avoid cuts next to clumps of conifer. Avian predators concealed in the conifers will prey heavily on grouse broods eating insects in the opening caused by cutting. Also, burn the slash and brush or otherwise remove or distribute it so that it is not piled, to reduce concealment for grouse predators. Like aspen, other forest types also can be managed for grouse habitat. It is just easier (faster) with aspen. The most crucial component seems to be vertical stem density to protect grouse from avian predators. Such cover should be about 2,000 stems over 5 feet tall per acre, within 300 feet of a good food supply, such as male aspen trees, hazel, birch, oak, witch hazel, cherry, and hop hornbeam.

If a lack of suitable logs for drumming by male grouse during spring courtship is a possible limiting factor, and it could be, then large enough trees should be felled or brought in. A suitable drumming log is 10 to 14 inches in diameter at the large end. It should be on level ground, 2 to 3 feet from a guard object such as the stump from which the log was cut, the trunk of another tree, or the flared roots of a wind-thrown tree. The log should provide the drumming male with a relatively unobstructed view for a radius of 50 to 60 feet. About 60 to 170 stems (5,000-17,000 stems per acre) of small trees and shrubs should be 8 to 30 feet tall within a radius of 10 to 12 feet of the log to reduce avian predation. Several mature male aspen should occur within sight of the log. (You can estimate stem density by using a rope 11 feet 9 inches long as the radius of a circle, count the stems over 5 feet tall in that circle—which is 0.01 acre—and multiply by 100. Do that a few times to get a decent average of stem density, i.e., number of stems per acre.)

Modifications to enhance deer and woodcock populations include openings in the forest. About 1 to 5 percent of the forest should be maintained in permanent herbaceous openings. No specific openings construction is needed other than those created from clearcutting aspen and the maintenance of existing fields, log landings, road system, and wetlands.

### Northern Hardwoods

Northern hardwoods are shade-tolerant tree species consisting mainly of sugar maple, red maple, and basswood, and less commonly yellow birch, white ash, black ash, black cherry, northern red oak, paper birch, beech, elm, red maple, silver maple, and some white pine, hemlock, and balsam fir, depending on site conditions. They usually lack substantial ground and shrub layers due to a closed canopy and low sunlight penetration. The ground layer is mainly herbaceous, covered in winter by a layer of snow. Thus, as with most coniferous stands, northern hardwoods tend to be devoid of most ground-dwelling and shrub-dwelling species of wildlife for lack of food, and in winter, unlike coniferous stands, for lack of thermal cover mainly, but even hiding cover. Only the canopy in summer supports relatively large numbers of wildlife, mainly birds, bats, and northern flying squirrels. A paucity of mast species limits use by other species of tree squirrels.

Because the oak component of the northern hardwood forest usually is small, oaks should not be cut. The acorn yield will be suppressed if northern hardwoods crowd the oak, as will seedling establishment. A group selection cut around such oaks would improve their vigor, branching, acorn production, and probably seedling establishment.

Most northern hardwoods should be managed with uneven-aged (all-aged) silviculture involving selection cuts (Table 3.1), and at least 1 portion of northern hardwoods should be managed with even-aged silviculture involving clearcuts, if you have the acreage. This variety of management would improve the variety and density of wildlife in your area. A clearcut will produce a greater variety of plant species and much browse and soft mast in a short time but often not good timber, unlike selection cuts. A long-lived brush/grass/forb community will result from the clearcut, which provides excellent summer wildlife habitat. All the even-aged silvicultural systems (clearcut, shelterwood, seed tree) enhance habitat for forest-edge species such as deer and ruffed grouse better than the uneven-aged systems (single tree selection, group selection).

| Table 3.1. Hardwoods to be left after a selection cut. (Klessig and Kroenke 1999) | | |
|---|---|---|
| Diameter | Trees left per acre | |
| (inches) | Number | Percent |
| 2-4 | 202 | 63 |
| 5-9 | 65 | 20 |
| 10-14 | 28 | 9 |
| 15-19 | 17 | 5 |
| 20-24 | 8 | 3 |
| Total | 320 | 100 |

Some species of songbirds are unaffected by logging in northern hardwoods, some increase, and some decrease, but responses are short-lived relative to the long intervals between cuts. Rare species of birds in undisturbed forests are greatly reduced or eliminated by logging.

Improvement cuts are recommended for hardwood sites next to winter shelter for deer because of supplemental browse produced. A sapling-sized (1 to 5 inch dbh) stand of northern hardwoods produces 26 to 46 pounds of fresh browse per square foot of basal area if all competing trees are cut within 6 feet of selected crop trees. Islands of conifers should be left intact to enhance diversity and provide winter thermal cover, unless next to an opening where raptors concealed in the conifers could prey on grouse more readily. All mast (nut-producing) and den trees should be left standing. So, inspect your trees before you cut.

You might want to preserve most of your large sugar maples and red maples for their esthetic quality of color in the fall, and for production of maple syrup in the spring. Heavy thinning will eventually produce tapping trees with a broad crown (Table 3.2).

# MORE WILDLIFE ON YOUR LAND

Table 3.2. Maples to be left after thinning and harvest.
(Klessig and Kroenke 1999)

| Average diameter of canopy trees (inches) | Trees left per acre Number | Trees left per acre Percent | Average distance between trunks of canopy trees (feet) |
|---|---|---|---|
| 6 | 210 | 34 | 14 |
| 8 | 145 | 23 | 17 |
| 10 | 110 | 18 | 20 |
| 12 | 85 | 14 | 23 |
| 14 | 70 | 11 | 25 |

Because northern hardwoods are the most extensive and least productive forest type for wildlife, site conversion, especially to aspen where clones exist, should be done in some areas. Cut the northern hardwoods and leave the aspen, oaks, and conifers to develop and spread.

## Oak/Hickory

Turkeys and oaks go together. So do squirrels and oaks.

Oak trees provide more food and cover to birds and mammals than any other woody plant except perhaps *Rubus* (raspberry, blackberry, dewberry, etc.). In addition, oaks have relatively open canopies that allow shrubs, grass, and forbs to flourish below, which also provide food and cover. Insects hide among the leaves and in the deep-furrowed bark. Ground litter beneath oaks supports various reptiles, amphibians, insects, and other wildlife.

Because oak is prized as timber and firewood, oak woods are being decimated and often replaced with shade-tolerant trees such as maple and ash. Oaks are fire tolerant, but suppression of fire allows other competing trees to develop.

Oaks do not bear acorns until about 25 years old, and then produce a good crop only every 3 to 5 years. The older bigger trees produce the most mast (nuts). About 80 species of oak exist in the U.S. and Canada. All occur in 2 general groups: the white oak group or the red (black) oak group (see Mast Trees in Chapter 2). Acorns from oaks in the white oak group require 1 year to mature, those in the red oak group require 2 years. Acorns from the white oak group have less tannin and are more palatable to most wildlife than acorns from the red oak group. In areas where oak wilt is a problem, another reason to favor the white oak group is that it is less susceptible to oak wilt—a serious threat that kills large numbers of oaks in the red oak group. But because of annual fluctuations in acorn crops, a variety of oaks in your woodlot is best. Hickories, mainly shagbark, usually grow with oak, have similar needs, and produce hickory nuts, which many species of wildlife, and humans, eat.

Before you cut, remember that oaks are slow growers, so replacement is slow, so do not cut too many. The most common method to regenerate oak is by shelterwood cutting. Like clearcutting, shelterwood cutting allows sunlight to penetrate the canopy so that the ground and shrub layers can develop, but shelterwood cutting does this only partially—which is what oaks prefer. For a shelterwood cut, first harvest 30 to 60 percent of the trees in your woods, leaving the healthiest and best acorn producers to provide food for wildlife and seed for your next generation of oaks. You might have to graze the woods lightly, conduct a controlled burn, or apply herbicide to control competing plants growing with the seedling oaks in the increased sunlight. Get some help or advice from your local wildlife manager before trying weed control. About 3 to 8 years later, harvest about half of the remaining trees, leaving the best acorn producers to develop into old growth and snags.

| 9 | 2 | 11 | 4 | 13 | 6 | 15 | 8 |
|---|---|----|---|----|---|----|---|
| 1 | 10 | 3 | 12 | 5 | 14 | 7 | 16 |

| 1 | 9 | 2 | 10 |
|---|---|---|----|
| 11 | 3 | 12 | 4 |
| 5 | 13 | 6 | 14 |
| 15 | 7 | 16 | 8 |

**Figure 3.2** *Cutting sequences (designated numerically) in oak/hickory to benefit tree squirrels by avoiding adjacent clearcuts on rectangular or square units. (Nixon and Hansen 1987)*

Tree squirrels can be used as featured species representative of some other wildlife species needing large old oaks. Thus, the use of shelterwood cuts or even clearcuts in your woodlot should include well-dispersed cuttings for the optimal cutting pattern (Fig. 3.2). The interval for cutting half of your woodlot or stand within it varies with the size of your woodlot, the size of the cut, and the rotation length (Table 3.3). After half of the woodlot or stand has been cut, the clearcuts might have to be deferred once during each rotation to avoid creating adjacent stands (if no edge effect is desired), each less than 40 years old (Table 3.4).

In mixed hardwood woodlots, selectively remove most of the non-oak trees to encourage oak. Since periodically-thinned stands produce more acorns than unthinned stands, vigorous trees should be favored during the first precommercial thinning, especially for white oaks where 30 percent of the trees might bear 90 percent of the acorns. Thinning also increases the abundance of

**Table 3.3. Minimum clearcutting intervals (in years), for cutting 50% of the oak woodlot, for various woodlot sizes, cut sizes, and rotation lengths.** (Nixon and Hansen 1987, modified from Roach and Gingrich 1968)

| Size of cut (ac) | Rotation length for 20-acre woodlot (yr) | | | Rotation length for 40-acre woodlot (yr) | | | Rotation length for 60-acre woodlot (yr) | | |
|---|---|---|---|---|---|---|---|---|---|
| | 60 | 80 | 100 | 60 | 80 | 100 | 60 | 80 | 100 |
| 2 | 6 | 8 | 10 | 3 | 4 | 5 | 2 | 2 | 3 |
| 3 | 9 | 12 | 15 | 4 | 6 | 7 | 3 | 4 | 5 |
| 4 | 12 | 16 | 20 | 6 | 8 | 10 | 4 | 5 | 6 |
| 5 | 15 | 20 | 25 | 7 | 10 | 12 | 5 | 6 | 8 |

**Table 3.4. Deferred cutting interval (in years) needed after 50% of the oak woodlot has been cut, to avoid adjacent stands, both of which are less than 40 years old.** (Nixon and Hansen 1987)

| Size of cut (ac) | Rotation length for 20-acre woodlot (yr) | | | Rotation length for 40-acre woodlot (yr) | | | Rotation length for 60-acre woodlot (yr) | | |
|---|---|---|---|---|---|---|---|---|---|
| | 60 | 80 | 100 | 60 | 80 | 100 | 60 | 80 | 100 |
| 2 | 22 | 16 | 10 | 16 | 8 | 0 | 16 | 8 | 4 |
| 3 | 31 | 28 | 25 | 24 | 16 | 12 | 16 | 8 | 0 |
| 4 | 28 | 24 | 20 | 22 | 16 | 10 | 20 | 15 | 10 |
| 5 | 25 | 20 | 15 | 19 | 10 | 4 | 20 | 16 | 8 |

NOTE: The deferral is needed only once during each rotation, after 50% (none adjacent) in the unit has been cut.

summer logging is best because scarification favors regeneration of spruce.

If your area is large enough, you might be able to use shelterwood cuts or clearcuts (see Southern Pines and Western Conifers in this chapter).

## Southern Pines

One of the most responsive wildlife species to management of southern pines is bobwhite quail, although such management also produces deer, rabbits, and various other wildlife species. The key is a good understory of abundant annual weeds, especially legumes, and a good mixture of food and cover.

Best management practices for quail habitat involve fire, timber, harvest, and harrowing in open areas. If you have crowded, unmanaged pine stands, you should prescribe burn about every 3 years in winter to control brush and mid-story hardwoods. Then selectively harvest undesirable hardwoods for pulp or firewood, thin the pines by harvesting pulpwood or sawtimber, and cut slower-growing, poorly-formed, or insect-infested pines, except leave trees with cavities for wildlife to use. You might want to preserve islands of hardwoods to provide some variety that would be attractive to various wildlife in an otherwise monoculture of pine. As a rule of thumb, you should thin whenever tree limbs touch or overlap limbs of adjacent trees. For quail habitat, what you really want is a stocking rate about 25 percent less than desirable for optimum wood production. The goal is a sparse, open canopy so that plenty of light can penetrate to the forest floor to stimulate growth of the ground layer of vegetation to include such food-producers as blackberry, raspberry, and honeysuckle. Without such light, pine forests will have virtually no ground layer, and be a rather sterile wildlife habitat. You can enhance the pine habitat for quail by harrowing nearby open areas in winter to produce desirable food-producing annual weeds the next summer, such as ragweed, beggar-weed, and partridge pea.

Remember that quail are creatures of the edge. If you can manage to arrange the cover on your land so that coverts are formed (see Chapter 2), you will have more coveys of quail to hunt or view in the fall. For quail, that's cover, covert, and covey.

Pine stands can be regenerated by (1) planting preferably (for wildlife) on a spacing of 8 by 10 feet or 10 by 10 feet to enhance production of understory vegetation; (2) direct seeding by aircraft or by hand with a cyclone seeder; (3) 2-cut shelterwood system of harvest highly recommended for small woodlot owners. Before the first cut, prescribe burn the understory to reduce competition for establishing pine seedlings. Then harvest 50 percent of the trees, leaving the best (shelterwood) trees to produce the seedlings with the best genetics. Or you can harvest so that 30 to 50 trees per acre are left if they are 12 inches dbh, 25 to 40 trees per acre if 14 inches dbh, or 20 to 30 trees if 16 inches dbh. Then about 5 years later, after pine seedlings are well established, harvest the rest. The damage done then to seedlings will be unimportant.

If clearcutting is used, as it often is with southern pine and other conifers elsewhere in North America, irregularly shaped narrow clearcuts of 10 to 20 acres are best, up to 350 yards wide, which is roughly twice as far as deer like to move from the forest edge, which means they will enter the clearcut area from each side and thus use the entire open area for grazing. Deer can overbrowse smaller areas. You have to do some careful long-range planning to distribute clearcut areas wisely for wildlife, for once set, the pattern is difficult and expensive to change. You should distribute cutting units so that all stages of plant succession, i.e., all stand conditions, are within the deer's home range of about $1/2$ square mile. That means a deer should have simultaneous access to the seedling stage, sapling stage, pole timber stage, and mature timber stage. On a 40-year rotation that means you should clearcut each unit within the range every 10 years. Do not make consecutive cuts back to back, for your edge effect will disappear. Cuts should be separated by an uncut strip $1/8$ to $1/4$ mile wide. Otherwise do not try this method if you have insufficient land; stick to shelterwood cuts or group selection cuts instead.

After a clearcut, site preparation generally should involve roller chopping and burning for establishing pine, as it is fairly cheap. Deer food is scarce under a closed canopy of young pines. Seedlings should be planted or thinned to a spacing of 8 feet, or 10 feet by 10 feet.

As the canopy closes, thin saplings to a basal area of 60 square feet per acre; 70 to 80 square feet per acre might be a more reasonable compromise with timber production (see Cutting Strategy and Mast Trees in Chapter 2). To maximize yield of understory forage, you should thin every 5 to 8 years, but no later than 10 years.

You should exclude fire from your pine stands until the trees are about 15 to 20 feet tall. Then prescribe burn every 3 to 5 years depending on fuel accumulation. Too little fuel will not carry the fire. Too much fuel can be hazardous.

Prescribed burning is a standard tool for deer, turkey, and quail management in the South. It will also reduce costs of preparing recently logged areas for tree planting, and reduce wildfire hazards. You will need to run a low intensity surface fire through a stand, preferably in winter, for various reasons.

In hardwood forests, burn before the acorns fall, to encourage new oaks to develop and to protect the acorn food source. That also will kill undesirable thin-barked trees such as red maple, and allow the oaks to dominate.

You will need a permit and the advice and help of your local wildlife manager for burning.

## Western Conifers

Western conifers tend to be harvested by clearcutting—if you have enough land so that after you clearcut an area, most of your land is still forested in various structural stages. In fact, patchcuts of 20 acres are best, which means you should have at least 140 acres of woods to do this. The formula for laying out clearcuts (patchcuts) to manage timber to produce wildlife is 1/R, where R is the desired stand rotation in decades. So if your plan is to harvest your trees in a 70-year rotation, that's 7 decades. So $1/7$ of your area should be clearcut every 10 years. And the cut should be about 20 acres, which would be $1/7$ of your wooded area, with the clearcuts scattered throughout. Do not clearcut slopes steeper than 15 percent.

Actually, the size of the clearcut is not as important as the width. The longer and narrower it is, the more wildlife home ranges will be affected. Based on the needs of deer and elk, your cutting units should be 1.5 to 2 times as long as they are wide, but no wider than about 350 yards for deer and elk, and 400 yards for moose.

Keep in mind what is called the **non-adjacency constraint**; succeeding clearcuts should not be adjacent to each other, for that will minimize edge effect—just the opposite of what you want. In fact, you will have maximum edge contrast when you place your clearcuts next to stands of mid-rotation age (Fig. 3.5). It is true that highest edge contrast will occur when a clearcut occurs next to a stand of mature sawtimber (or old growth). But the next stand to be cut would be the mature sawtimber stand, and then you would have low edge contrast between the previous clearcut and the recent clearcut.

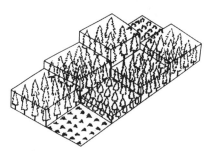

**Figure 3.5** *When integrated over 2 or more rotations, the maximum age difference between adjacent stands will occur if clearcuts are placed next to stands of mid-rotation age. (Harris 1984)*

If you do not distribute your clearcuts properly to maximize edge effect, then at least leave a **"leave strip"** (corridor) of trees and shrubs at least 6 yards wide for every 140 yards long the clearcut is to be, or leave a clump of trees $1/4$ to $1/2$ acre in size for every 5 to 10 acres clearcut (see Fig 3.4) to benefit many edge species of wildlife, including moose. If you schedule a new clearcut parallel to a similar cut made less than 10 years earlier, be sure to separate the sites by a wooded buffer at least as wide as the average width of the 2 cut areas (Fig. 3.6). To improve variety of

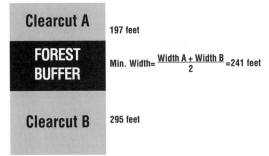

Clearcut A — 197 feet

FOREST BUFFER — Min. Width= $\frac{\text{Width A} + \text{Width B}}{2}$ =241 feet

Clearcut B — 295 feet

**Figure 3.6** *Method to determine the width of a forest buffer between 2 clearcuts less than 10 years old. (Connecticut Department of Environmental Protection 1989)*

habitat, retain stands of tree species different from the species being cut. Prescribe burn slash to increase the yield of nutritious forage, reduce fuel load, and open cones of lodgepole pine, but leave some slash piles for wildlife cover (see Dead Wood in Chapter 2). Also be sure to leave a reserve of trees and shrubs around fawning areas, mineral licks, aquatic areas, and other sensitive areas (see Fig. 3.3).

If your wooded area is too small to support clearcuts, use group selection cuts (see Chapter 2) or shelterwood cuts (see Southern Pines in this chapter).

**Conifer Plantations**

Plantations are bad news for wildlife, for the monoculture of a single tree species, closed canopy, self-pruning lack of vertical structure, no ground or shrub layers, and acidic soils produce a sterile environment. Still, if you must have a tree plantation for economic reasons, there are ways and means to enhance that environment for wildlife.

Various wildlife species make heavy use of young conifer plantations in summer because ground vegetation is still present for forage and insects and the trees are large enough for cover even for deer. After that stage, the canopy closes, ground and shrub layers disappear, and wildlife use declines drastically.

Let's start with planting. If site preparation is needed, roller chopping and burning is cheapest and best for wildlife. If Christmas trees are not an objective, plant the trees on a 10-foot or 12-foot spacing rather than a 6-foot spacing. This allows longer retention of lower branches and herbaceous cover. A spacing of 20 by 20 feet is much better for wildlife. A reasonable compromise between wildlife and timber production would be a spacing of 8 by 10 feet.

Visual diversity within the plantation can be improved by planting at different time intervals (Fig. 3.7) or planting a mixture of species. You might need to contact a tree nursery about using tree shelters to protect seedlings.

**Figure 3.7** *A planted stand with vertical structure established by planting groups of trees at time intervals. (Adapted from Hunter 1990)*

You can design block plantings in a checkerboard pattern of at least 2 species, each block having 4 or more rows of 4 trees each (Fig. 3.8). Or, you can plant blocks of each tree species in rows (Fig. 3.9) or in an aligned or staggered fashion (Fig. 3.10 and 3.11).

**Figure 3.8** *Checkerboard planting. (Perkins undated, Ohlsson et al. 1982)*

**Figure 3.9** *Row group planting. (Perkins undated, Ohlsson et al. 1982)*

**Figure 3.10** *Aligned row planting (top) and interplanting (bottom). (Perkins undated, Ohlsson et al. 1982)*

**Figure 3.11** *Staggered row planting. (Perkins undated, Ohlsson et al. 1982)*

If you are thinking about using a field or newly clearcut area of 40 acres or so for trees, you might want to plant about 30 acres of it and leave the rest to natural forest regeneration. If the opened area is smaller, say about 10 acres, you could plant it as in Figs. 3.12 and 3.13, or as in Fig. 3.14 if larger than 10 acres. You could plant long, narrow openings as in Fig. 3.15.

You can reduce wind chill and snow depth in a pine plantation by planting several rows of spruce around the perimeter. Retain hardwood thickets of aspen, cherry, hawthorne, and the like within plantations, as well as clumps of berry-producing shrubs like raspberry, salmonberry, and elderberry.

You should thin your plantation when the branches of adjacent trees touch

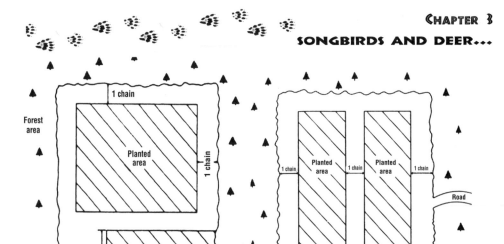

**Figure 3.12.** *Possible pattern for planting a 10-acre forest opening next to a road. (Rutske 1969)*

**Figure 3.13.** *Possible pattern for planting a 10-acre forest opening not next to a road. (Rutske 1969)*

or start to overlap. Thin in a fashion that opens the canopy and destroys the row effect. Sometimes, depending on tree species and site index (growth rate), a precommercial and a commercial thinning are necessary. For wildlife production, you should thin early enough to maintain a vigorous understory. Commercial thinning is delayed until the plantation is in the pole size and sawlog size, and benefits wildlife while improving growth of remaining trees. During commercial thinning, undesirable trees are culled. But do not remove all the dying trees, for wildlife needs some of them as snags and ultimately logs (see Dead Wood in Chapter 2).

Use the herringbone and chevron patterns of thinning rather than the line pattern (Fig. 3.16) to remove fewer rows (spines) of trees and leave short

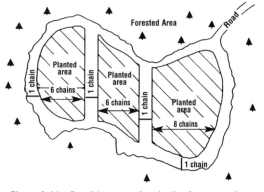

**Figure 3.14.** *Possible pattern for planting forest openings larger than 10 acres. (Rutske 1969)*

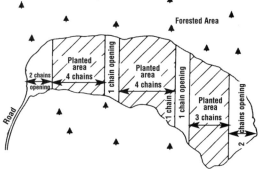

**Figure 3.15.** *Possible pattern for planting long, narrow forest openings with conifers. (Rutske 1969)*

**45**

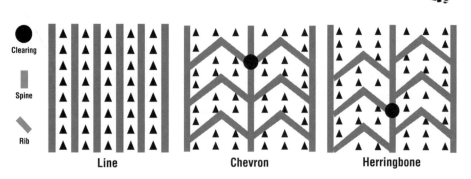

● Clearing

▮ Spine

◢ Rib

**Line**  **Chevron**  **Herringbone**

**Figure 3.16.** *With the herringbone and chevron patterns of tree thinning in conifer plantations, small clearings are formed at the juncture of each rib and spine.  (Anderson 1989)*

side rows (ribs) attached to each spine in the plantation. The juncture of each spine and rib forms an opening that is enlarged when corner trees are removed, thus benefiting wildlife as new plants colonize the small openings.

Do not prune the trees. That reduces vertical structure, especially for perching, nesting, and cover in the reduced ground and shrub layers. Instead, restrict pruning to selected crop trees within the stand so that some structure remains.

Pine plantations and often other conifer plantations tend to be harvested for pulpwood. Clearcutting often is the harvest method used, but a 2-cut shelterwood system is better for owners of small woodlots (see Southern Pines in this chapter).

Turkey vulture

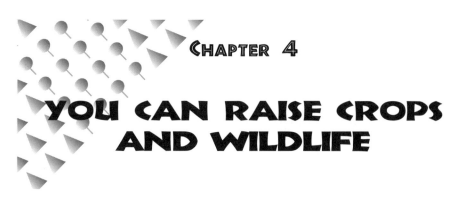

# CHAPTER 4

# YOU CAN RAISE CROPS AND WILDLIFE

It is a compromise, though. The cropland itself is a simple monoculture of a field full of a single plant species, which ultimately is harvested. Such a simplistic "ecosystem" is lousy wildlife habitat. But there are things you can do to improve it and also the adjoining habitats not harvested, such as fence rows.

Formerly, small family farms contained diverse crops and crop rotation interspersed with hedgerows, odd areas, and other wild areas. Since then, much habitat loss has resulted from "clean farming": fence row to fence row farming, clean fence rows, row crops instead of cover crops, etc. Plus, farms have gotten larger, with larger fields and fewer fence rows especially in flat areas. All of that has reduced wildlife habitat diversity; hence wildlife population diversity and density have been reduced too.

## Fertilizers and Pesticides

Use fertilizers only when soil nutrients are low. That means doing a periodic check of your soil by giving your county agent a small sample of it for laboratory analysis. Then the county agent can advise you if you should fertilize, and what kind and how much to apply.

If you are trying to establish perennial grasses in dryland situations, or a grass/legume mixture, do not use nitrate fertilizers. Because fertilizer can cause non-point pollution, do not use fertilizer near streams, lakes, wetlands, and riparian areas, and never use excess fertilizer anywhere. For habitat management, use fertilizers in non-cultivated areas of your farm, such as pastures, odd areas, and field borders.

Use of pesticides is touchy business (see Herbicide in Chapter 7). Unlike fertilizers, pesticides can kill wildlife, alter its reproductive and other behavior, or have deleterious effects on wildlife by screwing up its ecosystem. Furthermore, insecticides will kill your honeybees and those of your neighbors, and herbicides and insecticides will contaminate the honey, all of which is a major financial concern for folks producing honey from apiaries. So you really must be careful. Generally, herbicides are less toxic than insecticides, but guarded use of any pesticide is still needed. The hazard of a pesticide can result from its toxicity, application rate, time of application, type of formulation and spray mixture, persistence in the environment, environmental conditions, and bio-concentration in food chains.

So—if you want to use pesticides, here are some dos and don'ts:

1. Use pesticides only where needed and where benefits outweigh potential hazards.
2. Treat the smallest area possible.
3. Apply herbicides only when potential hazards to wildlife are lowest.
4. Avoid using chemicals during the nesting season (April-July).
5. Avoid treatments near wildlife concentration areas (e.g., goose feeding sites).
6. Avoid treatments during presence of wildlife (migration periods and concentrations).
7. Avoid treatments near riparian areas and in specific habitats (e.g., birds nesting in alfalfa).
8. Avoid treating non-tilled weedy areas (field borders, fence rows, ditches, odd areas). On farms these areas usually receive top wildlife use.
9. Avoid using highly toxic insecticides in center-pivot irrigation systems due to drift potential and lack of control of application rates.
10. Identify the problem weeds.
11. Use the safest herbicide registered, and buy only from reputable dealers.
12. Use biodegradable, short-lived pesticides, if possible.
13. Apply uniformly only at recommended rates, and mix only as much chemical as needed.
14. Use water-based sprays rather than oil solutions or water-oil emulsions.
15. Follow directions on the label.
16. Avoid drift by avoiding windy days and setting sprayer for coarse spray.
17. Choose the proper application equipment, clothing, and respirator, with trained personnel, certified and licensed, if required.
18. Avoid prolonged breathing of vapors or contact with eyes, skin, or clothing.
19. Clean application equipment; wash and change clothes.
20. Post signs in treated areas and notify residents ahead of time, as some might be allergic to pesticides.

If your soil is porous (sandy), pesticides will percolate through faster and possibly contaminate the groundwater, which fills your, and your neighbors', wells. If your soil is not porous and contains too much clay, silt, or organic matter, pesticides might be retained too long.

Use of pesticides is tricky business. Do not use them unless you absolutely have to, and then be extremely cautious and intelligent about it.

## Conservation Tillage

More and more farmers are switching to conservation tillage, sometimes called crop residue management, which leaves protective amounts of residue on the soil surface to reduce wind and water erosion. Conservation tillage can range from **reduced-till**, which leaves about 20 percent of the previous year's crop residue, to **no-till**, which leaves about 90 percent of the previous year's crop residue on the soil surface. Variants include **ridge-till**, in which a ridge is cultivated along each row and seeds are planted on the ridge the next year, and **mulch tillage**, in which other implements are used between harvest and planting. **Fallowing** means leaving stubble, especially of wheat, standing overwinter, which also reduces wind and water erosion. To reduce nest and brood destruction in fallowed fields, weeds should be controlled with an undercutter plow without a mulch treader.

Because conservation tillage results in fewer passes across the field by farm machinery, nest destruction is reduced. And the remaining residue provides cover and food to wildlife. Studies show greater wildlife use of fields under conservation tillage than conventional tillage, including production of ducks, pheasants, and grassland songbirds. But any cultivation of stubble usually is done around May when nest destruction would be highest. Such field management might cause a higher than usual hit on wildlife, and thus result in an ecological trap. If conservation tillage attracts nesting birds from other fields, and then you come along and plow the hell out of the field, you will cause higher-than-normal nest destruction because you sucked the birds into your field with your conservation tillage in the first place and then destroyed their nests in the spring with your plowing. Many birds will re-nest, but subsequent clutches always are smaller. Neither will this technique increase your wildlife production if you use more chemicals for weed and insect control to compensate for reduced tillage, or if your conservation tillage creates incentive for you to cultivate previously unplowed areas, which are far more productive habitat than conservation-tilled fields.

## Crop Rotation

A system of crop rotation that controls weeds with minimum tillage and also conserves soil moisture is called **eco-fallow**, for example, a 3-year rotation of wheat in year 1, a row crop (e.g., sorghum) in year 2, and fallow in year 3 where corn or grain sorghum is planted directly into herbicide-treated stubble. Some nest losses might occur, but re-nests will not be jeopardized by farming operations. By rotating sharecropping and prescribed burning among fields on a 6-year schedule, various states of succession are maintained in the various fields (Fig. 4.1). Such habitat variety is attractive to various species of wildlife associated with different developmental stages of fields.

Your crop rotations probably will include corn, small grains, and legumes like soybeans, clover, and alfalfa. Small grains and alfalfa can reduce soil erosion a lot. Moreover, alfalfa and other legumes in the rotation can save you fertilizer costs because they replace nitrogen to the soil that corn and other grains use up. Rotations also reduce your use of pesticides by naturally breaking the cycle

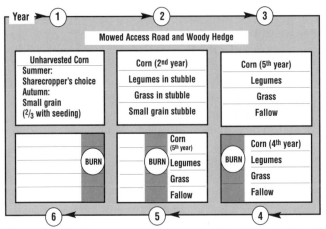

**Figure 4.1.** *Habitat management for terrestrial wildlife in Illinois. Developmental stages of succession are maintained by rotating sharecropping activity and prescribed burning among fields on a 6-year schedule. Note the great diversity of habitat resulting when 6 contiguous fields are in the rotation. (Bailey 1984)*

of insects, diseases, and weeds.

## Crop Diversity

You can enhance your habitat for wildlife, and thus your wildlife populations, by small field size (3-12 acres), high crop diversity (more than 4 crops), good interspersion of them for high contrast of vertical structure between them (i.e., a field of low crops next to a field of tall crops), and by leaving about 25 percent of the whole farm in non-cultivated permanent cover (Fig. 4.2). For pheasants and associated wildlife, for example, farmland habitat plans can be simple with large fields (Fig. 4.3), or complex (Fig. 4.4). Cover crops vary in value to wildlife (Table 4.1).

If you farm your area intensively with row crops, you should use grass meadows and fields of small grains to improve habitat, by interspersing them between, and rotating them with, your row crops. If you can, use legumes such as beans, peas, and alfalfa in your crop rotation to enhance soil nutrients and wildlife. That arrangement can reduce your income somewhat, but your satisfaction with your land management will increase as the benefits to wildlife and its response to your land management

| Table 4.1. Value of native habitats and crops for food and cover requirements of pheasants. (Guthery et al. 1984) | | | | |
|---|---|---|---|---|
| Cover type | Food | Nesting | Brooding | Wintering |
| Playa | Fair | Excellent | Excellent | Excellent |
| Roadsides | Fair | Excellent | Excellent | Poor |
| Weedy tailwater pits | Fair | Good | Good | Fair |
| Weedy equipment parking areas | Fair | Good | Good | Fair |
| Corn | Excellent | Poor | Fair | Fair* |
| Grain sorghum | Excellent | Poor | Fair | Excellent |
| Forage sorghum | Fair | Poor | Excellent | Poor |
| Wheat | Good | Excellent | Good | Poor |
| Cotton | Poor | Poor | Fair | Poor |
| Soybeans | Good | Poor | Fair | Poor |
| Sugar beets | Poor | Poor | Good | Poor |
| Alfalfa | Fair | Good | Good | Poor |
| Vegetables | Fair | Poor | Fair | Poor |
| Rangeland | Poor | Fair | Poor | Poor |
| *Corn is poor winter cover if all stubble is removed. | | | | |

increase. You might explore government incentives, such as reduced property tax or CRP (Conservation Reserve Program), or remuneration from hunting clubs for exclusive hunting rights (see Chapters 11 and 12). If you do not use small grains and grass meadows in your row-crop rotation, you will force broods of birds to range over an area 3 times larger than otherwise, exposing them to much higher mortality.

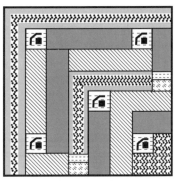

**Figure 4.2.** *A design to modify a quarter-section of northeastern Colorado tablelands for pheasants and other wildlife using chemical fallow and minimum tillage of wheat to increase nesting cover. (Rutherford and Snyder 1983)*

**Figure 4.3.** *A simplified habitat management plan for wildlife next to a playa lake. Fields should be at least 100 acres. Upland plants are left or planted around the playa basin. (Guthery et al. 1984)*

### Organic Farming

Organic farming has pros and cons. If done properly, it can improve compatibility between crop and livestock production and wildlife production. Organic farmers avoid fertilizers and pesticides, usually use less inversion tillage (complete plowing), use greater crop diversity and more crop rotation (especially legumes like peas or beans which add nitrogen to the soil), use small grains and meadows more extensively, and include livestock as an integral component of the field operation. Studies generally show increased wildlife production with organic farming, usually due to the increased diversity of crops and increased areas of cover, brooding, and feeding sites. But you can have deleterious effects on wildlife if your organic farm operation involves more frequent cultivation for weed control than conventional farming uses, with inopportune mowing; then you would have an ecological trap as described for conservation tillage.

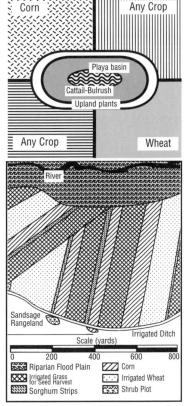

**Figure 4.4.** *A hypothetical arrangement of irrigated land along a river bottom managed with primary emphasis on pheasants and other nesting birds. (Rutherford and Snyder 1983)*

### Fall Plowing and Winter Cover Crops

You want more wildlife on your land? Do not plow in the fall. I know it speeds up the drying of your land and reduces plowing during spring. But it sure is bad news for wildlife and increases soil erosion from wind and water. On a windy day your fine topsoil will form into a dust cloud and blow into the next county—an obvious sign of mismanagement. And imagine what a 40-acre field plowed bare of vegetation must look like to a pheasant in winter. It is a huge barren frozen wasteland! If you must plow in the fall, plow only some of the field, and leave some unplowed borders or strips for spring tillage. Also, remember that the right-of-way for most 2-lane roads is 66 feet, i.e., 33 feet to each side of the centerline. Do not cultivate any of that in the road shoulder like some folks do illegally. That's public land; leave it alone for wildlife. Remember, you must compromise if you want more wildlife on your land.

Use winter cover crops, such as winter wheat, wherever the harvesting of crops leaves relatively bare soil. Canada geese and other species of wildlife love that stuff as food and cover, if it is tall enough. In spring, plow it under as soon as you can work the land, to reduce possible depletion of water for the grain crop and to add green manure to the soil.

### Contour Farming and Strip Cropping

If you have a lot of hills on your farm, you will want to plant your crops on the contour of those hills, and use strip cropping by alternating a strip of row crops with a strip of hay or small grains. That will prevent your topsoil from eroding down the hill, and provide some habitat diversity for wildlife. The strips of row crops and grain or hay should be about the same width. You will need several strips on long, moderately steep slopes.

### Grass Waterway, Grade Stabilization Structure, and Water Control Basin

You might have hilly enough land whereby water tends to drain along a certain pattern. That is a natural drainage way. To prevent erosion and provide cover for small animals, grade and shape the drainage way to form a smooth, shallow channel, and then plant it immediately to sod-forming grasses. The vegetation also can absorb some chemicals and nutrients in the runoff water.

If the drainage way is too steep, you might need a grade stabilization structure (small dam/retention wall) at the bottom to prevent a gully from forming. Or instead, you might build a small earthen embankment at the bottom of the drainage way to store runoff temporarily in a water and sediment control basin (see Chapter 8). The basin releases water slowly, usually through infiltration or a pipe outlet and tile line. This system can provide habitat including a water source for wildlife. See your NRCS (Natural Resources Conservation Service) representative for advice.

### Shoreline Stabilization

If you have a stream bank or lakeshore that is eroding for whatever reason (e.g., fishing, grazing, etc.), stop that reason first. Then reshape the shoreline,

#  YOU CAN RAISE CROPS AND WILDLIFE

maybe replace the topsoil, and seed it, or maybe protect it with rock riprap, or seed it with bioengineering materials. But rock riprap eliminates habitat and is expensive, overused, unsightly, and easy to install incorrectly. Just offshore, use wave-breaking devices protruding a few inches above the normal water level: coconut-fiber logs (coir), jute, bundled hardwood brush, rock within filter fabric, plywood, or double layers of plastic fence. Stake everything in place. The coir mats also can be installed directly against the shoreline. Plant seedlings within the fibers and behind the breakers. Watch them grow as the fiber decomposes. Coir products vary in thickness, and come in mats, carpets, pallets, and blankets from 3 to 7 feet wide and up to 160 feet long. In some states and provinces, you must obtain a permit from the state or provincial wildlife agency to use wave-breaking devices below the ordinary high-water mark in public waters.

Above the shoreline, flatten the slope to 2:1 (horizontal:vertical) or flatter, if practical. You might need a state/provincial or local permit. Use a grader or hand tools, depending on the size of the job. Keep soil out of the water with a silt fence or floating silt curtain. Seed. Then stake coir, jute, or wood-fiber blankets over the soil until plants establish. Or plant seedlings through openings in the fabric. You can use mulch, such as straw, to reduce erosion and increase moisture and insulation for young plants. You can spray "tackifiers" over it to "glue" it to the ground.

You also can use bundles of live branches, called wattles, up and down the bank to reduce erosion. During dormancy in late fall or early spring, cut live branches less than 1.5 inches in diameter of willow, alder, dogwood, elderberry, meadowsweet, arrowwood, nannyberry, etc., and tie them at each end and middle into bundles 6 to 8 feet long and 6 to 8 inches in diameter. Stake the bundles into trenches 6 to 8 inches deep 3 to 4 feet apart horizontally, and cover almost completely with soil.

You also can place layers of brush, 1 to 2 inches thick, 3 to 4 feet long, 20 inches almost horizontally into the soil of a 2:1 bank, spaced 3 to 5 feet apart vertically, perhaps interspersed with jute or coir fabric. Cover the branches with soil, leaving the tips protruding, and they will sprout to hold soil in place and intercept water.

Another method to stabilize a shoreline is by installing live willow posts. Use a power auger to drill holes about 2 feet below the low-water level of a flat shoreline, and at 4-foot intervals. Place willow 2 to 4 inches thick and 6 to 10 feet long into the holes, cover the holes with soil, and watch the willow sprout. Willow posts also can be used as stakes for erosion-control fabrics.

You might have to fit a special wood structure, called a lunker, into the bank to stabilize it, which also provides fish habitat. Stabilizing the shoreline protects water quality, improves fish habitat, and provides habitat for small animals. You will probably have to fence livestock out of the newly stabilized area (see Chapter 9).

If the bare bank seems natural, be careful about aggressively doing something about it. The U.S. Forest Service and some state conservation agencies have found that their aggressive erosion control efforts have eliminated mud banks essential for nesting by wood turtles. In other words, some natural disturbance of shorelines is desirable for some species of wildlife.

## Food Plots

You should not substitute food plots for other better methods of habitat management. But food can be a limiting factor for some wildlife populations, especially in winter. If other habitat requirements are met, plantings of nutritious foods can supplement inadequate natural supplies, increase wildlife populations by improving wildlife health and productivity and reducing mortality, increase distribution, and increase viewing opportunities. Disadvantages include concentrating wildlife, which increases the potential for predation and disease transmission, attracting pests such as blackbirds and feral hogs, and expense.

Fruits, leaves, acorns, other nuts and seeds, insects, and other prey animals provide plenty of food for wildlife in late spring, summer, and fall. Various annual weeds and grasses such as ragweed, smartweed, foxtail, thistle, and sunflower are important. In late fall and before the snow falls, untilled fields provide food for critters such as quail, pheasants, doves, squirrels, rabbits, mice, and deer. Fields of hay and clover provide food and cover. But under a layer of snow, such habitat disappears for all except mice. Mice? Sure. Think through the food chain. Mice attract various predators for viewing: hawks, owls, fox, coyote, skunk, weasel, raccoon, and snakes.

If natural food becomes exhausted, wildlife will use the food plots to put on body fat which can sustain animals for days or even weeks without food, thus pulling them through a tough time. Without it, a tough winter can cause hypothermia or death from exposure, or else the animal will enter the spring breeding season in poor shape. For species like quail, wild turkey, and pheasant, stressed hens will lay smaller clutches and delay nesting so that a second clutch will not be laid if the first nest is destroyed. Also, such stressed hens are more likely to die from the normal summer stresses of heat, disease, and even molting, thus reducing survival rates of their dependent chicks too.

Instead of going to the additional effort and expense to establish a food plot, you could convert odd areas or abandoned cropland to food plots, or simply reserve areas already cultivated, such as field borders or corners, as food plots. You also could plant foods between riparian areas and woody plantings (Fig. 4.5). Place your food plots near some sort of shelter so they will not completely drift over with snow. Look for places next to permanent cover such as windbreaks, woodlots, clumps of trees and shrubs, or marsh.

Food plots should be rectangular to linear in shape, about 0.5 to 5 acres for game birds and songbirds, and about 10 to 20 acres for deer. For quail, you need about 1 food plot for every 80 acres of your farm, spaced no further than 1,200 feet apart; for pheasants, make it 1 plot every 150 acres, spaced no

# YOU CAN RAISE CROPS AND WILDLIFE

more than 1,500 feet apart; for deer, make it 1 plot every 600 acres. Use these guidelines for other wildlife.

Cereal grains, grain sorghum, and legumes are the plants most useful for wildlife (Tables 4.2, 4.3). Grain sorghum is better than corn because sorghum grows better without irrigation, its seed is smaller (better for small birds), most granivorous birds like it, and its energy content is similar to that of corn. Deer and larger birds such as turkeys and pheasants prefer corn. Prepare the seedbed, fertilize, and plant just as you would for any other crop.

Sometimes it takes 3 or more years to attract wildlife to your food plot or to develop a new flock or a new feeding tradition. So do not be impatient if results are skimpy at first. Your local soil office, wildlife manager, or Pheasants Forever chapter (or the like) can help.

## Linear Habitat

Winter is deadly business for wildlife. Inadequate cover or inadequate food then is a killer, for winter is merciless. Most of the annual mortality to a wildlife population occurs over winter. You have various means at your disposal for thwarting or modifying winter effects.

If you fly over your farm in a Cessna airplane, or just look at an air photo, you will see that your land and your neighbor's land are laid out like a patchwork quilt of cropland, pastures, woodlots,

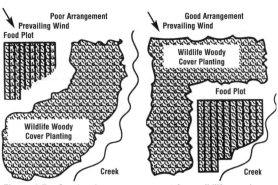

**Figure 4.5.** *Good and poor arrangement for a wildlife woody cover planting and food plot. (Henderson 1987)*

**Table 4.2. Principal plants for wildlife food plots. (Payne and Bryant 1998)**

| Upland wildlife species | Plants for food plots |
|---|---|
| Granivorous songbirds | Sunflower |
| | Sorghum |
| | Millet |
| Mourning dove | Millet |
| | Grain sorghum |
| | Sunflower |
| Bobwhite quail | Grain sorghum |
| | Corn |
| | Sunflower |
| Pheasant | Corn |
| | Grain sorghum |
| | Alfalfa |
| | Soybeans |
| Cottontail rabbit | Legumes (alfalfa, clovers, sweet clover, wheat/barley, vetch); Grass (bluegrass, wheat-grass, timothy); Annual grains (wheat, rye, triticale) |
| Deer and Turkey | Legumes (alfalfa, clovers, sweet clovers, vetch, peas, cow peas); Grain sorghum; Annual grains (wheat, oats, triticale) |

Note: Local soils, precipitation, temperature extremes, and elevation influence success of plants.

Table 4.3. Some considerations in selecting grain for use in food and food/cover plantings. (Rutherford and Snyder 1983)

| Grain type | Species or variety | Site preferences and applications | Planting recommendations | Value to wildlife | Problems and limitations | Comments and treatments |
|---|---|---|---|---|---|---|
| Sorghum | Grain sorghum | Does best in sandy loams with at least 15 in. annual precipitation. Summer fallow or irrigation preferred. | Disk and maybe use a pesticide about May 1. Plant around June 1 in rows 24-36 in. wide at 2-4 lb./ac. Combine with forage sorghums in most sites at 1/3 normal rate. | Food and limited feeding cover. Attains 2-3 ft. height in dryland sites. | Lodges under high winds and wet snow. Blackbirds consume in some locations. | Select early-maturing, lodge-resistant, dark-seeded varieties. Don't drill in less than 20-in. rows. Can be used in combination with forage sorghums, millets, and corn. Summer fallowing recommended on dry-land sites. |
| Tall sorghums | Forage sorghum (canes), Sudan grasses, hybrids of above, broomcorn | Same as above. | Same as above. Combine with grain sorghums. Sudan seed should be planted at 15-20 lb./ac. Plant at 2/3 normal rate when combining with milo. | Serves mainly as protective overstory for feeding and as tall feeding cover during heavy snows. | Might get too tall under irrigation to allow hunter use. Lodges at 1-3 ft. height under heavy snow. Sudan is fine-stemmed and shorter. Food value often marginal. | Select early-maturing, lodge-resistant, dark-seeded varieties. Use hybrid forage sorghums or sorghum-Sudan crosses on most sites. The grain-forage mixture is highly recommended for plains upland gamebird use. Use a summer-fallow/planted/idle-3-yr. rotation on dryland sites. |
| Cereal grains (winter annuals) | Rye | Adapted to use on sandy, poor soils with at least 15 in. annual precipitation. | Summer-fallow and drill in rows 10-14 in. wide at about 30 lb./ac. in Sept. | Late fall/winter green food. Seed not preferred. Limited late spring nesting attains 2.5-3.5 ft. height. | Provides little over-winter cover 1st yr. Subject to ergot (poisonous fungus) in seed heads. Lodges under heavy snow with limited winter cover value. Volunteers back readily. | Use sweep tillage to undercut in late summer after it matures to promote volunteer regrowth if not already present. Leave 2nd year for winter food/cover and nesting/brood use. |
| | Wheat (winter) | Better loam soils with minimum 15 in. annual precipitation. | Same as above. Seed at 30-40 lb./ac. | Late fall/winter green food. High protein seed. Provides marginal late spring nesting with 2-3 ft. height. | No winter cover 1st year. Lodges with limited cover value. | Same as above. Heads can be clipped after maturity to increase lodge resistance. Does not volunteer as readily as rye so sweep tillage undercutting might be necessary most years. |
| | Triticale (wheat-rye hybrid) | Same as for rye and wheat. | Same as for wheat. | Excellent green fall growth for winter greens. Better quality seed than rye but attains taller growth than rye. (Mainly for pheasants and grouse.) | Same as for wheat and rye. Not subject to ergot. | Recommended as a replacement for rye on poorer soils. Treat like rye or wheat, allowing to stand over a 2nd winter or longer if volunteering can be retained. |
| | Winter barley | Same as for wheat but adapted to high-alkaline sites. | Same as for wheat and rye. Seed at 50-80 lb./ac. | Same as above but seed not as highly preferred as wheat. | Same as for wheat. | Same as for wheat. |
| Cereal grains (spring annuals) | Spring wheat, spring oats, spring barley | Plant on loamy to sandy soils receiving 15 in. annual precipitation or more and use barley in high-alkaline soils. | Plant in early to mid-April in plains region in 10- to 14-inch-wide drill rows. | Limited midsummer nesting and brood cover. Fall/winter food and limited feeding cover. | Will not stand up under heavy snows to provide protective feeding cover. | Use sweep tillage, undercutting in subsequent springs to attain volunteer regrowth with minimum tillage while retaining residual for nesting/brood cover. |
| Millets | Proso | Sandy loams to loams in sites receiving 12 in. or more annual precipitation. | Plant June 1-30 in rows 20-24 in. wide at 12-20 lb./ac. Maybe use a herbicide about 1 month before planting. | Late summer dove food. Waterfowl food when flooded or planted next to water. | No cover value of its own and not recommended for upland game birds other than doves, except when added to sorghum mixtures. Flattened and buried under winter snows. | Plant small amounts in combination with grain sorghum and forage sorghum for late summer/early fall and spring consumption. |
| | Foxtail (German) | Same as above. | Same as above. | Same as above. | Produces more forage but less and smaller seed than Proso (Proso recommended). | Can be broadcast in disturbance tillage strips to supplement naturally occurring annuals. |
| | Japanese | Sandy wet sites. | Plant in late May or early June. | Mainly for waterfowl in wet sites or sites to be flooded. Limited use by doves and quail. | Same as for Proso. | Irrigate or temporarily flood to germinate and keep soil wet, if possible. Almost like barnyard grass. |

# YOU CAN RAISE CROPS AND WILDLIFE

**Table 4.3.** *(Continued)*

| Grain type | Species or variety | Site preferences and applications | Planting recommendations | Value to wildlife | Problems and limitations | Comments and treatments |
|---|---|---|---|---|---|---|
| Buckwheat | Tame buckwheat | Variable sandy to loam with 15 in. annual precipitation. Irrigation preferred. | Plant June 1-15 at 36-50 lb./ac. | Same as for millets, especially Japanese. Mainly for waterfowl. | Same as for millets. Seed doesn't persist. | Can be used to supplement forbs in disturbance-tillage sites in rangelands and riparian zones. |
| Sunflower | Numerous varieties available | Better loam soils with at least 15 in. annual precipitation. Irrigation preferred. | Plant in rows 24-42 in. wide in May or early June. | Large nutritious seeds. | Stands are too open to provide feeding protection in fall and winter. Seeds devastated by blackbirds and other passerines. Requires 1 or more post- planting cultivations. Insect problems common. | Not recommended for seeding except in mixtures with corn, sorghums, or spring grains. Prevents use of herbicides in corn, sorghums, and millets, so use opportunities limited. |
| Safflower | | Same as for sunflower. | Same as for sunflower. Broadcast at 25 lb./ac. | Seeds and limited cover. | Has not been evaluated in Colorado. | Possibly could be seeded in combination with sunflower, buckwheat, and field peas, but evaluations needed. |
| Legumes | Field peas | Loam soils with 15 in. or more annual precipitation; irrigation preferred. | Plant in combination with spring cereal grains or sunflowers. Seed at up to 60 lb./ac. Use either with drilled grains or row crops. | Mainly in flooded sites for waterfowl. No cover value in fall or winter. | Value restricted to doves and waterfowl when planted alone. Must be planted in combination with other vegetation for use by quail, pheasants, and grouse. | |
| | Hairy vetch | Better sandhill sites with 15 in. or more annual precipitation. | Seed in 14- to 24- in. rows in early May at 40-45 lb./ac. Plant in combination with sweet clover. | Provides fall/winter greens and seeds for prairie grouse and cottontails. | No important cover value other than for nesting and broods. | Biennial but tends to reseed readily, especially if shallow tillage is applied every few years. Can be seeded in combination with sweet clover, small grains (spring annuals), or sunflowers and safflowers. |

and wetlands. If these are isolated from each other, they have reduced value for wildlife because wildlife will be isolated in a particular habitat type. For example, species such as bobwhite quail and rabbits will not venture far from their main cover type to feed, loaf, or nest. Thus, other suitable cover on the other side of a plowed field will go unused by such animals because they will not walk or fly across the open field. You can connect such isolated habitats (woodlots are a good example too) with corridors of linear habitat such as field borders, fence rows, hedgerows, windbreaks, and riparian strips (see Fig.1.1 and see Corridors in Chapter 2).

## Field Borders

An abrupt edge between field and woods is not as good for wildlife habitat as a gradual transition between the two (see Fig. 2.4). You can encourage such a feathered edge by letting nature alone or by speeding it up with planting or removing some trees and shrubs. (See Woodlot Borders and Other Brushy Areas in Chapter 2.)

One of the simplest ways to provide herbaceous food and cover is to run a fence diagonally across the corner of a pasture to keep out the cows. You also can plant a suitable grass/legume mixture in a strip at least 5 yards wide along the edge of some crop fields. You also can plant these field borders with (1) native warm-season grasses such as big bluestem, little bluestem, Indian grass, switch grass, and blue-joint grass, or (2) cool-season grasses and legumes such as smooth brome grass, timothy, tall wheat-grass, intermediate wheat-grass, and alfalfa. You should mow this border 8 inches high in late summer the first year; then mow half of it every 2 to 4 years in late summer. Late summer means between August 1, and September 1, i.e., after virtually all nesting is completed and still in time to allow enough growth of grasses and forbs used as residual vegetation by early nesters the following spring. Field borders of alfalfa benefit some grassland birds and game birds. The wider your border is, the less nest predation will occur. Your wildlife will benefit with increased food and cover if you leave or plant 2 to 5 rows or a strip 3 to 10 yards wide of unharvested grain crops next to fence rows and wooded areas. But doing so is unpopular with many farmers.

Sometimes the only thing you have to do is let a 30-foot wide strip of field next to your woods revegetate. Just leave it alone and watch the grasses and "weeds" develop. Weeds? Not to wildlife. For instance, monarch butterflies need milkweed, bobwhites relish poison ivy berries and ragweed seed, goldfinches like bull thistle seeds, chickadees eat the insect larvae in the swollen stems of goldenrod, bobolinks and meadowlarks nest in the weedy cover, and so forth. These "weeds" actually are forbs, i.e., broad-leafed herbaceous plants. But 30 feet of it? That's not much, especially when you consider that crops planted within 20 feet or so of a woods often grow poorly anyway because adjacent trees root out—competing for moisture.

You can speed up the succession of this strip by planting trees and shrubs if you have the time and money. Initially, you might have to protect these saplings from hungry deer and rabbits by encircling the saplings with hardware cloth or plastic tree guards. Any shrubs or small trees will do if they will provide browse, insects, nuts and other seeds, and berries and other fruit, such as hazelnut, black cherry, choke cherry, pin cherry, wild plum, apple, crabapple, dogwood, Juneberry (serviceberry), nannyberry, high-bush cranberry, ninebark, elderberry, raspberry, salmonberry, huckleberry, blueberry, etc.

## Fence Rows and Hedgerows

In some areas of the country, so-called "clean" farming has reduced the last traces of wildlife habitat to what is left in fence rows. Even these offer nothing if completely cleaned. Farmers need to recognize the extensive use wildlife makes of fence rows. For example, studies in Iowa show 12 bird species use herbaceous fence rows, 38 use fence rows with scattered trees and shrubs, and 48 bird species use fence rows with continuous trees and shrubs! Farmers should preserve, maintain, and restore their fence rows. Remember that you are interested in producing more wildlife on your land, perhaps while farming it. So compromise a bit.

Your fence rows should be at least 10 feet wide, and developed so that you create mosaics through mowing and woodcutting, and retain or create

CHAPTER 4

# YOU CAN RAISE CROPS AND WILDLIFE

occasional snags at least 18 inches wide and 30 feet tall, although even smaller snags are heavily used. Maintain the logs and dead branches too. The branches are especially useful if piled up, with the big branches on the bottom. To encourage shrubs, especially raspberry, and protect the dead wood in the fence row, do not burn it or graze it. Shrubs will develop naturally from seeds in droppings from birds perching on the fence or in the trees.

If you really want a lot of wildlife, devote more of your land to it. Make your fence rows 25 to 50 feet wide, and plant the area on each side of the fence with wildlife trees and shrubs and mixed native grasses. Diversify by leaving occasional gaps in the tree and shrub plantings, and then plant vines and place brush piles in the gaps. Put the trees in the middle along the fence, and the shrubs on the outside so that you maximize the fence row as a travel lane for wildlife, along with its other wildlife uses. Space the shrubs at least 3 feet apart, and the larger trees such as evergreens 10 to 12 feet apart.

In some areas, glaciated areas mainly, farmers have to pick stone (rocks) from their fields almost annually, as frost heave brings more rock to the surface. Farmers deposit these rocks along fence rows, along field borders, and in a large pile in the field if the fence row is too far away. Small mammals and reptiles will burrow among these rocks. If you live where you must pick stone, allow trees and shrubs to grow among the rock pile or along its edge to improve habitat for wildlife, especially birds.

Lone trees often exist in large pastures and other fields. Protect these. They are heavily used mainly as resting and observation perches by some birds flying across the area, including hawks looking for mice in your field.

If you protect your fence rows, they will naturally develop into hedgerows. But let's say you want a hedgerow where no fence row exists. All you have to do is plow or disk a 10-foot strip along where you want it. Then stick in some fence posts right down the center of the strip you plowed or disked, not too deep so you can remove them easily later, and then connect them with twine or wire about 3 feet high. The birds will do the rest. They will perch on the line, and the seed in their droppings will take root below. Keep this in mind: for high populations of bobwhite quail and cottontails, you need about 200 yards of woody hedge or fence for every 40 acres of open country.

If you want to speed up the process, plant. Plant food-producing shrubs or a shrub-conifer mix. After site preparation, stick in 2 to 4 shrub stems per hole, with the holes spaced 1 to 2 yards apart, or 1 conifer per hole, the holes spaced 1 to 3 yards apart. Space the shrub rows 2 yards apart and the conifer rows 3 yards apart, so that unbroken cover will result in 8 to 12 years. You will have to thin the conifers at 10 to 15 years. You will get a hedgerow about 7 yards wide with 1 row of shrubs and 2 rows of conifers. You will have to protect it from grazing and fire. Keep your hedgerows about 4.5 feet high.

If you plant shrubs only, you need at least 4 rows 8 yards long spaced 2 yards apart, planted in early spring. To encourage their development, begin weed control the first or second year with herbicides or cultivation, mulching, clipping, and hand weeding.

If you live in hilly or mountainous country, plant your hedgerows on south-facing slopes first, with your second choice being the east- or west-facing slopes. On level ditch banks, the north and west edges are better. If you have slopes over 3 to 4 percent steep, separate your hedgerow from your row crops with a sodded border 2 yards wide. If you can do it, arrange your fields, hedgerows, access roads, and gates in a triangle (Fig. 4.6). If the hedgerow competes with crops for soil moisture, cut the roots of the hedgerow at its field edge with a root pruner. If your hedgerow will cross a stream, space the shrubs somewhat further apart at the stream crossing so that a vigorous grass/forb understory can develop for erosion control.

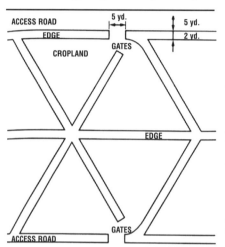

**Figure 4.6.** *Recommended arrangement of hedgerows. (Powers 1979)*

Plant the hedgerow with the food-producing shrubs previously mentioned. If you want spring colors and fragrances, plant crabapples, elderberries, and the like. For fall reds and purples, plant dogwoods, viburnums, sumacs, and the like. To garnish the white and gray of winter, the red bark of red-osier dogwood, neon-red of high-bush cranberry, and the like are attractive. Species of shrubs to plant vary regionally (e.g., Appendix V). See your local wildlife manager for more advice and even to obtain planting stock, or visit a nursery featuring wildlife plants. Every state has such nurseries.

You can revitalize an old hedgerow by cutting back the large overgrown old shrubs in small sections at a time every 5 or 10 years so that wildlife can use the food and cover in the uncut sections while the cut sections recover. You also should cut out undesirable plants such as non-native buckthorn and perhaps prickly ash, and maybe spot-treat with brush killer or other appropriate herbicide. Box elder is a prolific tree, but not a bad wildlife tree unless it comes in too thick and displaces other plants, thus reducing habitat variability. Then, girdle some of the box elders, because the dead trees provide nesting, roosting, and feeding sites for many songbirds.

## Windbreaks

You are cross-country skiing, and the sharp wind is raw against the face.

# YOU CAN RAISE CROPS AND WILDLIFE

**Figure 4.7.** *Cross-section of an effective shelterbelt offering good wildlife cover. Note the abundance of grasses and small shrubs growing near ground level. The arrows indicate prevailing wind direction. (Poston and Schmidt 1981)*

With relief, you realize that you will soon be in the shelter of the belt of trees planted years ago to break the wind. Shortly you get there, and sure enough, the windchill eases. And you are not the only one there for the same reason. You can see a few chickadees hanging around too, and you guess correctly that other wildlife also is using this windbreak for cover, as the cottontail tracks reveal.

Windbreaks, also called shelterbelts, are designed to protect farm buildings from winter winds and snow (Fig. 4.7), and farm fields from wind erosion where the winds can sweep across broad stretches of open field. Such a belt of trees also serves as (1) habitat that attracts wildlife species able to survive in small areas, (2) unique habitat that contrasts with pastures and cropland, and (3) a corridor of habitat linking other types of wooded habitat used by dispersing animals and migrating birds.

Changing land-use patterns have caused a decline in shelterbelts. Many are being removed to accommodate circular irrigation units, and others are allowed to deteriorate, despite their value as wind erosion reducers, snow catchers, and wildlife habitat. Existing shelterbelts should be preserved. Keep reminding yourself that you need to compromise sometimes if you want more wildlife on your land.

There are 2 kinds of windbreaks: the farmstead shelterbelt and the field windbreak. The farmstead shelterbelt is shaped like an "L", with the corner of the "L" aimed at the prevailing wind (Fig. 4.8). Its main purpose is to protect the farmhouse and other buildings from excessive winds that sweep across the extensive fields, especially in winter, and to act as a snow fence to keep deep snow from accumulating around the buildings. Its secondary purpose is to provide habitat for wildlife.

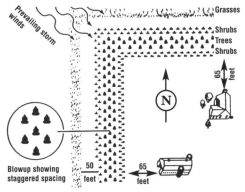

**Figure 4.8.** *Typical shelterbelt layout. (Judd et al. 1998, Henderson 1987)*

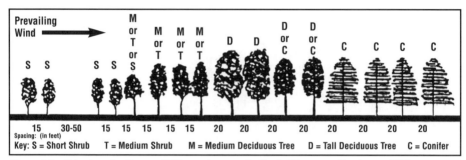

**Figure 4.9.** *Side view of a 16-row wildlife woody cover planting in Minnesota. (Henderson 1987)*

A shelterbelt that you plant near your house and barn will work with just 3 rows of trees. But you can enhance it for ground-dwelling wildlife, and thus wildlife viewing from your house, if you add a few more rows of shrubs and trees.

Windbreaks vary from 1 to 16 rows (Fig. 4.9). In northern regions, you need more rows for thermal protection and to control drifting snow. For example, in Texas and Oklahoma, 2- to 4-row shelterbelts are common; in South Dakota and Minnesota, an 8-row shelterbelt might be needed; in North Dakota and Manitoba, a 16-row shelterbelt might be needed. Regardless of region, the wider the shelterbelt, the better it is for wildlife. By planting a variety of different trees and shrubs, you could use a 10-row shelterbelt or some smaller combination of it for snow accumulation and for wildlife habitat.

A good compromise in size, with wildlife benefits, is a 7-row shelterbelt (Fig. 4.10). Starting at the west and/or north side, plant 2 rows of wildlife shrubs, such as Juneberry, ninebark, dogwood, or 1 of the viburnums. In addition to producing food, these shrubs will trap much of the snow before it reaches the main body of the shelterbelt, which should be about 45 feet away. Not only will the winter cover of the shelterbelt be improved this way, but snow damage to the trees will be reduced.

Now for the trees in the main body of the shelterbelt—plant 3 rows of tall-growing trees, with all 3 rows being evergreens or the middle row being fast-growing leafy trees. Good candidates for the middle row might be box elder, green ash, white pine, and red pine. The 2 outer rows should consist of trees such as white spruce or Norway spruce, which can take the shade and still retain the low branches, which reduces windchill and provides excellent cover in winter and summer for ground-dwelling mammals and birds. Plant the rows about 15 feet apart, and stagger the trees for maximum wind protection and growth (see Fig. 4.8)

Now, about 15 feet on the inside of the last of these 3 rows of tall-growing trees, plant a row of tall-growing shrubs or small trees such as silky dogwood or 1 of the crabapples, about 6 feet apart. Then, about 10 feet inside

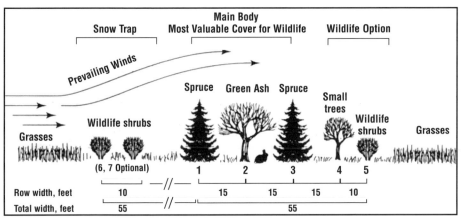

**Figure 4.10.** *Cross section of a 7-row shelterbelt with wildlife values. (Judd et al. 1998, Henderson 1987)*

of this row, plant a row of short shrubs 3 or 4 feet apart.

Finally, on each side of your newly-established shelterbelt, allow seed-bearing forbs to grow, such as giant ragweed, fireweed, and sunflowers, along with tall grasses such as switch grass, big bluestem, Indian grass, and wheat grass. These all provide good winter cover as well as food.

In time, thinning might be needed, but preferably not, if the correct spacing between rows and plants is maintained during planting. The 7-row shelterbelt is certainly better than the typical 3-row farm shelterbelt. But if time or money is a problem, a 5-row design, without the snow trap, is adequate.

Older designs for farmstead shelterbelts had tall hardwood trees in the central rows, with close spacing of the trees and shrubs contributing to excessive drifting of snow into the farmyard and a relatively short lifespan of the shelterbelt. Nowadays, the shelterbelt is built to last at least 100 years and to do a better job in reducing drifting snow. Accordingly, the tallest trees should be in the outside rows and all trees and shrubs should be spaced wider. One of the best farmstead shelterbelts is an arrangement of 10 rows of trees and shrubs (Table 4.4).

Farmstead shelterbelts should be located 65 to 100 feet away from the farm buildings, on the side(s) with the prevailing storm winds (usually west and north) (see Fig. 4.8). This type of shelterbelt will need an area 210 to 225 feet wide. Trees should be spaced 20 feet apart in rows 20 feet apart (30 feet apart for rows of silver maple). Shrubs should be spaced 4 to 6 feet apart in rows 15 feet apart. Stagger the trees and shrubs in each row, i.e., do not plant 1 row next to another with the tree or shrub in 1 row lined up with the tree or shrub in the adjacent row.

The other type of windbreak—a field windbreak—is a straight line of trees, rather than "L" shaped. It is well away from the farm buildings, on the edge of open fields. Its main purpose is to reduce wind erosion of soil. Good

**Table 4.4. Suggested arrangement of a 10-row farm shelterbelt.** (Henderson 1987)

| Row* | | Example 1 | Example 2 | Example 3 | Example 4 |
|---|---|---|---|---|---|
| 1 (outside) | (1) | Silver maple<br>Hybrid poplar | Silver maple<br>Hybrid poplar | Silver maple<br>Hybrid poplar | Silver maple<br>Hybrid poplar |
| 2 | (2) | Male box elder<br>Hybrid poplar | Male box elder<br>Hybrid poplar | Male box elder<br>Hybrid poplar | Male box elder<br>Hybrid poplar |
| 3 | (3) | Green ash | Hackberry<br>Hybrid poplar | Male box elder<br>Green ash | Hackberry<br>Hybrid poplar |
| 4 | (4) | Hackberry<br>Green ash | Hackberry | Black cherry, Black walnut, Butternut, Amur choke cherry, Cockspur hawthorn, Bitternut hickory, Bur oak, Scarlet oak, White oak | Black cherry, Black walnut, Butternut, Amur choke cherry, Cockspur hawthorn, Bitternut hickory, Bur oak, Scarlet oak, White oak |
| 5 | | Black cherry, Black walnut, Butternut, Amur choke cherry, Cockspur hawthorn, Bitternut hickory, Bur oak, Scarlet oak, White oak | Black cherry, Black walnut, Butternut, Amur choke cherry, Cockspur hawthorn, Bitternut hickory, Bur oak, Scarlet oak, White oak | Same as Row 4 | Same as Row 4 |
| 6 | | Same as Row 5 | Same as Row 5 | Green ash<br>Norway spruce | Norway spruce |
| 7 | (5) | Douglas-fir<br>Norway spruce | Douglas-fir<br>Norway spruce | Douglas-fir<br>Norway spruce | Douglas-fir<br>Norway spruce |
| 8 | (6) | White spruce<br>Black Hills spruce<br>Douglas-fir<br>Norway spruce | White spruce<br>Black Hills spruce<br>Douglas-fir<br>Norway spruce | White spruce<br>Black Hills spruce | White spruce<br>Black Hills spruce |
| 9 | (7) | White spruce | White spruce | Eastern red cedar<br>White spruce<br>Black Hills spruce | Eastern red cedar<br>White spruce<br>Black Hills spruce |
| | (8) | Red-osier dogwood<br>Gray dogwood<br>Juneberry<br>High-bush cranberry<br>Elderberry<br>Red splendor or crabapple<br>Pin cherry<br>Meteor cherry<br>Hazel | Red-osier dogwood<br>Gray dogwood<br>Juneberry<br>High-bush cranberry<br>Elderberry<br>Red splendor or crabapple<br>Pin cherry<br>Meteor cherry<br>Hazel | Red-osier dogwood<br>Gray dogwood<br>Juneberry<br>High-bush cranberry<br>Elderberry<br>Red splendor or crabapple<br>Pin cherry<br>Meteor cherry<br>Hazel | Red-osier dogwood<br>Gray dogwood<br>Juneberry<br>High-bush cranberry<br>Elderberry, Red splendor or crabapple<br>Pin cherry<br>Meteor cherry<br>Hazel |
| | (9) | Same as Row 8 | Same as Row 8 | Same as Row 8 | Same as Row 8 |
| 10 | (10) | Wild plum<br>Choke cherry | Wild plum<br>Choke cherry | Wild plum<br>Choke cherry | Wild plum<br>Choke cherry |

* Rows 5 and 6 of food-producing trees are omitted if row (8) and (9) of food-producing shrubs are included.

field windbreaks improve crop yields through the effects of evenly distributed snow and reduced drying, as well as reduced soil erosion. The effects of a field windbreak extend 10 to 15 times the height of the windbreak. That would be 300 to 450 feet downwind from a windbreak 30 feet high. But if the spacing of the trees or the species used is improper, snow will not be distributed uniformly over the field.

The best field windbreak is 1 row of green ash or similar trees spaced 10 feet apart with the row more or less at a right angle to the prevailing wind. Other species can be used, e.g., Black Hills spruce, red cedar, white pine, hackberry, jack pine, white cedar, Norway spruce, ponderosa pine, red pine, Siouxland cottonwood, white ash, white spruce, golden willow, black ash, and others. You will attract more wildlife to the field windbreak by planting raspberry and wild grape, although in time these will appear on their own, as birds that perch in the trees deposit the seeds in their droppings.

If you plant your windbreak in an undulating design (Fig. 4.11), your

# YOU CAN RAISE CROPS AND WILDLIFE

wildlife will be protected from view on 3 sides when entering the open areas.

**Figure 4.11.** *Undulating design of windbreaks that protect wildlife from view on 3 sides in opening. (PFRA Tree Nursery undated.)*

Species of shrubs and trees to plant vary regionally. Talk to your local state wildlife manager or county agent, or contact your local NRCS (Natural Resources Conservation Service) or FSA (Farm Service Agency) office for the best trees and shrubs to plant with your soil and climate conditions. Here are some more tips.

1. Locate shelterbelts on the north side of cropland rather than pastureland, especially near row crop fields that will not be fall plowed. This helps keep snow from burying the stubble, which increases its value to wildlife.
2. Plant your shelterbelts so that they are not isolated islands of habitat, i.e., connect them to existing permanent cover such as woodlots, ravines, and marshes. Your wildlife thus can move from area to area with less exposure by using your shelterbelt as a travel lane.
3. If you plant small shelterbelts on the north or west side of your farm lanes, not only will wildlife use the shelterbelts as travel lanes, but also the trees will serve as a snow fence which keeps snow from piling up in the lanes so you can use them for travel in winter, perhaps with the tractor towing the manure spreader.
4. When trees die in the shelterbelt, leave them alone; these snags serve for denning, perching, and foraging by wildlife.
5. When branches drop off and trees fall down in a shelterbelt, leave the branches, logs, and stumps for use by wildlife.
6. Leave rows of standing crops, such as corn, sorghum, and sunflowers, unharvested next to the shelterbelt, or provide food plots or artificial feeders next to it.
7. Use no-tillage or minimum-tillage farming on cropland next to shelterbelts.
8. Do not let your livestock graze in the shelterbelt.

One more "word" about shelterbelts. Do not put them in large, open natural grasslands. Same thing for hedges. They do not belong there. Shelterbelts fragment such grasslands. That is prairie country and prairie wildlife needs extensive, unfragmented grasslands.

## Odd Areas

I bet you have some odd areas around—areas you cannot cultivate and that are not in your woodlot. Such areas include gullies, rock outcrops, rock piles, bare knobs, sinkholes, gravel pits, borrow pits, fence corners, eroded areas in crop fields, and even pieces of good land cut off from the rest of the field by a gully, drainage ditch, or stream. The only thing you might have to do with these is protect them from cattle grazing and fire. You could run a fence diagonally between the corners of your fields, about 100 to 150 feet from each corner post. You will create an enclosed undisturbed triangle of grasses, shrubs, and other cover for exclusive use by wildlife.

But some of these spots are going to need food and cover plants. You should put at least half of each odd area in good ground cover of grasses and legumes (see Chapter 5). Put another 20 percent of the odd area in spruce trees and about 30 percent in deciduous fruit-bearing shrubs and small trees, such as crabapple, wild plum, choke cherry, and Juneberry. Sometimes these deciduous woody plants start by themselves (with the aid of birds). You might have to mow the grass/legume mixture about every 2 or 3 years or so to discourage invading woody plants. Set the mower 10 inches high and mow only in August, to reduce loss of nests and to allow time for growth of cover in fall for early spring nesters. You might have to spot-treat undesirables such as prickly ash and buckthorn with herbicides to eliminate sprouting.

Also, your abandoned outbuildings, including old barns and homesteads, create great wildlife habitat, believe it or not. So do not remove these to "tidy up" the farm, or you will be decreasing the very wildlife population you are trying to increase. The old attitude toward clean farming as a good idea, was a bad idea—a very bad idea. These old barns and other agricultural buildings are a part of our rich heritage. Barn owls use them, barn swallows use them, bats use them (these bats and swallows feed exclusively on your insects), etc. Thick tangles of weeds around the old dilapidated buildings add to the food and cover value. You will find that this attracts rabbits, quail, turkeys, pheasants, chipmunks, woodchucks, badgers, foxes, bobcats, raccoons, opossums, weasels, and skunks, providing nice opportunities for binoculars, camera, and gun.

If you are lucky enough to have a wet depression or two in your fields, leave a little upland cover around them. You will be surprised at how much you will increase the variety of wildlife, especially songbirds, with so little effort around these little wet areas.

### Center-Pivot Irrigation

Some of these things have that wicked timed arm that extends to irrigate the corners of the field, from the circular swing of the main arm. That should not be allowed. Protect the corners as wildlife habitat, for an entire huge field is being taken away from them. Maybe even plant trees, shrubs, forbs, and grasses attractive to wildlife (Fig. 4.12), or build brush piles in some corners. Leave some rows of crop unharvested next to the corner cover. In a quarter-section (160 acres) irrigation system, about $1/2$ to $3/4$ acre is

# YOU CAN RAISE CROPS AND WILDLIFE

generally adequate, preferably of corn, milo, or a forage sorghum with a large seed head. And do not overuse pesticides in your irrigation system, for that not only kills honeybees and the insect food base for many birds, but it can poison some species of wildlife and contaminate the local water supply for them.

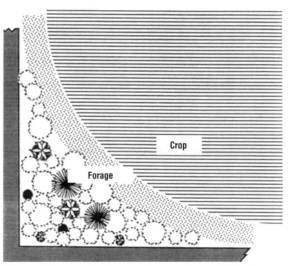

**Figure 4.12.** *Planting trees, shrubs, grasses, and forbs to create wildlife habitat for odd areas of a center-pivot irrigating system. (Henderson 1984)*

## Pastures

You can produce vital food and cover for wildlife by properly managing your pastures, hayfields, and forage crops. Such management depends on the type of disturbance (grazing and/or mowing), timing of disturbance, and forage type (e.g., hay, oats, wheat).

We know that if you live in Illinois, for example, and cut your hay between June 7 and 21, you will destroy most of your hen pheasants and their nests. Cutting earlier before most of them nest, even if the hay is not as tall as you would like, and cutting a second crop later, would be your best compromise. If you cannot mow early and do not want to wait until later, your best compromise would be to raise the mowbar so that 10 inches of stubble remains after mowing. Otherwise you will kill your pheasants, your grassland songbirds, and various other wildlife, too, while eliminating their nesting cover. If nothing else, start mowing in the center of the field and spiral outward, to give fledging birds a chance to escape.

Controlled grazing can be used to improve habitat for grassland wildlife if invasion by shrubs is a problem, for livestock will eat and kill much of the shrubs. But keeping the livestock too long on a pasture will eliminate cover and food for your grassland wildlife. Control is the answer. **Controlled grazing**, it's called. One method of controlled grazing is to use rest-rotation with four pastures (Fig. 4.13).

In general, most of the grazing of your pastures should be done between June 15 and September 15. This allows your nesting cover to develop in spring, and residual nesting cover to develop in late summer and early fall for early nesters the following spring. If you want to have ducks, pheasants, prairie chickens, other grassland birds, rabbits, and other mammals reproducing on your property, you should remove livestock pastured during

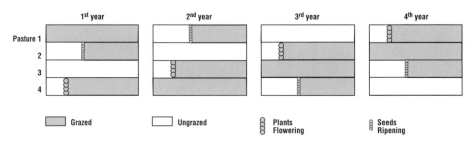

**Figure 4.13.** *A grazing plan, using rest-rotation with 4 pastures. (Poston and Schmidt 1981)*

the growing season when at least 50 percent of the annual herbage still remains, based on the key grasses and forbs eaten. If you pasture livestock during the dormant season, remove them when at least 35 percent of the annual herbage still remains (see Chapter 5).

Pronghorn

# CHAPTER 5

# PASTURES FOR LIVESTOCK AND WILDLIFE

## PRAIRIES, GRASSLAND, AND SAVANNAH

A prairie is essentially a large grassland. It consists of grasses and forbs almost exclusively. A savanna is a grassland with occasional trees here and there. If they are mostly oaks, it is an oak savanna; if mostly pine, it is a pine barrens which is also a savanna. A savanna is really a transition land between forest and prairie, with at least 1 tree per acre but less than 50 percent canopy closure.

Prairie, grassland, and savanna are highly threatened, even endangered, habitats, along with much of their associated wildlife. Why? Because people turn them into agricultural land and housing development because it is easy and cheap to do compared to, say, forests and wetlands. And they are protected from fire. Of course, you say. But these habitats are absolutely dependent on fire, even the oak savanna, for these oaks are resistant to fire. Fire suppression actually destroys these habitats. Take an oak savanna, for example. Even if no one cuts the trees and plows the land or builds houses on it, fire suppression leads to a brushy woodland. Then, so much for the savanna and its wildlife. And do not build a golf course in your fields, with their water needs and fertilizer and pesticide loads. The world does not need another golf course at the expense of natural areas.

Furthermore, remnant patches will not entirely do. Some grassland birds and other wildlife, like their forest counterparts, are size-dependent. That means they absolutely need large unfragmented areas of habitat for a successful (viable) breeding community. How much of **that** is around?

By rights, grassland restoration should be at least 75 acres in size and maybe as large as 250 acres to benefit wildlife species most sensitive to grassland fragmentation. But plantings less than 50 acres will still help other grassland wildlife. As with wildlife in other habitats, each grassland bird species has a particular range of habitat conditions to which it is well suited. While pure prairie wildlife species such as bison and pronghorns require vast prairie, species such as elk are edge species involving forest management and grassland management.

Most private landowners do not have large enough areas or otherwise cannot afford to restore large areas to prairie or savanna. So let's do what we can.

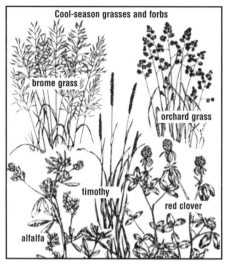

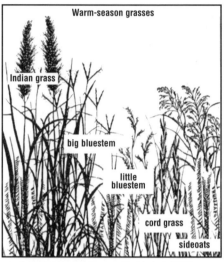

Figure 5.1. *Examples of cool-season grasses and forbs, and warm-season grasses. (Judd et al. 1998)*

## Prairie and Other Grassland

Grasses are either **bunch grasses** or **sod grasses**, i.e., they grow in bunches, or as a carpet of sod such as lawn grass. They also can be divided into warm-season grasses and cool-season grasses (Fig. 5.1). **Warm-season grasses** are the native prairie grasses, such as big bluestem, little bluestem, Indiangrass, switch grass, sideoats grama, prairie cordgrass, and prairie dropseed, that thrive under the heat of late summer. They should be mixed with forbs, i.e., colorful native wildflowers (Fig. 5.2). **Cool-season grasses**, such as timothy, orchard grass, brome grass, tall wheat-grass, and intermediate wheat-grass, tend to be introduced aliens and are valued as wildlife cover because they provide cover early in the season and are easy to establish. But they tend to mat down under snow, rain, and wind, and in time lose vigor.

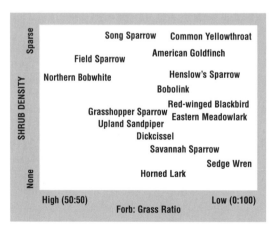

Figure 5.2. *Shrub density and forb abundance relative to distribution of grassland birds. (Herkert et al. 1993)*

Is hayfield good grassland for wildlife? It certainly would be if the hay is not cut before July 15 to ensure that most grassland birds have nested. But it **is** cut before then, so your birds die, so a hayfield is actually an ecological trap that attracts birds away from other fields for nesting and then

# ✻ PASTURES FOR LIVESTOCK AND WILDLIFE

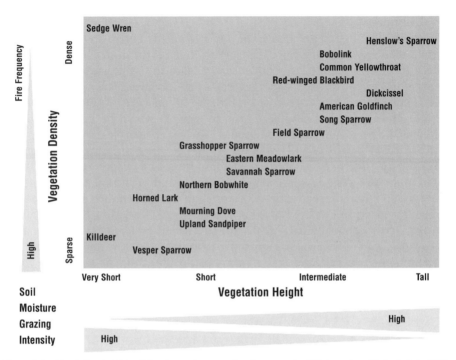

**Figure 5.3.** *Vegetation height and density preferences of various grassland bird species. (Herkert et al. 1993)*

kills them. (See Pastures in Chapter 4.)

Warm-season grasses hold up better and thus make better wildlife cover. Plus they are native, esthetically pleasing, and can make good forage although they can take 3 to 5 years to establish. But then they need little attention and can live indefinitely—a major benefit over cool-season grasses.

Then there is the difference between tall and short native warm-season grasses. You want areas of each, to maximize grassland bird species diversity (Fig. 5.3). Recommended tall grasses include big bluestem, Indiangrass, and switch grass. Recommended short grasses include little bluestem, sideoats grama, prairie dropseed, green needlegrass, and western wheat-grass. Also, include forbs in the seed mixture for both a **short-grass prairie** and a **tall-grass prairie**. When establishing a tall-grass prairie, also include shorter grass seed in the mix. The wildlife agency for each state and province has a list of sources for seed and other plant stock for wildlife plantings.

Be sure to check with the U.S. Natural Resources Conservation Service and the Farm Services Agency about their Conservation Reserve Program (CRP) and the Grassland Reserve Program (GRP) for monetary assistance in establishing and maintaining grasslands (see Chapter 12).

### Establishment

First of all, if you can spare the land, avoid fragmenting any existing grassland or savanna you have. Preservation is better than establishment—unless you have non-native cool-season grasses that you want to convert to a native prairie of warm-season grasses and associated forbs.

Let's say you **do** want to convert a field or old pasture or an area of former crops back into prairie. The best area to convert would be next to another field of some sort—not next to a woods (Fig. 5.4). The area surrounding your new prairie or savanna will certainly influence what animals use it. Better to have your prairie or savanna next to an area of low edge contrast. Then, try to make the area as square as possible (round is better), to reduce edge effect, although a big rectangle is better than a small square. Here, a woody or brushy fence line is terrible, for the range of predators like opossums, skunks, and raccoons is extended with the travel lanes provided by brushy fence rows, and such predators are big nest destroyers, often including the nesting hen. It is better to keep your prairie plantings at least 100 yards from your woods and buildings, with cropland or pasture in between.

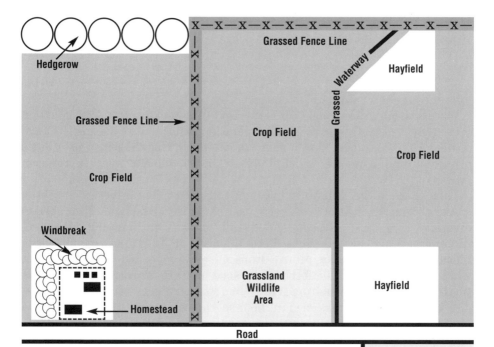

**Figure 5.4.** *Where a single large grassland wildlife area cannot be established, a small one should be located next to hayfields preferably, or other low-contrast areas, some distance from the homestead, woods, and hedgerow, but connected to other grassy areas by a grassed waterway or deliberately established grassed corridor. (Herkert et al. 1993)*

# ❄ PASTURES FOR LIVESTOCK AND WILDLIFE

Your land is likely to be fragmented, so if you plan to manage several grassy areas for wildlife, keep them as close together as possible.

Actually, isolated shrubs or small shrubby patches or isolated small trees less than 10 feet tall within your grassland, but less than 5 percent of it, will benefit the shrub/grassland bird species, and be used as perches or singing posts by grassland birds although they do not need them. But if you see cowbirds perching in the woody stuff, get rid of it. Cowbirds are parasitic nesters, i.e., they lay their eggs in the nests of other bird species, which is bad news, and they will perch in the woody stuff to scan the surrounding grassland for such nests.

## Seeding

To keep it simple, there are 2 basic methods. If you have steep slopes and sandy soils, use the no-till method to reduce erosion. With a special seed drill you sow the seed directly into an old hayfield or into the residue left after harvesting a crop (see Conservation Tillage in Chapter 4).

Otherwise, use the clean seedbed method of plowing and then disking the soil to free it of the previous year's crop residue. You might have to plow or disk a hayfield several times. You want a firm, well-packed seedbed free of clods, but do not overwork fine soils or they will dry out and become crusty. You want good seed-to-soil contact so that air pockets will not kill the new roots; therefore, before you seed, drag behind your tractor a cylinder on wheels called a cultipacker to firm your soil.

You should design one area that will have 5 strips of grassland, each strip 5 to 10 feet wide, so that each year you plow 1 strip in sequence, such as 2-4-1-3-5 or 1-3-5-2-4 (Fig. 5.5). You will slow down shrub invasion, and let nature take its course. The first year you will get favorite bird food and cover plants such as poverty grass, panic grasses, lambs-quarter, ragweed, and smartweed. By the third year you will get a mixture of grasses and forbs such as daisies, asters, goldenrods, and milkweed.

If your grassland is at least 5 acres, you will want to use some type of seed drill for planting. Warm-season grass seed is fluffy and will clog some types of drills. Check with your local

**Figure 5.5.** *Plowing pattern to develop natural grassland strips for grassland birds. (Ohlsson et al. 1982)*

wildlife manager about which mechanical seeders are available in your area.

Plant the seed $1/4$ inch deep. If your seeder does not have a roller, go over the field again with a cultipacker to ensure good seed-to-soil contact.

You can seed large fields fast with an air seeder that blows seed onto the soil from booms rigged on a truck. Air seeders do not clog even with various seed sizes, but you still need to cultipack after seeding.

For small areas or backyard plots, you can use a cyclone spreader for broadcast seeding, or just spread seed by hand. You will have to have a clean-tilled seedbed, though. Just use a spade or rototiller, and then smooth it with a rake before seeding and again after seeding. You will still have to pack the site firmly with a roller, or tamp it with your feet for good seed-to-soil contact.

Generally, plant the seed of your grasses, legumes, and wildflowers in spring when soil moisture is high. Fall is okay if moisture conditions are suitable. And for best results, plant a grass/legume mixture—not just one species—for the variety of height and density and species most attractive to grassland wildlife, including insects so necessary in the food chain (for example, Table 5.1). Use about 3 to 5 pounds of seed per acre. Also for best results, make sure the seed you will use originates within 100 miles north or south and 250 miles east or west of your property.

Native prairie grasses and wildflowers do not need fertilizer. Also, avoid herbicides, for they usually kill more than you want. But weed control is needed during the year of establishment. Do it by mowing after July 1, to about 10 inches high, to destroy the seed crop. You might have to mow the first 2 or 3 years if weeds persist.

Table 5.1. Grassland seed mixtures recommended for areas where these plants grow. (Meyer 1987)

| Grassland | Seeding rates, lb/ac | | Seeding date | Site | Soil |
|---|---|---|---|---|---|
| | Pure stand | Mixed stand | | | |
| Introduced cool-season grasses and legumes | | | < May 15 or August 10–Sept. 20 | All sites suited to farming | Moist, well drained |
| Tall wheat-grass | | | | | |
| Intermediate wheat-grass | 11 | 4.5 | | | |
| Alfalfa* | 10 | 4 | | | |
| Yellow sweetclover* | 4 | 1 | | | |
| | 3 | 0.5 | | | |
| Tall, native warm-season grasses | | | June 1-15 | Lowlands, bottomlands, nearly level plains | Deep, fine, well drained to moderately drained |
| Big bluestem | 11 | 5 | | | |
| Indiangrass | 10 | 3 | | | |
| Switch grass | 5 | 1 | | | |
| Mid-height native grasses | | | <May 15 | Uplands, rolling plains with moderate to steep slopes | Moderately deep, medium-textured, well drained |
| Green needlegrass | 10 | 4 | | | |
| Western wheat-grass | 12 | 4 | | | |
| Sideoats grama | 9 | 3 | | | |
| Little bluestem | 6.7 | 1 | | | |
| * Introduced species. | | | | | |

# ⚙ PASTURES FOR LIVESTOCK AND WILDLIFE

## Maintenance

Mow every 3 to 4 years during August. This allows nesting birds to fledge. It also allows some growth in the fall to provide winter cover, residual vegetation for early nesters in spring, and accumulated dead grass for nesting and other cover.

An alternative to mowing is a prescribed burn every 3 years in early spring. It is best to burn $1/3$ of your grassland each year so that the $2/3$ unburned area remains for nesting birds and other wildlife. Prairies have evolved and adapted to burning as the principle disturbance factor that keeps a prairie a prairie. Burning rejuvenates the prairie plants and suppresses growth of unwanted woody plants and grasses. It is efficient and economical. But get advice and help from your local wildlife manager.

You can enhance the quality of your established CRP and GRP lands (see Chapter 12) by strip-disking fireguards around the margins of your fields in early spring or even late winter. That will enable you to conduct occasional controlled burns. That will also increase edge, and stimulate growth of broad-leaved annuals (forbs). You will see your pheasant population and other grassland wildlife populations increase. Also, try interseeding perennial legumes and other forbs into recently burned grass stands. That can be effective. So too will interspersing grass/legume strips on intensively farmed croplands; use the CRP and GRP for this.

Herbivory and prairies also evolved together, especially bison grazing. Livestock can substitute for bison, but you must be careful here. Bison migrated and were not confined on 1 area like livestock are. Overgrazing can destroy your grassland. You must use **controlled** grazing if you use it at all. Divide your grassland pasture into 3 sections called **paddocks** by using a lightweight movable fence. Let the livestock in a paddock until about 50 percent of the plant growth is removed, but at least a 10-inch height of grasses remains. You will produce this with about 1 cow for every 2 acres. Then move them into the next paddock, and so on. This is a rotational grazing system. But do not graze after August to allow vegetation to regrow before dormancy. (Also see Pastures in Chapter 4, especially Fig. 4.13.)

## Savanna

Contact your local wildlife manager and together take a look at your woods. If the wildlifer determines that your woods used to be an oak savanna, you might want to restore it to that condition. That will require cutting the non-savanna woody shrubs and trees (save the oaks), spot-treating the tree stumps with a suitable herbicide to prevent sprouting, and then burning in the spring. Burning will be needed annually until most undesirable vegetation is removed. Then plant with a grass/forb mixture of warm-season grasses (see Prairie and Other Grassland) and burn it each year to control non-savanna species until the native species reestablish. Then burn the area every 3 to 5 years. If you happen to have a natural savanna, also maintain it by a prescribed burn every 3 to 5 years when enough dead grass fuel builds up. You will need a burning permit. Prescribed burning is a great tool, and you will usually use headfires and backfires. But it is complicated business that can be difficult to control, and even dangerous. Use the fire tool, but not by yourself. Use common sense, and get help from your local professional wildlife manager.

Bison

# CHAPTER 6

# WHAT'S A RIPARIAN AREA?

What's a riparian area? Only just your most productive and important wildlife area, that's what: songbirds, wood ducks, other birds, deer, other mammals, reptiles, and amphibians. You might not have any riparian area if you do not have a stream running through your property. You might not have any, even with a stream running through your property—if you have cut all the woody stuff next to it or allowed your cows to graze the shoreline.

Let's say you have a stream on your property surrounded by woody vegetation (Fig. 6.1). That's the **riparian zone**. How do you improve it for

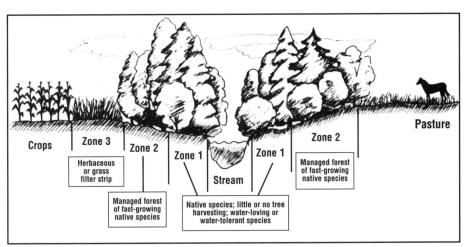

**Figure 6.1.** *A riparian forest buffer includes zone 1, the area closest to the water body or course, and zone 2, the area next to and up gradient of zone 1. Trees and shrubs in zone 1 provide important wildlife habitat, litter fall for aquatic organisms, and shading to lower water temperature. This zone helps stabilize stream banks and shorelines. Trees and shrubs in zone 2 (along with zone 1) intercept sediment, nutrients, pesticides, and other pollutants in surface and subsurface water flows. Zone 2 can be managed to provide timber, wood fiber, and horticultural products. A third zone, zone 3, is established if periodic and excessive water flows, erosion, and sediment from upslope fields or tracts are anticipated. Zone 3 is generally of herbaceous plants and a diversion or terrace, if needed. This zone provides a "first defense" to assure proper functioning of zones 1 and 2. (U.S. Natural Resources Conservation Service 1998)*

wildlife? Protect it! You should have at least 30 yards of riparian vegetation on each side of the stream. Can't spare that much, you say? Too bad. Then spare what you can. Whatever you do, do not cut the stuff—and keep the cows out. I have seen narrow trout streams entering someone's property and becoming wide, shallow, slow, and warm. Why? Because the farmer let the cows have access to it any place they wanted. That caused the stream banks to break down and the soil to enter the stream, thus making it shallow and widening it, resulting in slower, shallower, warmer water, with increased fertility from direct cow manure and indirect cow manure from rain runoff into the stream. And the stream is muddy. No trout can even live there for lack of oxygen and cold temperature, much less reproduce there. And even if the trees have been left standing, which often they have not, the cows have trampled things and eaten everything up to 6 feet high. That's no good. Plus the trees would help shade the stream, cooling it. Plus branches would fall into the stream at times, becoming what is called coarse woody debris. That furnishes cover for aquatic insects needed by trout and other fish, as well as cover for the fish themselves—all of which then attracts other wildlife for cover or food, including frogs, turtles, birds, and mammals.

So here is what you do. Protect whatever you have. Fence it off from grazing; allow the cows access to the stream, for drinking only, at 1 or 2 small locations a few yards wide. Run the fence into the stream if necessary, so that the cows cannot wade around behind it (see Fig. 8.1 for ideas). Always remember that in most cases the stream water and stream bottom are a public resource, not private.

If the stream runs through a field, do the same thing, and then plant riparian trees and shrubs between fence and stream. Suitable species to plant include willow, cottonwood, aspen, red maple, silver maple, river birch, water birch, black ash, white cedar, hemlock, balsam fir, black spruce, cypress, dogwood, serviceberry, alder. Plant them on the outside bends of the stream (Fig. 6.2). Other woody species, such as raspberry and elderberry, will seed in through bird droppings. Species of forbs, grasses, and sedges will establish from wind-borne or animal-borne sources. The best thing to do is examine a nearby riparian area to see what is growing along the stream there. That is the best guide about what to transplant into your area.

You also can protect your riparian areas from overgrazing of livestock by adjusting the distribution of livestock (i.e., stocking rates and location), pasture design, livestock access points, amount of use, timing of use, duration of use, frequency of use, and kind of livestock. By fencing off your riparian area, your loss of forage there would be inconsequential because little is produced there compared to open field or range. But fencing and maintenance are expensive and can restrict movement of big game if not done right. You should use fencing to protect the small riparian area around springs and seeps, and then pipe the water to adjacent areas if needed by livestock for drinking (see Chapter 9). Sometimes the terrain will allow you

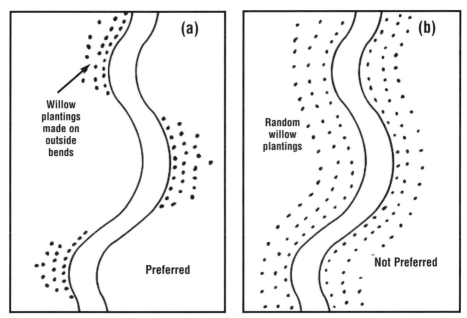

**Figure 6.2.** *Willow cuttings arranged to provide stream bank protection. Selective arrangement in (a) is preferred and more cost-effective than random arrangement in (b). (Melton et al. 1987)*

to regulate the natural trailing and loafing of livestock in riparian areas. For example, you can fence gaps relative to gullies, cliffs, and other natural barriers that tend to funnel livestock into riparian areas. You also can place trees, brush, or rocks (at least 10 to 20 inches in diameter) along stream banks. Livestock are less inclined to trample or loaf in rocky areas used as water gaps to the stream. Fenced riparian areas will need an occasional rocky water gap to the stream to allow drinking but reduce loafing and trampling (see Fig. 8.1). You could suspend panels of corrugated metal roofing over the stream from wire strung across the stream. Such a structure will allow debris to pass by swinging with the flow of water, while preventing livestock from wading too far in the stream.

To avoid extensive fencing of large riparian areas, you can attract livestock away from riparian areas by creating shade and water developments, and placing rubbing posts, oilers, salt, hay, grain, molasses, and other supplements only in upland areas at least 400 yards, and preferably twice that far, away from riparian areas and intermittent drainages.

You should locate the entrances to your pastures and livestock-handling facilities well away from your riparian areas, especially if you have drinking water located somewhere else. Also, if you plant palatable forage species well away from your riparian areas, or use prescribed burning to enhance forage production and palatability, your livestock will be less inclined to seek out your riparian areas. Frequent riding and herding also improve distribution of livestock and feeding opportunities, thus increasing calf crops. Another thing—some groups of cattle prefer riparian areas and some prefer the uplands. Keep an eye out to identify them and then selectively cull the cattle that prefer the riparian areas.

Minimize the number of times you move livestock through a riparian area. Locate stock driveways and trailing areas away from streamside zones. If you must move stock through, drive small groups of them slowly, perhaps over stock bridges or revetment at specific crossings. You might need to stabilize the shoreline (see Shoreline Stabilization in Chapter 4).

Alligator

# CHAPTER 7

# GOT ANY WETLANDS OR PONDS?

Wetlands come in a variety of types. Some are wooded swamps, with waterlogged soils during the growing season, often covered with shallow water, and swamp trees that can tolerate such conditions. Some are shrub swamps with conditions similar to wooded swamps, except swamp shrubs rather than swamp trees. Some are marshes of herbaceous plants, saturated soils, and usually standing shallow water. These marshes can be freshwater or saltwater, and shallow, intermediate, or deep. Some wetlands can be sedge meadows with saturated soils but no standing water except maybe in spring. Bogs have acidic water, dense mats of peat and sphagnum moss, and unusual plants such as the insect-eating pitcher plant and sundew. Fens are grassy wetlands of alkaline water fed by mineral-rich springs or groundwater.

Let's look at the shallow wetland marsh, the type you are likely to have. Like all wetland types, this is an extremely valuable wildlife habitat—probably the most productive habitat (along with riparian) on your property in terms of amount and variety of wildlife using it for breeding and other purposes. If you have such a marsh, count yourself lucky. If you do not, perhaps you can create one (see Chapter 8).

Much of your wetland management will attract shorebirds, wading birds, geese, and ducks. Two general categories of ducks exist: dabbling (puddle) ducks and diving ducks. The divers like bluebills, redheads, and canvasbacks, have their legs well back on their body to facilitate diving and swimming underwater in deep water. But that makes them unbalanced on land, so they nest close to the water in emergent vegetation. The dabblers, like mallards, teal, and wood ducks, have legs in the middle of their body, so they are well-balanced and often nest $1/4$ mile from the pond because their ducklings can walk to the water. Dabblers can dive, but usually do not, and feed in shallow water by tipping. The ducks you will likely attract will be dabblers, for your wetland and pond management will be shallow water management. From a distance you can tell what type of duck is using your pond by the way they take off from the water. If they jump off the water to fly, they are dabblers; if they flap their wings and run along the water surface to get airborne, they are divers.

## Protection

If you have a marsh, or any kind of wetland, all you have to do is protect it from

unnatural disturbance. Mostly, do not graze it excessively or at all (see Fig. 8.1). Marshes tend to have an area of shallow water with emergent plants, like cattail and sedge, growing in it, surrounded by a narrow or broad zone of marsh plants on the shoreline. That entire area constitutes your marsh, and needs your protection.

Ideally, what you want in the shallow water area of your marsh is a ratio of 50 percent open water and 50 percent of it with emergent vegetation scattered throughout, although keeping the ratio between 30 percent and 70 percent works. How deep should the water be? Eighteen inches is best for ducks and many other aquatic and semi-aquatic creatures.

Cattail is a valuable plant; for example, many marsh birds nest in it, muskrats feed on the roots and build houses with the stalks, and mink in turn feed on the muskrats. But cattail is an aggressive plant that can form extensive monotypic stands and eventually choke out your open water areas. Then it needs control. But cattail is a native species. The most common invasive wetland plants in the Midwest are alien: reed canary grass, giant reed grass (common reed), purple loosestrife, and buckthorn. All should be controlled.

If you have a grassy area rather than cattail or other marsh plants in the 100- to 200-foot area around your shallow water area, maintain it as such. That area will help protect the site from pollutants and be a visual and noise barrier. Your ducks and various shorebirds and grassland birds will nest in that stuff, so it is very valuable to them—and to you, too, if you want them to remain there every season and breed there. In fact, maintain more than 200 feet if you can spare it economically. Some ducks such as mallards will nest up to 1,200 feet from the water's edge, but 300 feet gets most of them. Even a narrow buffer around your wetland is better than none at all. The ratio of water to nesting cover is 1:4, i.e., if you have 1 acre of water, you should have 4 acres of nesting cover—some combination of sedge meadow, hayfield, or other grassy cover. But if you can spare it, at least 40 acres of grassy cover and/or sedge meadow is best because predators can find the duck nests much easier on smaller areas, and it is better in a block than in a narrow strip easy for predators to search. In any case, you will have to fence it off from cattle or sheep.

Protect your wetland, streams, and lakes from chemical pollution. These areas are downhill from most human habitation, and they act as a sink for the pesticides, fertilizers, and other chemicals we use. Reduce your use of chemicals near your wetland, and talk to your neighbors too about reducing use of chemicals. Maintain your septic system properly.

Excessive water draining uplands through drain pipes, culverts, and ditches can flood your important lowland plant communities and introduce your wetland to silt and chemicals such as manure, commercial fertilizer, salt, gas and oil, and pesticides. Divert such excessive water elsewhere, perhaps into a buffer zone before it enters your wetland, or spread it evenly over the landscape.

During any construction activity near your wetland, reduce siltation of your

wetland by using a silt curtain to trap silt below areas with bared soil. You can see how these are used along roadsides during road construction.

## Grazing

Grazing cows in the marsh can help control the rank vegetation such as cattail, common reed (giant reed grass), reed canary grass, bulrush, cordgrass, and willow by opening up the marsh through trampling and grazing. It works best after a prescribed burn when cattle will eat the new shoots. You should use cattle thus for 2 to 3 months in late winter and early spring, but definitely not during July, August, and September so that the vegetation can recover to provide residual nesting cover the following spring for early ground nesters such as prairie chickens, pheasants, grassland songbirds, shorebirds, and most ducks. Also, keep the cows away from the shoreline because removal of rank growth there will reduce or eliminate duck use of such windswept, wave-washed, unsheltered areas, and erosion will increase too.

## Trapping

Muskrats and nutria will help you maintain the preferred 1:1 ratio of open water to emergent vegetation by cutting some of the plants, especially cattail. So if you or someone else traps these critters for fur, do not overdo it—which is hard to do with such prolific species. But too many of these animals can result in an **eatout** whereby they remove too much vegetation for food and house construction. So some trapping might be necessary. You also might want to trap some of the main predators of your ducks and duck nests: raccoons, opossums, skunks, and foxes. Don't trap the otter, though, because they will feed voraciously on the carp and bullheads that muddy the water and reduce plant growth. (I heard a wildlife manager describe an otter as "a straight pipe.") In the South, alligators help keep raccoons, muskrats, nutria, and beaver in check.

## Mowing

To control cattail, you could mow or burn it in winter level to the ice, for during spring flooding, water will cover the stubble, destroying much of it. Cattail on the shoreline you should mow at ground level in June or July when carbohydrate reserves are low after the heads are well formed but not mature, and then mow 1 month later when the new growth is 2 to 3 feet high. Cutting common reed for 2 or 3 consecutive years will reduce its density for 8 to 10 years. You can use standard rotary mowers, including brush hogs and batwings, or sickle-bar mowers towed by standard farm tractors to cut brush such as willow and alder or herbaceous plants. Set the cutting bar to leave 4 to 6 inches of stubble in some areas for nesting and none in a few other areas for feeding birds such as robins and nesting for birds such as killdeer and horned larks. Do not mow until after July 15 when most ground-nesting birds have fledged, and before September 1, so that grasses and forbs will have time to rejuvenate to produce residual nesting cover in spring for ducks and other ground nesters. Ducks use the previous year's residual vegetation for nesting cover in spring before the new stuff greens up. You should mow $^1/_3$ of the area every year.

For brush control, use a brush hog to mow about 6 to 8 inches above ground in winter, when the ground is frozen.

## Burning

Your wetland also can be rejuvenated with a prescribed burn every 3 to 5 years. In a wetland, a prescribed burn (1) makes new green shoots, roots, and rhizomes of grasses and sedges available to geese; (2) exposes fallen seed for ducks; (3) reduces impenetrable stands of plants such as cattail, giant reed grass, reed canary grass, bulrush, sawgrass, and cordgrass, and promotes growth of good seed producers such as beggar's tick and smartweed; and (4) improves nesting area for waterfowl and shorebirds.

Burn about $^1/_3$ of the area every year. You will need permits and professional advice and help, so see your local wildlife manager.

## Herbicide

Be careful here (see Fertilizers and Pesticides in Chapter 4). Even a well-directed plant-specific stream or spray from a hand-held can will kill any adjacent plants it touches. Directly spraying 6 percent glyphosate (e.g., Roundup®, etc.) in early spring for 3 years will kill reed canary grass while minimizing damage to warm-season native plants (see Table 5.1)—if it is in small patches mixed with high-quality vegetation. When reed canary grass has become a monoculture, use a spray of 6 percent glyphosate, then burn 3 weeks later, or cultivate with a disc to stimulate germination, and spray again. But be careful not to confuse reed canary grass with the desirable native, blue-joint grass.

Purple loosestrife should be pulled out by hand if feasible, and the plants (with seed heads) burned. If it is too extensive for that, apply an appropriate hand-held herbicide. (You might be eligible to receive beetles from your department of natural resources, to help control the purple loosestrife if your site is over 4 acres and loaded with it.)

You can control buckthorn—both glossy and common—by pulling out the seedlings. If it is too big, cut the stem close to the ground and paint the cut immediately with a 50 percent solution of glyphosate.

## Adding Water

Generally speaking, you probably will not install a water control structure connecting your wetland to a stream, due to the expense and permits involved. But if you did—you could really have some fun managing your wetland—except that, once wetlands are altered like this, non-native plants tend to invade and habitat quality diminishes over time, even though you might attract waterfowl initially. Still, through timely water level manipulation you could control your aquatic plants better, as well as muskrats, nutria, and carp, and generally improve the whole wetland for wildlife, especially waterfowl and shorebirds. Through proper water level manipulation, undesirable aquatic plants can be decreased, and desirable food-producing aquatic plants can be increased. But that requires considerable knowledge and experience (See Dugouts and Diked Dugouts in Chapter 8).

If you have a low area where water tends to collect and then run off down a slight slope, dump a few loads of dirt there to contain it. That is a low-head dike, and it will hold the water, preventing it from running off, and even back it up some, thus creating a small pond for you and your wildlife. The wetland plants will develop in and around it on their own.

Before you add water, though, or do anything except consult a wildlife manager, you need to make a map of what you want your wetland to look like when it is finished.

If you have a low area on your property that holds sheet water for a while in spring, you have the makings of a wetland. Hire yourself a scraper to come in and enhance that area by scraping out a shallow area and hauling the fill to an upland site on your land; it is illegal to dump this stuff in a wetland even on your own property. (Most of the fill will be topsoil.) Do not go too deep—2 feet max for 75 percent of it, 1.5 feet is better. The wetland should resemble a shallow saucer. You are going to need a 1:10 slope to have the gentle shoreline you need. And do some bottom contouring with the scraper or even a road grader to develop low ridges and furrows in a washboard pattern 1 foot deep to provide flight paths for ducks, open water areas for duck broods, and some microtopography for a variety of aquatic plants. By rights, this should be done in irregular strips 10 to 20 yards wide, the strips about 75 yards apart, with gently sloping sides. In the shallow 75-yard strips, dig out a few randomly located areas of about 2.5 acres to a depth of 1 yard below the anticipated water level (called **normal pool**), with interconnecting channels dug 2 feet deep. This bottom contouring will reduce aggregations of breeding ducks and provide flight paths for diving ducks, which cannot jump off the water to fly like dabbling ducks.

You will need permits. Get some advice from your local wildlife manager, who might tell you that you need permits from your state or province, the U.S. Fish and Wildlife Service, the U.S. Natural Resources Conservation Service, and the U.S. Army Corps of Engineers, or the Canadian Wildlife Service.

While you are at it, leave an island or two in your new pond-to-be. Nesting success for ducks and geese is better on islands due to better protection from predators because the surrounding water acts like an impassable moat for them. They can be 0.1 to 1 acre in size (Fig. 7.1), with the point of the oval island into the wind to reduce erosion and as far from shore as feasible, for large ponds at least 300 feet. Add soil in layers, each layer compacted by the heavy

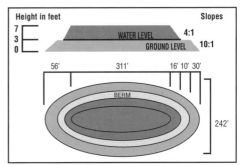

**Figure 7.1.** *A 1-acre island built in an oval shape with a rounded outline creates a more natural appearance. (Lokemoen and Messmer 1994)*

equipment being used. Add 4 to 6 inches of the original topsoil stockpiled for that purpose. Let the seed bank in the soil produce the plants if desirable plants were there initially, or seed with a grass/legume mixture (ask your local wildlife manager), and restore the desirable contours of the pond bottom (See islands in Chapter 8).

## Restoration

Get some background information before you do anything to your land or buy some land for its wetland potential. Talk to the owner or previous owner about any draining or filling he or she might have done, or about knowledge he or she might have about such alterations done by a previous owner. A neighbor and town historian could be helpful. Examine the abstract of your land to find out who the previous owners were and how much of your land was farmed, wooded, or wet in the old days. Some abstracts have that information. Make sure you have the legal description of your property: county, township, range, section. It should be on the survey map of your property, but you can get it from the county plat book in the library, county clerk's or assessor's offices, or even a real estate office.

Go to the nearest NRCS office (Natural Resources Conservation Service—the former Soil Conservation Service) and get a soils map and soils descriptions for your property. Have them explain where the hydric (wetland) soils are on your property. Also while you are at it, check with the Farm Services Agency to see if any recent and past air photos exist for your property. These are acquired about every 5 years, and some go back to the 1930s. The NRCS office also has Wetland Inventory maps on air photos, as do the various states and provinces. You will want to get those for your area.

Topographic maps also are useful, and your county might have maps with 2-foot contour intervals that provide much detail. (See Maps in Chapter 12.)

Draw a map of your own property. Use a compass and pacing to be fairly accurate. (Count the number of paces it takes you to walk 50 feet.) Identify special features (see Chapter 2). Take some photos at identifiable spots for before and after comparisons. Learn to identify some wetland plants that might be living along field borders or between cropped plants. These are clues to wetland soils. Learn to identify the invasive plants too. (See Inventory and Planning in Chapter 2.)

Now, compare all your maps and other information about your property, and try to make some sense of it all. Try to identify previous wetland areas for restoration. They might be obvious. Maybe not. And remember that any restoration cannot affect a neighbor's land, so you might need to hire a surveyor to survey your land to determine accurate property lines.

If you have a field that you know or can tell once was a wetland, and you live in the U.S., what you ought to do is restore the field to a wetland by contacting the NRCS and ask them about their Wetlands Reserve Program (WRP). There will be a federal representative in your state for sure, and maybe in your area. Among other things, the WRP offers payment for wetlands previously drained and

Elk

Wood frog

Garter snake eating American toad

Mourning
cloak

Snapping
turtle

Prairie chicken

Gray squirrel

Robin (juvenile)

Cottontail

Opossum

Juvenile red-tailed hawk eating a mallard

Bald eagle

Black bear (cinnamon color phase)

White-tailed deer

Mule deer

Wild turkey

White-tailed deer

Bighorn sheep

Newfoundland caribou

converted to agricultural use, pays up to all restoration costs, and you do not have to allow public access. Wetlands converted after 1985 are ineligible. If you do restore a former wetland that is now a field on your land, check Chapter 12 for help. Some of the things described in the previous section (Adding Water) apply here too. Again, check on permits.

If the wetland was filled in to produce your field, hire that scraper to come in and unfill it. But keep it shallow (18 to 24 inches max), with gently sloping sides (1:8 ratio, 1:10 is better). Get the financial help and advice of the WRP. Also, check with your state's or province's local wildlife manager, your state's representative from the U.S. Fish and Wildlife Service and U.S. Army Corp of Engineers, or your province's representative from the Canadian Wildlife Service.

If air photos of your property were taken in spring, frost heave might reveal outlines of drain tile lines. Otherwise, search any drainage ditches for outlet pipes, and work back with a tile probe and flagging stakes. You can buy a tile probe from a forestry or natural resources catalog, or with your computer, log onto the web with the key words "forestry suppliers" to locate natural resources equipment. Tile will be buried 3 to 3.5 feet underground, but might be just 1.5 feet deep if hand dug. Tile lines are parallel and generally 40 to 80 feet apart in mineral or clay soils, and 80 to 100 feet apart in sands or muck. Some tiles are 150 feet apart. With a backhoe, remove the lines and fill the trench. You can crush and rebury clay tiles. A less expensive but less effective method is to remove 50 feet of each line of tile, and simply fill in the hole. If you have neighbors serviced by the same tile line, or you want control of the water level, before filling in the hole you could fit the tile lines with special water control structures such as rise-tubes or perforated bypasses, so that the needs of both you and your neighbors are met. You will have to rest the elbow on 2 cement blocks or a small slab of concrete, with an antiseep collar around the horizontal tile pipe and a debris cover over the riser. Again, check out the WRP for direction and financial help with all of this, and check about permits to change things.

If an open drainage ditch drains the field you want to restore to the original wetland, you must fill in the ditch. Or plug it, which is easier and cheaper initially, but not as good. With mineral soils, the plug should fill in at least 100 feet of the ditch and be 33 percent above grade for settling. With organic soils, fill in at least 150 feet, 20 percent above grade. Use an 8 to 1 slope on the plug. It has to be a good bond too, or it will leak (Fig. 7.2). You need to remove the organic material from the ditch where you want to plug it, probably with a dragline or backhoe. Then use a dozer to push the old berm back into the ditch, or get a dump truck to bring in as much clay from a borrow site somewhere, and dump it in the

**Figure 7.2.** *Ditches were constructed to drain wetlands years ago. Plugging the ditch with a ditch plug of heavy soil allows water to collect in the wetland basin again. (Judd et al. 1998)*

ditch. Have a dozer run over it several times to compact it to 2 or 3 feet above the water level, top it with black dirt, and seed it. (See Shoreline Stabilization in Chapter 4.) You should cut a small spillway in one side of the plug to allow excess water to escape. If you anticipate that too much water will build up in the ditch too fast behind the plug, you will have to install a culvert too. Small tidewater bayous can be plugged like this in the South. Be sure to check about permits to do this. If your ditch is considered navigable, you will have a problem.

Get several estimates and recommendations before settling on a contractor to do your restoration. Then discuss which equipment will be used, and if it is well-maintained to minimize oil leaks, etc. Equipment should be steam cleaned before entering your wetland, so that undesirable seeds are not inadvertently introduced. Contact "Diggers Hotline" to locate any underground cables or utility lines. Inform the contractor which sites you want undisturbed, perhaps by flagging them, and which routes equipment operators should use to enter and leave the site, where silt curtains should go, where excavated soil should be deposited and graded, and where water should be pumped if necessary. Inspect the operation daily, and do not make final payment until you are satisfied.

## Beaver Ponds

You should count yourself lucky if you have a beaver pond on your property. Sure, beaver can flood things and cut trees, but they are fascinating because it is the only animal that deliberately alters and improves its habitat for itself—and incidentally for many other animals too, from wood ducks to deer and great blue herons. Plus, they have interesting biology: they are monogamous, live in colonies, are territorial with only 1 colony per pond, leave castoreum scent on mud scent mounds as territorial markers, do not disperse and breed until 2 years of age, do not reach maximum productivity until age 4, breed in February in the lodge and have a gestation of 100 days so the 3 or 4 kits are born in May, can live 20 years, have an annual mortality of 25 percent, build dams, build lodges, store winter food during fall in a browse pile of deciduous tree branches in front of the lodge, swim out of 1 of the 2 plunge holes in the lodge to cut a stick under ice and water (lips close behind incisors so a mouthful of water is not taken while cutting) and take it into the lodge to peel off the bark and eat it and then shove the peeled stick under the ice, prefer aspen, and more. Trap them out with Conibear 330s if you have to, but keep them around if you can, perhaps by inserting a beaver pipe through the dam (Fig. 7.3). Save the preferred trees by armoring them with half-inch hardware cloth wrapped around the base, but bend in the top so birds cannot get in and get trapped.

Figure 7.3. *Clemson beaver pond leveler. (Cole et al. 1996)*

Let the beaver do the work and create a wetland for you. Then stand back and enjoy the variety of wildlife attracted to it, including the beaver themselves.

# CHAPTER 8

# FARM PONDS AND STOCK PONDS

You might have a farm pond already on your land, or a stock pond. If so, there are things you can do to improve it for wildlife. If not, you can build one. Farm ponds are used for watering stock, irrigation, fishing, and other recreation, but probably mostly for fishing. So they tend to be deeper and closer to buildings than waterfowl, for example, prefer and certain other wildlife too. Or maybe the farm pond was dug near a busy highway so that the fill could be used for a nearby overpass. So stock ponds, being more remote, tend to benefit wildlife more than farm ponds do, except livestock often use stock ponds so heavily that their wildlife habitat opportunities are compromised. But you can do something about that and still use your stock ponds and farm ponds the way you like (Table 8.1).

**Table 8.1. Evaluating past management programs, potential, and habitat improvement of stock ponds for brooding waterfowl.** (Evans and Kerbs 1977)

| HABITAT COMPONENT | RATING |
|---|---|
| 1. Size: | |
| a. Temporary water. | Unsuitable |
| b. Permanent water, <1 surface acre. | Inadequate |
| c. Permanent water, >1 surface acre. | Good |
| 2. Average shoreline slope, measured from existing water level: | |
| a. >3 ft./5 horizontal ft. | Unsuitable |
| b. 2-3 ft./5 horizontal ft. | Poor |
| c. 1-2 ft./5 horizontal ft. | Fair |
| d. 0-1 ft./5 horizontal ft. | Good |
| 3. Shoreline vegetation within 1 yd. of existing water level: | |
| a. 0-25% of the shoreline vegetation covered, or shoreline completely covered with tall rank vegetation with no open shoreline for brood resting sites. | Unsuitable |
| b. 25-50% vegetation covered. | Poor |
| c. 50-75% vegetation covered. | Fair |
| d. >75% vegetation covered, except as in "a". | Good |
| 4. Existing water conditions: | |
| a. Water level low with shoreline vegetation either absent or excessively trampled by livestock. | Poor |
| b. Water level low with a good cover of shoreline vegetation, or pond about half full. | Fair |
| c. Pond full or nearly full. | Good |
| 5. Food and cover plants (circle selected rank as follows): 0 = absent, 1 = rare, 2 = occasional, and 3 = common | |
| a. Pondweed. | 0  1  2  3 |
| b. Smartweed. | 0  1  2  3 |
| c. Spike-rush. | 0  1  2  3 |
| d. Bulrush. | 0  1  2  3 |
| e. Cattail. | 0  1  2  3 |
| f. Naiad. | 0  1  2  3 |
| g. Buttercup. | 0  1  2  3 |
| h. Water milfoil. | 0  1  2  3 |
| i. Coontail. | 0  1  2  3 |
| j. Chara (stonewort). | 0  1  2  3 |
| 6. Emergent and aquatic vegetation (refer to ranking of plants in item 5): | |
| a. No plant listed is ranked above the rare (1) category. | Unsuitable |
| b. No plant listed in "a" through "d" is ranked as common, but enough emergent and aquatic vegetation exists to rank some of the 10 listed species above the category. Listed plant species occupy <25 percent of the area of water<2 ft. deep. | Poor |
| c. Of the plants listed in "a" through "d", 1 or more, and preferably 2, are common on the pond. Aquatic and emergent vegetation occupies 25 to 50 percent of the water area <2 ft. deep. | Fair |
| d. Of the plants listed, 5 or more occupy >50 percent of the water area <2 ft. deep (except as in "e"). Of the species listed in "a" through "d", 2 or more are common on the pond. | Good |
| e. Pond is completely or nearly completely covered with emergent and aquatic vegetation (choked). | Unsuitable |

## Improving Your Pond
### Plants

Size up your pond for plants. Probably, aquatic plants have pioneered into it and you do not have to do anything. But your pond might be too isolated from a seed source for that to have happened, in which case you will have to transplant some. In late summer the water level might be low enough to expose suitable sites for transplanting rootstock. What to plant? See what is growing in natural ponds or wetlands nearby, and get permission to transplant some of the stuff into your pond, especially smartweed and spike-rush, so that ultimately emergent vegetation covers 30 to 50 percent of your pond. You also want less than 10 percent of the shoreline bare, about 33 percent of it rimmed with shrubs, and most of it uncultivated and ungrazed. Best development of vegetation takes at least 5 years.

If your pond has too many plants, especially algae and duckweed, it is too fertile. You have too much fertilizer running into it from your surrounding land. Do not fertilize so close to the pond (no pesticides either) and make sure the surrounding area is vegetated enough to prevent manure from draining into it with rain or snow runoff, or you will have a slimy mess as your pond clogs with algae and other plants (see Chapter 7 and Shoreline Stabilization in Chapter 4).

In fact, the land surrounding your pond should be part of your pond management strategy. If you want ducks or shorebirds to nest there in addition to your grassland birds including ring-necked pheasants, you need 4 times as much grassland as you have pond. So if your pond is 1 acre, you need 4 acres of grassland next to it. You will probably have to fence it off from your cattle if your stocking rate is high (see Fencing in Chapter 9), except for access points to drink (Fig. 8.1), because cattle tend to congregate around a water source, resulting in overgrazing there. The duck population on your stock ponds will increase with a stocking rate of 37 cattle-days per year, or somewhere up to 3 acres per AUM (animal unit month), because that will increase your grassy shorelines and your brushy and emergent shorelines preferred by duck broods. Also, nearby fields of small grain will be used for food by nesting hens. (An animal unit month equals a cow and calf grazing in an area for 1 month.)

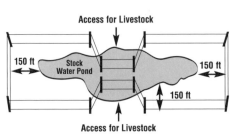

**Figure 8.1.** *Fencing design around a pond to prevent livestock from trampling shoreline vegetation. (Payne and Bryant 1998)*

### Rocks and Logs

Along the north shore of ponds of at least 1 acre, place rock piles of riprap.

# FARM PONDS AND STOCK PONDS

Such an area will be used for sunning by your reptiles—turtles, lizards, and snakes—and as shelter by some of your amphibians, especially bullfrogs and salamanders. If you want more amphibians, keep fish out of some of your stock ponds. Place some brush piles and tree branches in water 2 feet deep or less for egg laying. Place some tree branches along at least 25 percent of the total pond bank. In most ponds, place 5 to 10 logs (cedar, preferably), 5 to 8 feet long and 6 inches wide, with part of the log in the water and most of the underside touching the bottom. If you live in country with large rocks, place a few relatively flat ones in the pond so that they stick out around the shoreline.

## Islands on Ice

Nesting success of ducks, geese, and other birds is better on islands because the water serves as a barrier to many mammalian predators like opossums, skunks, foxes, and even raccoons. Even though your pond is already standing, you can still build an island if you live in the north. Wait until there is at least 1 or 2 feet of ice on the pond (Table 8.2), then either remove some of the ice and dump dirt in the hole created, or dump a bunch of dirt on the ice in the center of the pond away from emergent vegetation. It is probably too costly to

| Table 8.2. Amount of ice needed to support various loads.(Messmer et al. 1986) | |
| --- | --- |
| Thickness of ice,* inches | Permissible load |
| <2 | Stay off. |
| 2 | One person on foot. |
| 3 | Group of people in single file. |
| 7.5 | 2-ton truck gross or car or snowmobile. |
| 8 | 2.5-ton truck gross. |
| 10 | 3.5-ton truck gross. |
| 12 | 8-ton truck gross. |

*Ice must be twice as thick if it is soft and slushy. Water flowing beneath ice impedes freezing in rivers (especially in the main channel), in lakes at inlets and outlets, and around beaver lodges.

build islands in water over 3 or 4 feet deep. You will want an island somewhere between 36 square yards (e.g., 6 x 6) and 1,000 square yards (e.g., 25 x 40). Depending on how deep the pond is, you might have to build the island over 2 or 3 years if the dirt does not protrude as an island after the ice melts. Once it does, you will have to add topsoil the next winter so that you can go out by boat in spring to plant it with a suitable grass/legume mixture. (Also see Fig. 7.1.) Ask your local wildlife manager about a suitable mixture to plant. (See Adding Water in Chapter 7.)

You also could dump rocks (6 inch diameter preferably) on the ice. About 20 cubic yards of rock and/or gravel dumped on the ice in about 16 inches of water will yield an island of about 20 square yards at waterline once the ice melts. Then add topsoil the next winter and seed to a grass/legume mixture the following spring.

## Starting from Scratch
## Dugouts and Diked Dugouts

Maybe all you need to do is dig a hole with a dragline or backhoe in an area with a high water table, and let it fill with groundwater. Such ponds are

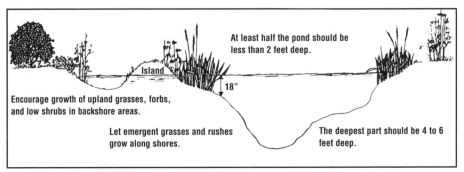

**Figure 8.2.** *Dugout (cross-section). (Poston and Schmidt 1981)*

sometimes called **dugouts**. If you dig the pond at the base of a hill, it will catch runoff from rainwater or snowmelt too. A good location for a dugout often is a natural pothole or intermittent lake bed. Do not locate them in wet or muddy areas because large animals will have difficulty getting to the water. Stock ponds tend to run small—somewhere between 0.1 acre and 0.25 acre. Farm ponds are larger, often several acres. Most are rectangular. Some are dug up to 12 feet deep, mostly for fish. But that is way too deep for ducks and other birds and mammals. By rights, about half the pond should be about 2 feet deep. And the shoreline slope should be about 7:1 to encourage growth of aquatic plants that supply food and cover, with grasses planted on the bank, and a rest-rotation grazing system used (see Fig. 4.13) or fencing placed at least 40 feet back with access points for livestock (see Fig. 8.1). In addition, you should have the 4:1 ratio of grassland cover surrounding your pond, i.e., 4 acres of grassland for every acre of pond.

Start with a sketch and notes about depth, location of spoil, and bottom slopes and contours. Make the shorelines irregular, such as a kidney-shaped pond, or crescent-shaped, rounded-L, dogleg, or oak-leaf—anything except square, rectangular, or round to produce more edge (Fig 8.2 and 8.3). Save the topsoil! Pile it nearby. Then have the subsoil bulldozed around the edge and piled into at least 1 island in the middle, with the rest of the subsoil spread and landscaped around the edge of your pond-to-be. Then have the saved topsoil spread over the subsoil on the island(s) and the edge. Then seed it with a suitable grass/legume mixture.

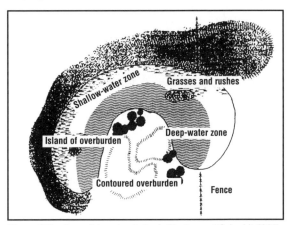

**Figure 8.3.** *Dugout (overhead view). (Poston and Schmidt 1981)*

# FARM PONDS AND STOCK PONDS

Make improvements as discussed under "Improving Your Pond" in this chapter, and you will be all set.

Now, if your pond-to-be is on somewhat of a slope, deposit the excavated subsoil, from the borrow pit, on the downhill side to form a dike. This type of pond is sometimes referred to as a **diked dugout**. During wet years, the dike backs the water into the surrounding area. A dense growth of emergent vegetation usually results, providing excellent feeding and brood-rearing areas for waterfowl, as well as habitat for other wetland wildlife. During dry years, the dugout area will retain water for survival of broods of ducks nearing flight stage. The dike should have a spillway (trough) cut around it 2 feet lower than the top of

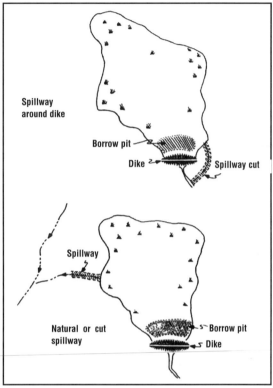

**Figure 8.4.** Common development of retention reservoirs. (Atlantic Waterfowl Council 1972)

the dike so that excess water from a heavy rain can escape without overtopping the dike and washing it out (Fig. 8.4). Apply topsoil to the spillway and seed it with a good grass mixture for stability.

Maybe you do not have to dig out soil for your pond. Maybe, if the slope of your land is adequate, all you have to do is build a dike across the downhill side and let runoff water from rain and snow do the rest. Such a pond is sometimes called a **retention reservoir**. If the watershed (area draining into your pond-to-be) is less than 25 acres, you will not even have to put a control structure in the dike, i.e., a culvert usually, that you can open and shut. Large watersheds generally require a water control structure in the dike, unless part of the flow can be diverted. A control structure tends to complicate matters somewhat, including expense, but it does make things more interesting because you have more flexibility in your control over the water level, and can get involved in water level manipulation to improve habitat conditions, which can be complicated (See Adding Water in Chapter 7). If you build your pond in an upland where the watershed is too small, your pond will fail to fill adequately or even dry up in summer because only runoff (surface) water is used, rather than groundwater too.

But let's keep it simple. If your watershed is less than 25 acres on gently rolling land, build a dike that is about 2 yards wide at the top, with a 3:1 slope. Material from the dike comes from the "borrow pit" dug into the pond just behind the dike for that purpose. The height of the dike will vary with how far you want to back up the water retained by it. As a general rule, you need about 10 acres of watershed for each acre of pond. Thus, if you figure that the watershed that will drain runoff water (rain or snow) into your pond is 25 acres, your pond can be 2.5 acres. And about half of your pond should be 2 feet deep or less for maximum use by waterfowl, shorebirds, wading birds, and other wetland wildlife. You can get by with a smaller watershed for your pond if the watershed is mostly pasture and cropland, but you will need a large watershed if it is mostly woodland or brush land. You should talk to a

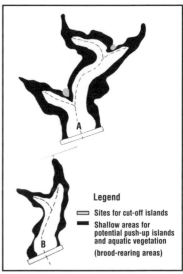

**Figure 8.5.** *Potential sites for construction of islands in retention reservoirs. (Eng et al. 1979.) Site A is better than B because A has more shallow water and potential sites for islands with about the same size dike.*

wildlife manager and a soil scientist about all this, especially the water-holding capacity of your soil. Leaky soil, i.e., sandy soil, on the bottom of the pond will not hold water. Clay soils are best, i.e., soils with a lot of clay.

In any case, you will need a spillway 2 feet lower than the top of the dike, cut as a gentle trough into the top of the bank around 1 side of the dike usually, to get rid of excess water (see Fig. 8.4). Pave it with topsoil and seed it with a grass mixture for stability.

You might be lucky in having a site that contains side channels, which will be flooded to increase the shoreline/pond-area ratio after you build your dike (Fig. 8.5). Such a site also facilitates construction of cutoff islands (Figs. 8.6 and 8.7).

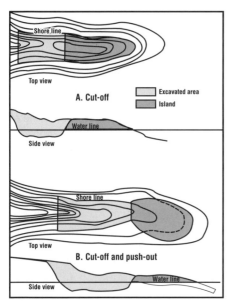

**Figure 8.6.** *Two methods for creating cut-off islands. (Eng et al. 1979)*

# FARM PONDS AND STOCK PONDS

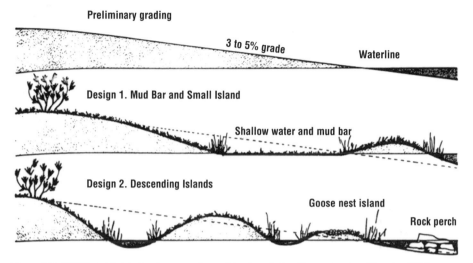

**Figure 8.7.** *Wildlife habitat design for arms of cove islands and shoreline peninsulas. (Stoecker 1982)*

## Islands

The time to develop your island(s) is before the water is present. Place your island as far from shore and emergent vegetation as possible to discourage predators. Building islands in water deeper than 3 or 4 feet probably is too costly. Small islands with low profiles are less attractive to predators; thus, your ducks will be more successful nesting there.

You could build a cut-off island from the end of a small peninsula cut off from the "mainland" by a dozer (Fig. 8.6 and 8.7) or a push-up island with soil scraped into a mound by a bulldozer (Fig. 8.8 and see Fig. 7.1). Push-up

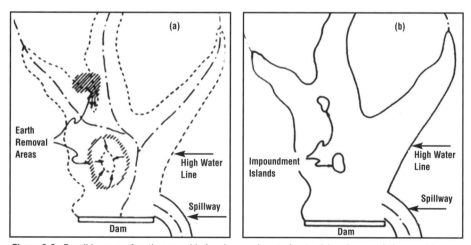

**Figure 8.8.** *Possible areas of earth removal before impoundment of water (a) and areas of placement to create islands after impoundment (b). (Jones 1975 in Ambrose et al. 1983)*

islands are easiest to build from natural high points of ground or from gentle slopes in the upper end of the pond. You can use a dozer to push up and compact material, or a scraper to move, dump, and compact material. Scrapers slope islands better, reducing wave erosion. Islands should be built in an oval, kidney, or peanut shape to create a natural appearance and reduce wave erosion, and point into the prevailing wind. In small ponds where little wave action is likely to occur, the slope can be 6:1 or 8:1 without a berm. When pushing up the island, save the topsoil and apply it to the top of the island before planting a suitable grass/legume mixture. Strive for 50 to 75 percent of the area to be covered by grasses, legumes, and other forbs over 1.5 feet tall, and low shrubs less than 4 feet tall, such as western snowberry, Wood's rose, and sweet fern.

Rock islands work too. Dump large rocks (about 6 inches in diameter) so that the pile will be 2 to 3 feet above water and 10 to 15 feet in diameter. Then cover with 2 to 3 feet of soil from the pond bottom or adjacent upland sites, and seed a grass/legume mixture.

Canada goose

# WHAT ABOUT THE BACKYARD AND ARTIFICIAL THINGS?

**Backyard Wildlife**

Books have been written on the subject of backyard or urban wildlife. (See Chapter 12). What you really need to do is go to your local library or get into bookstores or on the Internet and look up key words such as **urban wildlife** or **backyard wildlife** or **gardening with wildlife** or **nature and gardening** or **butterfly garden** or **backyard birds** or something like that, and see what is available, perhaps on amazon.com or barnesandnoble.com. Use your imagination in selecting key words. If your library does not have the book you want, ask the library to get you an inter-library loan. Also, check out any nature-type stores in your area—those that sell birdhouses, bird feeders, birdbaths, etc. These stores usually sell books about backyard wildlife. Also, check with the wildlife agency in your state or province for information on backyard wildlife. Two other good sources are the National Wildlife Federation, 8925 Leesburg Pike, Vienna, VA 22184, which has an information kit on *Backyard Wildlife* for your area, and the National Institute for Urban Wildlife, 10921 Trotting Ridge Way, Columbia, MD 21044, which has a series of information leaflets in the *Urban Wildlife Manager's Notebook*.

Generally, backyard habitat can be improved for attracting wildlife by planting a variety of things (Appendix VI, VII, VIII) and locating them in clumps and perhaps as a connecting corridor between adjacent trees, hedge, or pond, and a clump of plantings in your yard. Remember that berry- and nut-producing shrubs and trees produce food, and clumps of evergreens provide roosting and winter cover.

**Lawn Mowers and Driveways**

More land is used for lawns than for any single crop in the U.S. Let your beautiful and interesting wildflowers and shrubs grow. Do not tear them out and substitute with a sterile monoculture of Kentucky bluegrass. If you have already done it, please undo it. You might think that huge lawn looks nice, but it certainly does not to wildlife, or to lots of enlightened people either. Rural landowners seem to be the biggest culprits of this unproductive cultural practice, with its waste of time, energy, and money spent on watering lawns and on mower and fuel to cut the grass and pollute the air with a riding lawn mower, while polluting groundwater and wildlife from the chemicals in lawn pesticides and fertilizer. A lawn mower pollutes the air in 1 hour as much as a car in 350 miles, while increasing noise pollution, hearing loss, accidents, and gas consumption. Keep your lawn small and let the clippings lie when you mow, to recycle their nutrients for a vigorous lawn that then will need less, or no, extra fertilizer, pesticide, and water. You can landscape the entire area for wildlife, and it will look far more attractive and interesting than an ecologically sterile monoculture of real short grass. You do not have to have any lawn at all. Landscape for butterflies and birds with a combination of bark, rock, wildflowers, deciduous nut- and fruit-bearing shrubs and trees for food, and coniferous shrubs and trees for cover. Books have been written on this (see Chapter 12 and Appendix VI, VII, VIII). Get some ideas.

And that driveway—keep it narrow! Do not even pave it, unless you absolutely feel a physical urge to do so. Use crushed granite. It is far cheaper and far more environmentally friendly. And do not plop down asphalt and concrete all over the place. Keep it to a bare minimum. And do you really need a 4 or 5 car garage? With lawn, driveway, sidewalk, patio, garage slab— let your wild things grow. They are so much more variable, interesting, and beautiful than the artificial and sterile monoculture of Kentucky bluegrass, asphalt, and concrete that you do not really need, does not look as attractive, costs extra to install and maintain, and destroys wildlife habitat.

## Nest Structures

The main reason to put up nest structures is to observe the bird activity, and usually not because the birds need them. You would not know if they needed them unless you evaluated the habitat and censused the birds to determine if the bird species of interest are below carrying capacity, and that is beyond the call of duty for you. Not only that, but you should know that installing nest structures, maintaining them, and replacing nesting material annually is a tall order, in time, effort, and money. You will also have to clean out periodically undesirable critters like house sparrows, starlings, maybe grackles, and insects. Moreover, nest structures are not suitable substitutes for snags, den trees, and nest trees, which provide some 40 uses nest structures do not. Also, predators can learn to search for nest boxes, so you should install predator guards.

So that is the nasty side. The good side is that where suitable natural nesting sites are no longer present, artificial nesting structures will increase carrying capacity and provide increased opportunity to observe and enjoy bird activity. Good locations for birds using more open habitats include pastures and field borders, fence rows, shelterbelts, orchards, road, railroad, or power line rights-of-way, clearcut areas, and cemeteries. Good locations in

# WHAT ABOUT THE BACKYARD AND ARTIFICIAL THINGS?

woodland include woodland clearings and even the interior. Wood duck nest boxes can be used in marshes and ponds.

To reduce territorial conflicts, nest boxes should be spaced out, for example, 100 yards for bluebirds, 25 to 30 for tree swallows, about 2 to 3 per acre for small nest boxes, and 1 box per 5 acres for large ones.

Preferably, build them of rough-sawn red cedar, redwood, or bald cypress for durability, the wood $3/4$ inch thick (Table 9.1, Fig. 9.1, 9.2). Make the box so that you can open it either on top (Fig. 9.1) or on one side

**Table 9.1. Nest box dimensions and placement heights.** (Kalmbach and McAtee 1969, Mitchell 1988)

| Species | Box floor (in.) | Box depth (in.) | Entrance. height (in.)* | Entrance diameter (in.) | Box height (ft.) |
|---|---|---|---|---|---|
| American robin† | 7 x 8 | 8 | — | — | 6-15 |
| Eastern bluebird | 4 x 4 | 8-12 | 6-10 | 1 1/2 | 4-6 |
| Mountain bluebird | 5 x 5 | 8-12 | 6-10 | 1 1/2 | 4-6 |
| Western bluebird | 4 x 4 | 8-12 | 6-10 | 1 1/2 | 4-6 |
| Chickadees | 4 x 4 | 8-10 | 6-8 | 1 1/8 | 4-15 |
| Titmice | 4 x 4 | 8-10 | 6-8 | 1 1/4 | 5-15 |
| Ash-throated flycatcher | 6 x 6 | 8-10 | 6-8 | 1 1/2 | 5-15 |
| Great-crested flycatcher | 6 x 6 | 8-10 | 6-8 | 1 3/4 | 5-15 |
| Phoebes† | 6 x 6 | 6 | — | — | 8-12 |
| Brown-headed nuthatch | 4 x 4 | 8-10 | 6-8 | 1 1/4 | 5-15 |
| Pygmy nuthatch | 4 x 4 | 8-10 | 6-8 | 1 1/4 | 5-15 |
| Red-breasted nuthatch | 4 x 4 | 8-10 | 6-8 | 1 1/4 | 5-15 |
| White-breasted nuthatch | 4 x 4 | 8-10 | 6-8 | 1 3/8 | 5-15 |
| Prothonotory warbler | 5 x 5 | 6 | 4-5 | 1 3/8 | 4-8 |
| Barn swallow† | 6 x 6 | 6 | — | — | 8-12 |
| Purple martin | 6 x 6 | 6 | 1-2 | 2 1/2 | 6-20 |
| Tree swallow | 5 x 5 | 6-8 | 4-6 | 1 1/2 | 5-15 |
| Violet-green swallow | 5 x 5 | 6-8 | 4-6 | 1 1/2 | 5-15 |
| Downy woodpecker | 4 x 4 | 8-10 | 6-8 | 1 1/2 | 5-15 |
| Golden-fronted woodpecker | 6 x 6 | 12-15 | 9-12 | 2 | 10-20 |
| Hairy woodpecker | 6 x 6 | 12-15 | 9-12 | 1 1/2 | 8-20 |
| Lewis woodpecker | 7 x 7 | 16-18 | 14-16 | 2 1/2 | 12-20 |
| Northern flicker | 7 x 7 | 16-18 | 14-16 | 2 1/2 | 6-20 |
| Pileated woodpecker | 8 x 8 | 16-24 | 12-20 | 3 x 4 | 15-25 |
| Red-headed woodpecker | 6 x 6 | 12-15 | 9-12 | 2 | 10-20 |
| Yellow-bellied sapsucker | 6 x 6 | 12-15 | 9-12 | 1 1/2 | 10-20 |
| Bewick's wren | 4 x 4 | 6-8 | 4-6 | 1 1/4 | 5-10 |
| Carolina wren | 4 x 4 | 6-8 | 4-6 | 1 1/2 | 5-10 |
| House wren | 4 x 4 | 6-8 | 4-6 | 1 1/4 | 5-10 |
| Screech owl‡ | 8 x 8 | 12 x 15 | 9 x 12 | 3 | 10-30 |
| Saw-whet owl | 6 x 6 | 10 x 12 | 8 x 10 | 2 1/2 | 12-20 |
| Barn owl | 10 x 18 | 15 x 18 | 4 | 6 | 12-18 |
| Barred owl | 12 1/4 x 12 1/4 | 23 | 12 | 7 | 20-30 |
| Wood duck | 7 3/4 x 8 | 24 1/4 x 25 1/4 | 18 | 3 x 4 [a] | >3; >20 [a] |

*Height of entrance hole above nest box floor. †Use nesting shelf, which has open front.
‡Same dimensions for American kestrel. [a]Also for hooded merganser; 4 inches is width of oval hole. Entrance is 3 1/4 x 4 1/4 inches for common goldeneyes and 5 x 6 inches for common mergansers. Place nest at least 3 feet above water and about 20 feet above ground.

with only a pivot nail driven into front and back towards the top so that the side will pivot open (Fig. 9.2). It can be held closed with a screw and washer, screw eye, or even a double nail. Drill some drain holes in the bottom.

Predator guards can be purchased commercially or constructed (Fig. 9.3, 9.4, 9.5). You also can make a guard of hardware cloth that surrounds the box entrance and extends outward about 5 inches.

The best structures for wood ducks (excluding tree cavities) are a wooden box (see Table 9.1 and Fig. 9.3, 9.4, 9.5), a vertical metal box, a horizontal metal box, a plastic pail (Fig. 9.6), and a commercially available plastic Tom Tubbs structure. They will need a strip of $1/4$-inch hardware cloth attached inside from bottom of entrance hole to bottom of box, to allow ducklings a toehold for exit (Fig. 9.6).

Mount your nest boxes in the water or as close to it as possible, on posts, poles, pipes, or trees, but trees provide less security from climbing predators including fire ants. Especially do not use aspen trees near water, for beaver will cut them down to de-branch them and eat the bark as preferred food. Locate plastic boxes in full shade. Face the opening of the box toward the open water at 90 degrees to prevailing winds. Space them about 1 per acre.

## Bird Feeders and Birdbaths

Unlike birdhouses, bird feeders and baths are not so size-dependent and almost any will serve a variety of birds, for the most part. Purchase them locally or visit the store to get ideas on construction. For bird feeders, you will absolutely need a squirrel baffle, also available commercially. Incidentally, many songbirds are attracted by the sound of running water, so you might want to buy a birdbath or fountain with a pump, or rig up something yourself.

Installing several bird feeders reduces competition on any one. If house sparrows, starlings, cowbirds, or grackles are a problem, try going with pure sunflower seed rather than a seed mixture.

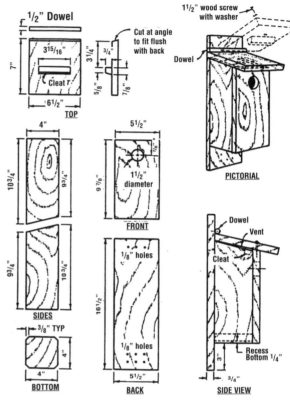

**Figure 9.1.** *Construction details for a top-opening songbird nest box. (Mitchell 1986)*

Discontinue feeding after August so migratory birds will not delay their migration. Begin again after the fall migration ends. Birds become accustomed to and even dependent on feeders, so once you start, keep it up or your birds will suffer, especially in winter. And clean them out regularly, or your birds could sicken and die of disease. Much information is available from books, state and provincial wildlife agencies, federal wildlife agencies, university extension services, local chapters of the National Audubon Society, National Wildlife Federation, and others.

## Perches and Roosts

Take a look and watch where your songbirds and certain other types land to perch. Notice how much they use dead limbs, not all birds certainly, but very many species. Unless the dead limbs pose a hazard, let them be! You want to see out a ways from your windows but too many branches block the view? Okay, remove some, but girdle others. They'll die but remain as low perches for close viewing and photographing your birds, while still allowing

# WHAT ABOUT THE BACKYARD AND ARTIFICIAL THINGS?

you to view the distant scene. Make a brush pile out of the severed branches, for some of your small birds will perch in the edge of it, and it will serve as cover for some of your small mammals, especially rabbits and chipmunks (see Brush Piles in Chapter 2). If you have a fence, it too will be heavily used as a perch (see Fencing in this chapter). So will your electric and telephone lines.

## Bat Houses

Again, like birdhouses, you might not **need** bat houses. But bats are fascinating critters. For one thing, bats are the **only** mammals that can fly! (Flying squirrels glide.) And the species in the U.S. and Canada feed almost exclusively on **your** insects. Anyway, build a bat house and sit back and enjoy watching them drop out of

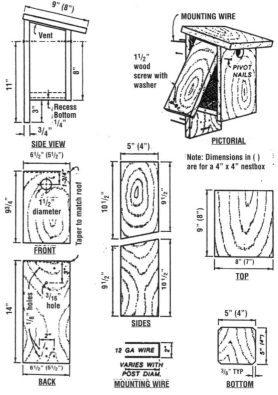

**Figure 9.2.** Construction details for a side-opening songbird nest box. (Zeleny 1976)

the bottom just after sunset when enough light still exists, and watch them go after your insects. Fascinating.

Use untreated, rough-sided lumber, galvanized nails, and roofing shingles on the roof (Fig. 9.7). You might want to cover the top half of the house with tar paper to create a temperature differential. You can build it large enough to house an entire colony. You can hang the house securely in various ways with nails, screws, hooks, and brackets. A big one might need a cross arm along the back for support. Attach it on a tree trunk 3 to 5 yards above ground, preferably near water, facing east to receive the morning sun and to protect it from the southern sun and prevailing winds.

## Burrows

You can have some fun and boost your carrying capacity for small mammals and even burrowing owls by installing burrow boxes of concrete or wood such as oak or tulip poplar or warp-resistant exterior plywood (Fig. 9.8). Use water-resistant lumber at least $3/4$ inch thick and nails or screws. You might need lumber $1^1/2$ inches thick for the tunnels leading into the box

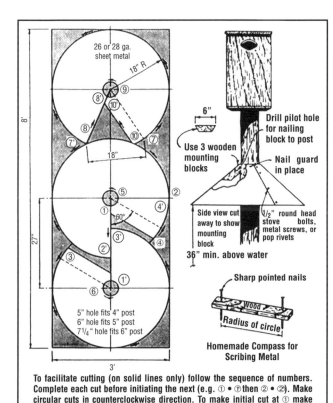

if you place the burrow in pastures where you might have cows stepping on them. But do not apply preservative like paint or creosote.

The box needs no bottom, but put a removable lid on it so that periodically you can inspect it to see if anything is occupying it and to clean it out. Bury the box about 6 inches deep to insulate it, or place it at ground level with the top covered by brush to help keep the box interior dark. Build a mound of soil around the entrance to help attract burrowing animals.

Place the box in well-drained soil near good cover such as a woods border or a weedy fence row. For

**Figure 9.3.** *Construction details for a cone predator guard made from sheet metal. (U.S. Fish and Wildlife Service 1976 in Ridlehuber and Teaford 1986)*

muskrats, place the box above high water in the back of your pond if it has emergent vegetation. On slopes or cut banks, place the box so that the entrance is slightly lower than the box itself, to reduce the chance of flooding. You will have the best luck with your artificial burrows in areas where the soil is hard or tightly packed, with few abandoned burrows, and where cover is sparse. Now and then, lift the lid to enjoy seeing what's inside—but not too often, or your animals will abandon it.

## Watering Devices

No big deal in the East, but in the West—a major limiting factor in many areas. So if you live in dry parts of the western United States or Canada, here is what you can do.

Springs, seeps, vernal pools, and ephemeral pools need protection from livestock (see Water in Chapter 2). So do stock ponds, farm ponds, riparian

# WHAT ABOUT THE BACKYARD AND ARTIFICIAL THINGS?

areas, and wetlands (see Chapter 6, 7, and 8). You have to make sure your water supply is permanent, or your wildlife will suffer, and maybe die when they rely on your water and find it gone. And installing a watering device without regard for the availability of food or cover is a waste of time and money. Do not place any watering device in gullies or arroyos; on sandy soils; close to a natural water source; in unnatural places like ridges or summits; near roads, trails, or other areas of human activity; and in localized spots called rain shadows where less rain falls, if the main source of water is to be from rain.

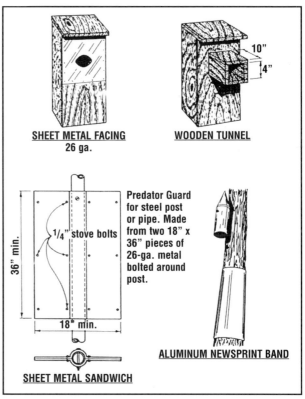

**Figure 9.4.** *Four types of predator guards commonly used with artificial duck nests. (Ridlehuber and Teaford 1986)*

Preferably, install a watering device in ecotones and coverts, protected from prevailing winds, and in locations accessible to target wildlife but not competing animals such as cattle or feral burros. Such animals disturb wildlife, and denude and trample shoreline plants as they come and go for drinking and as they tend to loaf around the watering device. Also, the watering device should not be located on wintering range for ungulates, where water might encourage animals to remain throughout summer, thus damaging the site from overuse.

You might have a lot of phreatophytes around—woody vegetation such as saltcedar tamarisk that sucks up water and transpires it through leaves constantly. Cut that stuff, and you should see some water conservation.

## Water Holes, Dugouts, Ponds, and Tenajas

Simple watering devices such as a water hole should be about 0.5 acre in size, and about 6 to 9 feet deep with gentle slopes, in a density of about 1 per square mile. If a basin exists already, you could trench runoff directly to it.

A dugout, or charco, is a stock pond used by watering livestock and also wildlife. It can be improved for wildlife as discussed in Chapter 8. You could build a rain-trap by using a storage pit (Fig. 9.9) or a storage bag. In plaza basins of the southern high plains, excavated dugouts are called "tailwater pits" locally because they receive overflow irrigation. Other types of ponds involving dikes also can be built or improved for wildlife as discussed in Chapters 7 and 8. For water holes and stock ponds, use fencing to restrict livestock to less than $1/4$ of the shoreline (see Fig 8.1).

A tenaja is a rock basin that holds water, from a few

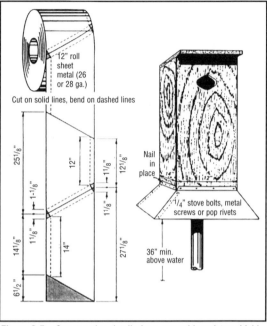

**Figure 9.5.** *Construction details for a pyramid predator shield made from sheet metal. (Ridlehuber and Teaford 1986)*

gallons to more than 25,000 gallons. You can increase the storage capacity by use of a sunshade to reduce evaporation. To do so, anchor eyebolts into

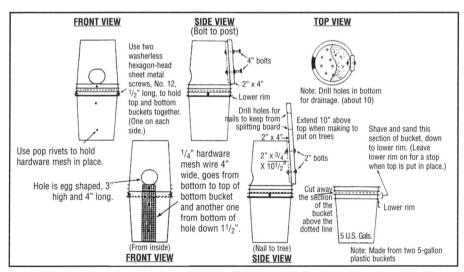

**Figure 9.6.** *Plastic bucket wood duck nest box. (U.S. Fish and Wildlife Service and personal communication Bill Meier, Wisconsin Department of Natural Resources.)*

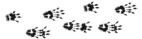
the canyon walls for attaching cables over the tenaja and then attach a shading material such as sheet metal to the cables. You could also build a small dam of impervious soil (with some clay) on the downhill side to hold more water. If the rock bottom and sides contain porous cracks, clean them, then use a sealer to prevent water loss.

## Springs and Seeps

Fence any natural spring or seep if you notice damage to it from wild and domestic ungulates.

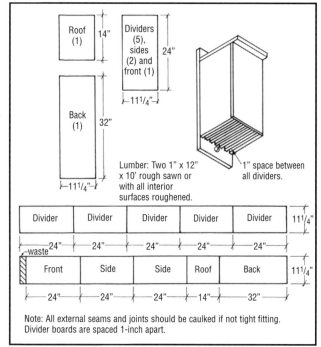

**Figure 9.7.** *Bat house. (Henderson 1992)*

You can connect it with a pipeline leading outside the fence to a protected tank away from the sensitive spring or seep area (Fig. 9.10). For dependability, a spring or seep often needs some sort of installation, which should be fenced against trampling by ungulates (Fig. 9.11). The installation can include a redwood spring box, open at top and bottom, installed at or near the spring or seep, with galvanized or plastic pipe (plastic is lighter for handling) at least 1.25 inches in diameter to lead the spring water away to

**Table 9.2. Size of apron needed for 600-, 700-, and 900-gallon guzzlers.** (Yoakum et al. 1980)

| Minimum annual rainfall (inches) | Square feet of collecting surface required | | | Apron dimension in feet | | | | | |
|---|---|---|---|---|---|---|---|---|---|
| | | | | Square | | | Circular (diameter) | | |
| | 600 gal. | 700 gal. | 900 gal. | 600 gal. | 700 gal. | 900 gal. | 600 gal. | 700 gal. | 900 gal. |
| 1 | 965 | 1,127 | 1,453 | 31 | 34 | 38 | 36 | 38 | 43 |
| 2 | 482 | 563 | 726 | 22 | 24 | 27 | 25 | 27 | 31 |
| 3 | 322 | 376 | 485 | 18 | 19 | 22 | 20 | 22 | 25 |
| 4 | 242 | 282 | 365 | 16 | 17 | 19 | 18 | 19 | 22 |
| 5 | 192 | 225 | 290 | 14 | 15 | 17 | 16 | 17 | 19 |
| 6 | 162 | 189 | 243 | 13 | 14 | 15 | 15 | 16 | 18 |
| 7 | 138 | 161 | 208 | 12 | 13 | 14 | 13 | 14 | 16 |
| 8 | 121 | 141 | 182 | 11 | 12 | 14 | 12 | 13 | 15 |
| 9 | 107 | 125 | 161 | 11 | 12 | 13 | 12 | 13 | 14 |
| 10 | 97 | 113 | 146 | 10 | 11 | 12 | 11 | 12 | 14 |
| 11 | 87 | 102 | 132 | 9 | 10 | 11 | 10 | 11 | 13 |
| 12 | 80 | 94 | 121 | 9 | 10 | 11 | 10 | 11 | 12 |

a trough. A "T" fitting attached inside the spring box will prevent debris from entering the pipe. Plastic pipe should be covered by soil to protect it from freezing, trampling, and rodent damage.

Another method you could use to develop a spring or seep into a single stream that will not freeze readily is to use plastic sheeting and perforated pipe covered with coarse gravel (Fig. 9.12). Dig a small pit a short distance below the source to collect the water and stimulate plant growth for wildlife. Fence out livestock at the source and at the pit.

## Guzzlers

A guzzler has 2 or 3 main components: (1) an apron to catch and channel water to (2) a cistern or storage tank which pipes water to (3) a basin (guzzler) from which wildlife drinks. Sometimes the apron leads directly to the drinking basin guzzler. The apron can be a large slick rock that diverts water to the cistern or guzzler (Fig. 9.13), or a hillside steep enough and cleared of enough debris for runoff to fill the guzzler. Artificial aprons usually are corrugated sheets of galvanized iron or fiberglass on an elevated roof-like structure pitched about 5 percent to catch rain and snow and divert the water to the cistern or guzzler (Fig. 9.14).

Generally, an apron 15 yards by 2 yards is fine for an area receiving 8 to 12 inches of precipitation per year. But you can determine the size of the apron for 600-, 700-, and 900-gallon guzzlers in areas of rainfall varying from 1 to 12 inches per year (Table 9.2).

Make the cistern of galvanized iron under the apron, which diverts most

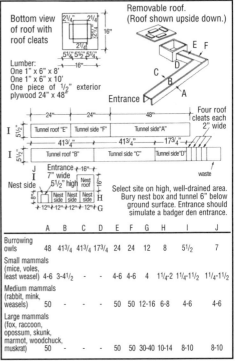

| | A | B | C | D | E | F | G | H | I | J |
|---|---|---|---|---|---|---|---|---|---|---|
| Burrowing owls | 48 | 41¾ | 41¾ | 17¾ | 24 | 24 | 12 | 8 | 5½ | 7 |
| Small mammals (mice, voles, least weasel) | 4-6 | 3-4½ | - | - | 4-6 | 4-6 | 4 | 1½-2 | 1½-1½ | 1¼-1½ |
| Medium mammals (rabbit, mink, weasels) | 50 | - | - | - | 50 | 50 | 12-16 | 6-8 | 4-6 | 4-6 |
| Large mammals (fox, raccoon, opossum, skunk, marmot, woodchuck, muskrat) | 50 | - | - | - | 50 | 50 | 30-40 | 10-14 | 8-10 | 8-10 |

**Figure 9.8.** *Generic design for artificial burrow for burrowing owls and ground-dwelling mammals. (Dimensions in inches.) (Henderson 1992, Herricks et al. 1982)*

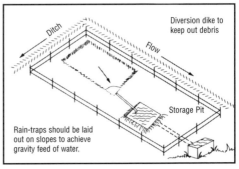

**Figure 9.9.** Design for a rain-trap that feeds a storage pit and trough. (Payne and Copes 1988)

of the water. You can also pipe or channel the water from apron to cistern if necessary, with screens to prevent debris from entering the cistern. But check screens regularly, and make sure the cistern is dark to inhibit sunlight and algae, facing north preferably, the open end away from the prevailing wind, buried to prevent freezing, and cleaned every 2 years.

The guzzler itself (drinking basin) can be a tank of prefabricated fiberglass, or a concrete tank, varying in size relative to the kinds, sizes, and numbers of animals using it, but usually about 28 to 30 inches in diameter and about 6 to 8 inches deep. You also can use a heavy-equipment tire with the top rim cut back for easier access, and with "corten" plate steel, concrete, or clay bottom (Fig. 9.15).

An 8-foot heavy-equipment tire holds 350 gallons of water and the black rubber absorbs enough heat to prevent freezing of water at night (Fig. 9.16). You should bury it in a hillside steep enough for runoff to be channeled into the tire, which serves as both

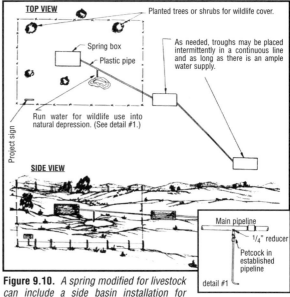

**Figure 9.10.** *A spring modified for livestock can include a side basin installation for chukars. (Nevada State Office, U.S. Bureau of Land Management in Yoakum et al. 1980.)*

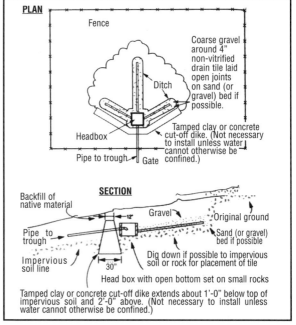

**Figure 9.11**. *Development designed to tap water in seeps or spring. (Payne and Copes 1998.)*

cistern and drinking basin. It can be covered low so that chukar partridge can drink but large animals cannot, or covered higher for all animals to drink. The shade decreases algae, temperature, and evaporation.

Water levels in the drinking basin usually can be controlled by a float valve in a container box separate from the basin itself. Bury this box and valve in the ground below the cistern.

Be sure to check with your local wildlife manager for additional information concerning guzzlers.

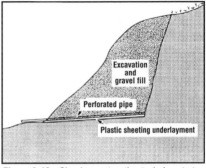

**Figure 9.12.** *Simple construction technique to tap springs and seeps. (Rutherford and Snyder 1983)*

## Pipelines, Spurlines, and Overflow Pipes

If you have some form of watering device for livestock or for other use, e.g., ponds, reservoirs, wells, or storage tanks, you probably can use a pipe and gravity flow to deliver water to drinking basins for wildlife (see Fig. 9.10). Unless gopher

**Figure 9.13.** *Slick-rock apron for guzzler (top), and water collecting aprons for self-filling wildlife watering facility (bottom). (U.S. Forest Service 1983)*

(1) Shape and smooth area.
(2) Cover evenly with dry cement at rate of 1 sack for each 50 sq. ft., except on heavy clay soils, where you should use 1 sack for each 30 sq. ft.
(3) Rake in thoroughly 2½ to 3 inches.
(4) Sprinkle thoroughly until soil is wet to a depth of 6 inches.
(5) Paint or spray with asphalt emulsion as soon as possible after cement is set, but always within 24 hours.

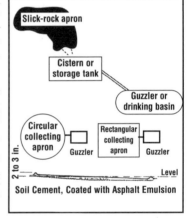

damage is a potential problem, use plastic pipe because it is lighter than galvanized pipe for transporting. You could even attach several spurlines off one pipeline to distribute water. But it is expensive and might need extra maintenance if you bury them for esthetics or have to prevent freezing or trampling.

If the drinking basin is subject to undue damage or disturbance from domestic, feral, or wild ungulates, you will have to fence it. Place the basin about 50 to 100 yards from the source. Use at least 20 inches of steel pipe at the source and the basin, with plastic pipe in between laid to grade to prevent air blocks. To regulate water levels in the drinking basin, you might need a float valve and container box.

You must have an overflow pipe on your livestock drinking troughs or storage tanks, or you will end up with drowned turkeys, quail, chukar, songbirds, and even small mammals trying to drink when the water level is low. All the overflow pipe has to do is let water run over to form a puddle. Better yet is to pipe the overflow water 50 to 100 yards away from the

# WHAT ABOUT THE BACKYARD AND ARTIFICIAL THINGS?

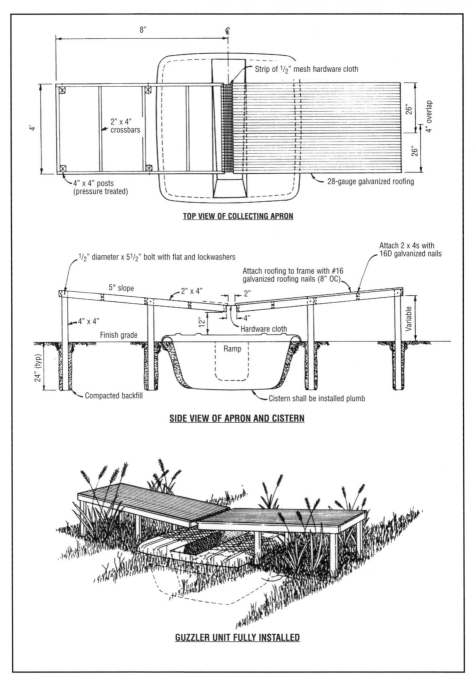

**Figure 9.14.** *Construction and assembly details for 2 collecting aprons that feed water to the guzzler. (Johnson and Jacobs 1986)*

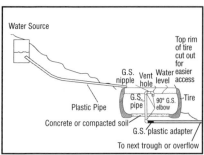

**Figure 9.15.** *Rubber tire trough watering system. (Payne and Bryant 1998)*

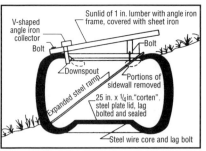

**Figure 9.16.** *A simple guzzler with a tire to catch runoff water from an upland slope. (Elderkin and Morris 1989)*

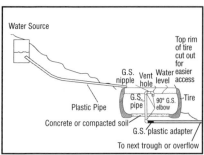

36" square opening for overflow pipe

12" x 2" redwood planking for float board

**WINDMILL AND WATERING TANK**

Note: (1) The objective of float boards is to help cut down the water evaporation in the tank, and (2) to give game birds, in the process of obtaining drinking water, a structure which can help them escape should they fall into the tank.

**TOP VIEW**

2" x 4" redwood

Water level
Float board
36"
square

16-gauge metal tank

**SIDE VIEW**

1½" galvanized overflow pipe to come within 2 inches of tank top.

**Figure 9.17.** *The simple round float board illustrated prevents drowning of wild birds by providing an area for them to drink at round water troughs. (Nevada State Office, U.S. Bureau of Land Management in Yoakum et al. 1980.)*

trough to the drinking basin for wildlife. Overflow pipes work especially well if you live in a dry region and you have a windmill that pumps livestock water into a large storage tank (Fig 9.17).

In areas of less than 30 inches annual precipitation, you might want to manage intensively for critters like bobwhite quail by installing temporary watering facilities (Fig. 9.18), in addition to pipelines, spurlines, and overflow pipes. Such facilities might increase your quail and some other wildlife populations by dispersing them into unused habitat. But you must be faithful in replenishing the water you have habituated the local wildlife to depend on; otherwise do not even think about doing this.

### Safety Devices and Special Features

To avoid drowning small birds and mammals and to enhance water availability, check regularly to make sure the water level is within 2 inches from the lip of the tank or trough. You must provide escape ramps or ladders so they cannot be damaged by domestic or wild ungulates (Figs. 9.19, 9.20, 9.21, 9.22, 9.23, 9.24).

### Fencing*

Most fences are designed to control livestock. Fences affect wildlife by (1) hindering their movements and

\* *I was captain of the fencing team in 1960-61 for the University of Wisconsin-Madison, but that was sword fighting (saber, epee, foil), not wire stringing.*

# WHAT ABOUT THE BACKYARD AND ARTIFICIAL THINGS?

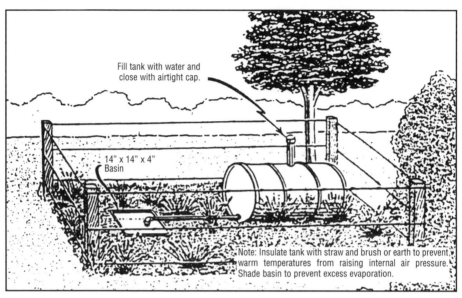

Fill tank with water and close with airtight cap.

14" x 14" x 4" Basin

Note: Insulate tank with straw and brush or earth to prevent warm temperatures from raising internal air pressure. Shade basin to prevent excess evaporation.

**Figure 9.18.** *Temporary wildlife watering facility. (U.S. Soil Conservation Service in Payne and Bryant 1998)*

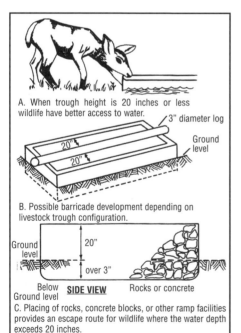

A. When trough height is 20 inches or less wildlife have better access to water.

3" diameter log

Ground level

20"

20"

B. Possible barricade development depending on livestock trough configuration.

Ground level

20"

over 3"

Below Ground level

**SIDE VIEW**

Rocks or concrete

C. Placing of rocks, concrete blocks, or other ramp facilities provides an escape route for wildlife where the water depth exceeds 20 inches.

**Figure 9.19.** *Design modifications beneficial to wildlife for water troughs constructed for domestic livestock. (Adapted from Wilson and Hannans 1977 in Yoakum et al. 1980.)*

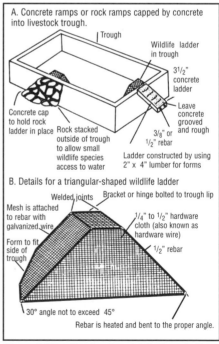

A. Concrete ramps or rock ramps capped by concrete into livestock trough.

Trough

Wildlife ladder in trough

$3^1/_2$" concrete ladder

Concrete cap to hold rock ladder in place

Rock stacked outside of trough to allow small wildlife species access to water

Leave concrete grooved and rough

$3/_8$" or $1/_2$" rebar

Ladder constructed by using 2" x 4" lumber for forms

B. Details for a triangular-shaped wildlife ladder

Welded joints

Bracket or hinge bolted to trough lip

Mesh is attached to rebar with galvanized wire

Form to fit side of trough

$1/_4$" to $1/_2$" hardware cloth (also known as hardware wire)

$1/_2$" rebar

30° angle not to exceed 45°

Rebar is heated and bent to the proper angle.

**Figure 9.20.** *Construction details for adapting a livestock water trough for wildlife use. (Wilson and Hannans 1977 in Yoakum et al. 1980)*

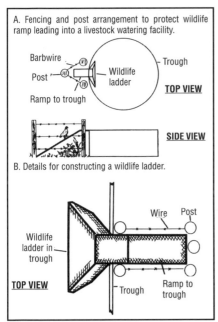

A. Fencing and post arrangement to protect wildlife ramp leading into a livestock watering facility.

Barbwire
Post
Wildlife ladder
Ramp to trough
Trough
**TOP VIEW**

**SIDE VIEW**

B. Details for constructing a wildlife ladder.

Wire   Post
Wildlife ladder in trough
**TOP VIEW**
Trough   Ramp to trough

**Figure 9.21.** *Plans for modifying a livestock water trough by providing both an outside and inside wildlife ladder. (Wilson and Hannans 1977 in Yoakum et al. 1980)*

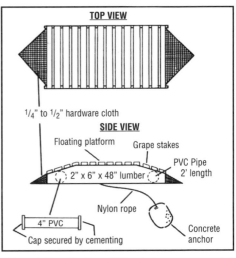

**TOP VIEW**

1/4" to 1/2" hardware cloth
**SIDE VIEW**
Floating platform   Grape stakes
PVC Pipe 2' length
2" x 6" x 48" lumber
Nylon rope
4" PVC
Cap secured by cementing
Concrete anchor

**Figure 9.22.** *Floating wildlife platform recommended for large open water storage tanks. (Wilson and Hannans 1977 in Yoakum et al. 1980)*

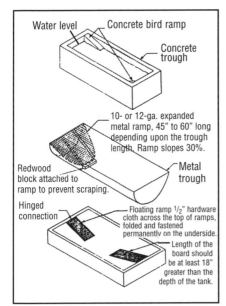

Water level   Concrete bird ramp
Concrete trough
10- or 12-ga. expanded metal ramp, 45" to 60" long depending upon the trough length. Ramp slopes 30%.
Redwood block attached to ramp to prevent scraping.
Metal trough
Hinged connection
Floating ramp 1/2" hardware cloth across the top of ramps, folded and fastened permanently on the underside.
Length of the board should be at least 18" greater than the depth of the tank.

**Figure 9.23.** *Trough bird ladder. (Payne and Copes 1988)*

home range, (2) entanglement and death, (3) concentrating livestock on critical wildlife habitat, (4) protecting wildlife habitat from overgrazing or trampling by livestock, and (5) excluding nuisance wildlife from such areas as cropland, orchards, airports, and highway rights-of-way.

Do not fence any more area than you have to. Paint the tops of fence posts white on new fencing so ungulates can see the new fence, and flag new fences with pieces of white cloth, which will eventually deteriorate. Do not use net or woven wire; wildlife cannot pass through. In areas of heavy seasonal movement by deer, elk, or moose, the preferred fence is any wood fence or a wire fence with poles as the top strand. Thus, a visual height berrier is obvious to wildlife for ease of passing without causing damage to fence or animal.

Avoid loose wire on a fence; it entangles wildlife easier than taut wire does.

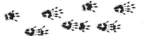
# WHAT ABOUT THE BACKYARD AND ARTIFICIAL THINGS?

Smooth wire will reduce injury to wildlife better than barbed wire will. So use all smooth wire; otherwise, replace the top and bottom strands of a barbed wire fence with smooth wire to facilitate movement of white-tailed deer, mule deer, elk, and moose which jump over, and pronghorns which crawl under. Deer also crawl under. The top 2 strands should be 12 inches apart to reduce the chance of entanglement when deer jump the fence (Fig. 9.25), and unlike fences used on pronghorn range, place wire fence stays every 8 feet apart to keep top wires from twisting around a deer's legs. Deer normally jump with their hind legs forward. Elk and moose drag their hind legs over the fence, and thus are less likely to become entangled. Set the bottom strand 18 inches above ground to allow deer and pronghorns to crawl under. Set the top strand no higher than 40 inches above ground to allow deer to jump over (Fig. 9.25). But with mountain sheep, a 3-strand fence is best, with wires spaced at 20, 15, and 4 inches. Otherwise,

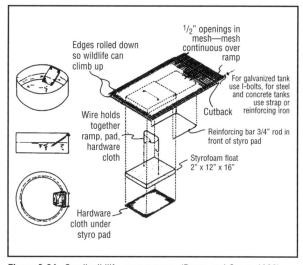

**Figure 9.24.** *Small wildlife escape ramp. (Payne and Copes 1988)*

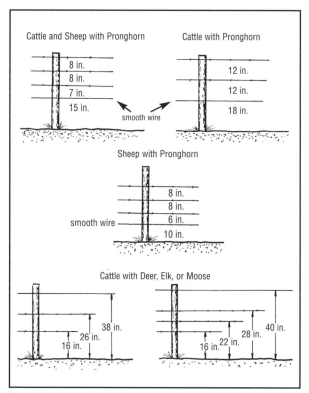

**Figure 9.25.** *Spacing of fence wire to accommodate wild ungulates and livestock. (Karsky 1988)*

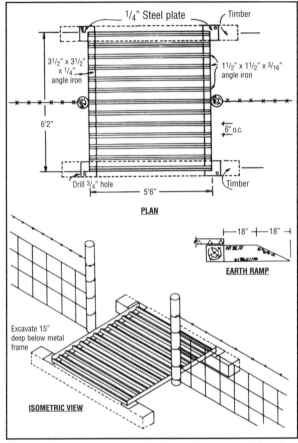

**Figure 9.26.** *Antelope pass specifications and recommended method of installation. (Mapston and ZoBell 1972 in Yoakum et al. 1980)*

sheep can stick their heads through the top 2 strands, but cannot crawl under or between.

Use as few strands of wire as possible. Three strands are better than 4, and 2 are better than 3.

If you decide against adjusting the bottom strand for pronghorns, then at least do not use fence stays in every section of the fence, to allow pronghorns to crawl through. You also could place a cattleguard as an antelope pass at the corners of the fence (Figs. 9.26 and 9.27), because pronghorns will be funneled by the fence to the corners often to die there in winter, unless your cattleguard is there for them to jump. Pronghorns are long jumpers, not high jumpers, for their natural habitat, prairie, does not have anything high for them to jump, and high jumping did not evolve with them for survival as it did for deer in the woods. However, pronghorn fawns often cannot jump the cattleguard, so do not use them if your fence otherwise allows pronghorns to slip through. You would be wiser to use a let-down fence (Fig. 9.28) to allow pronghorns and other wild ungulates to pass, especially during snow depths of 30 inches or more.

To encourage waterfowl to nest on your property near a wetland, fence livestock 30 to 60 yards away from the wetland, because waterfowl will use the grassy area for nesting.

Do not place a fence on a slope (Fig. 9.29). A fence in such a location is especially difficult for wildlife to cross. If you decide you have to run a fence on a hillside, run it up and down rather than on the contour.

In pronghorn range, help keep the fence relatively free of snow by locating

# WHAT ABOUT THE BACKYARD AND ARTIFICIAL THINGS?

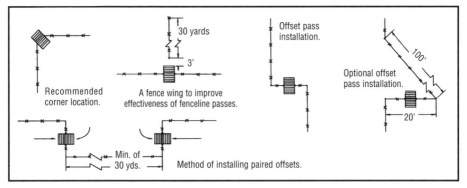

**Figure 9.27.** *Recommended methods for installing antelope passes. (Mapston and ZoBell 1972 in Yoakum et al. 1980)*

it in naturally windswept areas. You might have to determine that by reconnaissance the winter before you do the fencing.

Place fences at least 4 to 6 yards from the edge of brushy cover so that wildlife can see the fence and avoid getting tangled in it.

In farm country, leave a margin 4 to 6 yards wide of natural vegetation along a new fence line. Wildlife will use the natural cover as nesting and denning cover and a travel corridor along the open fields.

In wooded or brushy country, keep the sight line down the fence line to something less than 360 yards, i.e., put some kind of angle in it or run it around a rock pile or something. That way hunters and poachers cannot see and shoot so far down the fence line, and wildlife will not be so reluctant to approach the fence for crossing.

Place a snow fence such that you reduce snow depths in stands of shrubs that could be used by browsing deer, or that you create drifts to cover overused or newly-seeded areas.

If you want to keep deer or elk out of gardens, orchards, tree nurseries, etc., you must install a fence at least 6.5 feet high for deer and 8 feet high for elk. Keep the brush

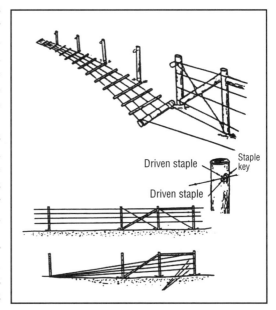

**Figure 9.28.** *Let-down fences to permit wildlife to cross. (Karsky 1988)*

trimmed away from the fence so that deer or elk do not try to jump brush and fence together.

You can fence bears away from beehives with a 5-strand electric fence about 60 inches high (Fig. 9.30).

Be sure to check with your local wildlife manager for additional information on fencing.

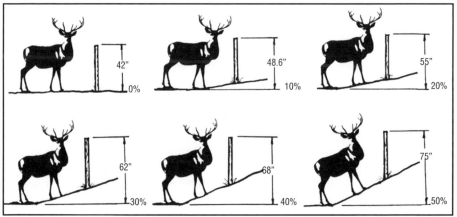

**Figure 9.29.** *The barrier height of any fence is increased for deer, elk, and moose with the increase of ground slope. (Karsky 1988)*

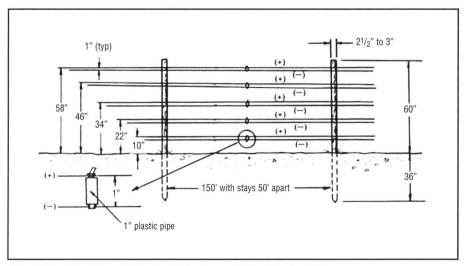

**Figure 9.30.** *A bear fence with 5 sets of hot and ground wires. (Karsky 1988)*

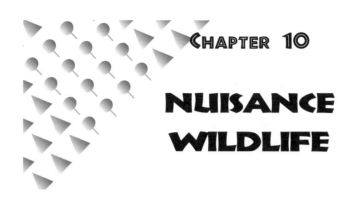

# CHAPTER 10

# NUISANCE WILDLIFE

## Sources of Information

You want to know what to do about nuisance wildlife? I cannot handle it well in this book. That is a book in itself. There is a lot of stuff on it out there. Every state and provincial agency and every state cooperative extension service (located at a state university) provides information on nuisance wildlife, so be sure to check with them. The most comprehensive of the books on nuisance wildlife is the (1997) *Prevention and Control of Wildlife Damage: A Handbook For People Who Deal With Wildlife Damage Problems,* S. E. Hygnstrom, G. E. Larson, and R. M. Timm, editors, and published by Diane Publishing Company, Upland, PA, and *Resolving Human-Wildlife Conflicts*, by M. Conover (2001) and published by Lewis Publishers, Boca Raton, FL.

Another good source is the out-of-print 1,150-page book (request inter-library loan) by M. Novak and others (1987), *Wild Furbearer Management and Conservation in North America*, published by the Ontario Ministry of Natural Resources, Toronto, with its highly illustrated Chapter 61 ("Traps and Trap Research" by M. Novak), Chapter 62 ("Techniques for Commercially Harvesting Furbearers" by J. A. Baker and P. M. Dwyer), and Chapter 63 ("Nuisance Furbearer Damage Control in Urban and Suburban Areas" by M. H. de Almeida). Another good source is Chapter 18 ("Identification and Control of Wildlife Damage" by R. A. Dolbeer, N. R. Holler, and D. W. Hawthorne), in T. A. Bookhout's (1994) *Research and Management Techniques for Wildlife and Habitats*, published by The Wildlife Society, Bethesda, MD. Also examine C. Rutledge's (1998) *Backyard Battle Plan: The Ultimate Guide to Controlling Wildlife Damage in Your Garden*, published by Viking Penguin, New York. You might also check with Animal Damage Control of the U.S. Department of Agriculture for information and other help, and the Internet.

For information about the economic status, biology, and management of nuisance and other mammals, see the 1,147-page (1982) *Wild Mammals of North America: Biology, Management, and Economics* edited by J. A.

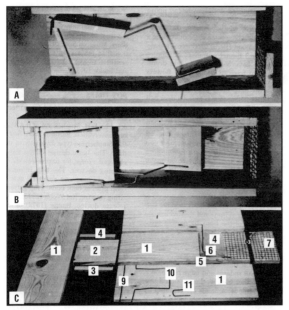

**Figure 10.1.** *Small mammal live trap, showing construction details. A. Trap with side removed. B. Trap with top removed. C. Parts of trap, numbered as diagrammed in Fig. 10.2. (from Mosby 1955 in Taber and Cowan 1969).*

Chapman and G. A. Feldhamer and published by Johns Hopkins University Press, Baltimore.

**Control**

Actually, 5 species of wildlife account for most of the nuisance complaints from urban and suburban homeowners: gray squirrels, cottontail rabbits, raccoons, white-tailed deer/mule deer, and Canada geese. Be sure to check the wildlife laws for your area, and obtain permits.

**Geese** are more inclined toward golf courses, parks, and areas landscaped around office and other buildings with storm water holding ponds. But you might have too many of them around your pond or wetland. You can discourage geese by planting clumps or patches of shrubs there, which geese avoid because they cannot see predators, or by leaving areas of tall grass, like switch grass, there.

You can do the following things to reduce nuisance problems from **gray squirrels**:

1. Exclude squirrels from your house and other buildings by repairing holes with boards, metal flashing, or hardware cloth. You also can attach screening over windows, vents, and chimneys, or smear fox urine (from stores selling trapping supplies) around them.
2. For your bird feeder, install a squirrel baffle (commercial or homemade) or buy a feeder with a counterweighted entrance. Also, your birds really like proso millet but squirrels do not, so try that as bird feed.
3. If you attach metal flashing (sheet metal) around isolated trees next to your house, you will keep squirrels from climbing them and jumping onto your roof.

You also can trap them with a rattrap baited with peanut butter, a commercial live trap, or build your own (Fig. 10.1 and 10.2), but first check with state and local laws about using them.

You can do the following things to reduce nuisance problems from

**cottontail rabbits**:

1. Put chicken-wire fence around your garden or other areas, 18 to 24 inches high, staked flush with the ground or buried a few inches.
2. Wrap hardware cloth 18 to 24 inches high around small trees. Fold and bend in the top so small birds cannot go in and get trapped.
3. Use commercial live traps or build your own (Fig. 10.1 and 10.2) (check

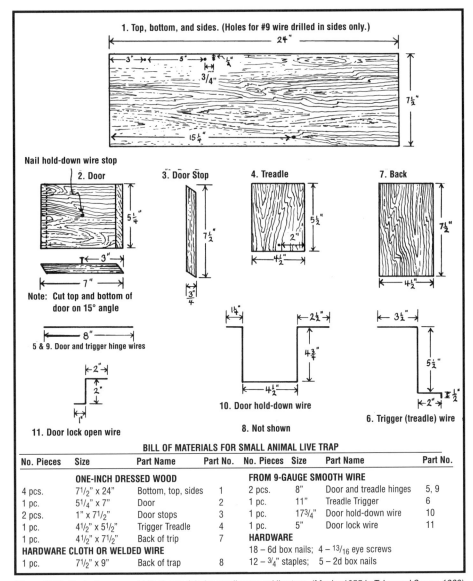

| No. Pieces | Size | Part Name | Part No. | No. Pieces | Size | Part Name | Part No. |
|---|---|---|---|---|---|---|---|
| **ONE-INCH DRESSED WOOD** | | | | **FROM 9-GAUGE SMOOTH WIRE** | | | |
| 4 pcs. | 7 1/2" x 24" | Bottom, top, sides | 1 | 2 pcs. | 8" | Door and treadle hinges | 5, 9 |
| 1 pc. | 5 1/4" x 7" | Door | 2 | 1 pc. | 11" | Treadle Trigger | 6 |
| 2 pcs. | 1" x 7 1/2" | Door stops | 3 | 1 pc. | 17 3/4" | Door hold-down wire | 10 |
| 1 pc. | 4 1/2" x 5 1/2" | Trigger Treadle | 4 | 1 pc. | 5" | Door lock wire | 11 |
| 1 pc. | 4 1/2" x 7 1/2" | Back of trip | 7 | **HARDWARE** | | | |
| **HARDWARE CLOTH OR WELDED WIRE** | | | | 18 – 6d box nails;  4 – 13/16 eye screws | | | |
| 1 pc. | 7 1/2" x 9" | Back of trap | 8 | 12 – 3/4" staples;  5 – 2d box nails | | | |

**Figure 10.2.** *Parts diagram and bill of materials for small mammal live trap. (Mosby 1955 in Taber and Cowan 1969)*

on state and local laws), if you have just 1 rabbit or 2 or 3, and release the rabbit at least 5 miles away, or eat it.

4. Try a commercial repellent, but results vary.

You can do the following things to reduce nuisance problems from **raccoons**:

1. Do not inadvertently or deliberately feed them pet food, scraps, etc.
2. Cover garbage cans with animal-proof covers.
3. Install animal-proof caps on chimneys and vents (phone a chimney sweep or carpenter to do this).
4. Use hardware cloth, grillwork, louvers, and other barriers to attics, undersides, etc., to deny raccoons access. Remember that raccoons are powerful.
5. They like to use storm-sewers for cover and maybe food, so make sure storm-sewer grates and covers fit securely.
6. Large trees with cavities or platform crotches will house raccoons. On such isolated trees, attach roofing metal around the trunk to prevent climbing.
7. Contact a professional wildlife control service, in the Yellow Pages.

Now, what about **deer**? That **is** a problem. Live trap them or drug them with a dartgun and move them out of there? Not hardly. Way too time consuming and expensive. To be bluntly honest, shooting them is **by far** the cheapest and most efficient and effective. But you cannot discharge firearms in the city limits. Best thing is to support a bow season in nearby green areas like certain large reserves to cut that deer population down. You can try commercial deer repellents around your plants, but results vary and are not 100 percent. Deer are beautiful, graceful animals, and fun to see. But they can pose problems. Fencing? Maybe so. See Chapter 9. For more information about deer control, refer to the book (1997) *Deer Proofing Your Yard and Garden* by R. M. Hart, Storey Communication, Pownal, VT.

A quick and dirty synopsis of control methods for some other animal problems follows, but, again, check laws for your area and obtain permits.

**Woodpeckers**: live traps, snap traps, shooting, frightening devices, exclusion (e.g., wire mesh).

**Gulls, crows, ravens, magpies, pigeons, and certain other birds**: overhead screening with wire grids, mechanical and chemical frightening agents, toxic baits, toxic perches, trapping, shooting, habitat modification.

**Bats**: exclusion (including use of devices such as nylon that allow bats to leave but not return, to be used in late summer after the young reach flight stage), repellents, traps, artificial roosts, toxicants.

**Chipmunks**: live traps, snap traps, toxic baits, repellents, shooting (BB or pellet gun, .22 with bird shot, shotgun), exclusion.

**Deer mice and meadow mice**: exclusion (screening), snap traps, live traps, toxic baits, seedling protection (plastic mesh), habitat modification.

**Pocket gophers**: kill traps (pocket gopher traps), toxic baits, fumigants, protective covering for cables and pipes, seedling protection (plastic mesh),

habitat modification (flood irrigation, crop rotation).

**Moles**: kill traps (harpoon, scissors, and choker traps), toxic bait, fumigants, repellents, insecticides (to remove food source), habitat modification (e.g., soil compaction).

**Beaver**: see Beaver Ponds in Chapter 7.

## Population Estimates of Rabbits and Squirrels

You can have some fun with your rabbits and squirrels while also doing some research to estimate their population size. Just buy some numbered self-piercing fingerling tags, size No. 1, and a No. 1 tag pliers from National Band and Tag, Newport, KY. Build 12 or more wooden box traps (Fig. 10.1 and 10.2) and place them 200 feet apart, in a grid pattern (use a magic marker to number each trap), because the effective trap radius is 100 feet for rabbits and squirrels. (My dad and I built 90 of these things once.) Use no bait for rabbits if you have good rabbit trails; just place the trap in the trail. (I caught 517 cottontails without bait in 7 months for my master's degree.) Otherwise, for rabbits and squirrels, use cracked corn or dried apple for bait. After catching a rabbit or squirrel, place an eartag properly in the eartag pliers so that the hole in the eartag is directly over the indentation of 1 jaw of the pliers, and then squeeze the eartag through the lower part of the ear where the cartilage is thick. But do not bend the ear over! And do not leave slack between ear and end of eartag, or a twig might catch it there and tear it out. Actually, rather than eartags, just apply some dye to the tail. That works, but you will not individualize your animals, so you will not be able to determine how long they live from year to year, or figure out home range if you use dye. But you can estimate population size.

Oh, yes. To get a rabbit out of the wooden trap, open the door, reach in, and firmly but gently grasp the rabbit by the hind legs and pull it out. They almost always face away from the door to look out through the wire end. If it faces the door, run you hand over the back, grasp the waist, pull the rabbit out head first, then grasp the legs with your other hand when you have the rabbit out of the trap. Then sit on the trap, place the rabbit across your thigh, hold its head firmly, and release the legs to free a hand for tagging. With its head held firmly, the rabbit will not kick, but you can place your free forearm across its back to help hold it while you position the ears and tags. Cottontail rabbits do not bite.

But squirrels do. So build yourself a handling cone out of $1/4$-inch hardware cloth. Shape it like an ice cream cone, but just large enough for a squirrel's body, so that it cannot turn around in it. Put a cotton wad in the end so the squirrel will not cut its nose. Take an old pillowcase, open the closed end, and sew the pillowcase onto the wide end of the handling cone (Fig. 10.3 and 10.4). Then place the pillowcase over the door end of the trap, press the door open right through the pillowcase, straighten out the pillowcase and handling cone so that the squirrel can see light through it, and grab the cloth right behind the handling cone when the squirrel sees daylight and makes a dash for it into

**Figure 10.3.** *Method of placing cloth handling cone over door of trap.*

the cone (Fig. 10.3 and 10.4). (Use a tweezers to pull the ear out through the mesh for tagging.)

The only thing is, you must check your trapline twice a day for squirrels or once a day for rabbits for several days in a row some time during September, October, and November when the animals are most trappable, and **you must not miss** doing this, or you will sustain some trap mortality, and that is inhumane and will screw things up besides. So be faithful at it or do not do it at all.

Anyway, after a few days when you have some marked animals running around in your population, calculate the population size one day by multiplying the number of animals caught that day times the total number of animals you have tagged in the area, and divide that by the number of returns (animals with dyed tails or eartags, i.e., retrapped animals) you caught that day. That is called the Lincoln Index, and was first used on fish. For example, let's say that after several days of trapping you tagged 11 rabbits. Then the day you decide to start your population estimate, you trap 10 rabbits, and 5 of them are retraps, i.e., already previously marked. You multiply 11 times 10, which is 110, and divide that by 5, for an estimate of 22 rabbits in the trapped area. If you used 11 traps with an effective trap radius of 100 feet, and therefore spaced the traps 200 feet apart in your woods, you sampled 440,000 square feet of habitat, which, divided by 43,560 square feet in an acre, is 10 acres. Hence, your population **density** is 2.2 rabbits per acre for **the entire** habitat like you sampled. It is not exact; it is a crude estimate, but it gives you some notion of what you have. You can compare different habitat types or different years in the same habitat. Just keep a yearly record. You also can calculate a crude home range for eartagged animals by recording the trap number each time the animal is caught, and connect the dots to each of those traps on a map. See how far the animals move and how much overlap in home range there is among animals. You will get good at it, have some fun, gain some knowledge, and perhaps alter your habitat to increase or decrease your animal density.

**Figure 10.4.** *An animal holding device can be made from a cone of hardware cloth or chicken wire attached to a cloth adapter. The end of a live trap is enclosed with the adapter, when the door is opened, the animal will run into the cone. (Taber and Cowan 1969)*

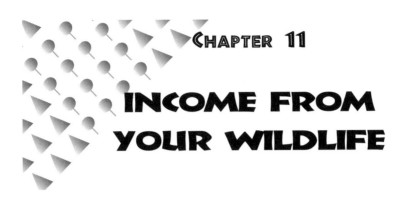

# CHAPTER 11

# INCOME FROM YOUR WILDLIFE

If you have made wildlife habitat improvements to your land, and your wildlife populations have responded favorably to them, you might want outside hunters to respond to your efforts with some monetary remuneration. If you do not have enough land to lease to private individuals or a rod and gun club, you could join in a **landowner cooperative** with adjacent landowners for the common purpose of leasing all the land together to form a larger unit. Check to see if your state or province requires you to buy a license to run a leasing operation.

If you have neighbors who have leased their land to hunters, talk to them to find out what they charge so that you can set a competitive price. If you do not have such neighbors, you could talk to the local rod and gun club to negotiate a lump-sum price or a price of your land per acre, or per hunter. You could charge additional fees for additional improvements or services provided.

In states like Texas, where private land holdings comprise large ranches, a lease might not have to be exclusively for hunting. The lease could be for **ecotourism**, i.e. leasing your land to individuals or groups interested in birdwatching, big game watching, wildlife photography, camping, hiking, horseback riding, canoeing, whitewater rafting, mountain biking, snowmobiling, snowshoeing, cross-country skiing, etc.

**Types of Hunting Leases**

Different types of hunting leases exist. (1) You could charge for a daily or weekend or weekly hunt by selling the hunter a daily or weekend or weekly permit. The hunting lease could be (2) seasonal for all game animals, (3) seasonal for specific game animals, e.g., deer only, (4) multi-year for all game animals, or (5) multi-year for specific game animals. With multi-year leases, hunters often are more willing to invest time, labor, and even money in leased property as a secure investment for several years. And you and the hunters will get to know each other, which builds trust over time. A "package" hunt lease, as with dove hunting, for example, often includes guides, lodging, and meals, and requires good management and marketing, but often yields a high rate of income return. As the landowner you could, of course, reserve some hunting rights for yourself and your family and friends.

## Hunting Lease Agreements

You will need a written hunting lease agreement (Appendix IX, X, XI), perhaps with optional clauses (Appendix XII). A handshake is not good enough, if for no other reason than liability for injury or property damage, but also to avoid misunderstanding or disagreement. A good hunting lease agreement will protect your interests and still be flexible enough to allow the hunters to enjoy themselves. Sometimes a short-term agreement might suffice (Appendix XIII). Occasionally you might want to give to the hunter, or the hunter might demand, a hunting access permit, i.e., written permission to hunt on your property (Appendix XIV), in case someone else challenges him.

You will find that leasing to local hunters or hunter organizations pays better dividends than leasing to distant folks, not necessarily in income, but in intangible benefits such as better public relations with neighbors, with no potential for local resentment caused by leasing to outsiders. Here are some things to think about:

- Get some **references** if you do not know the hunters or hunt club.
- Make sure the club is organized, governed by self-regulating bylaws, and **incorporated** so that the club representative (president, secretary, treasurer) can legally sign the lease agreement for the entire club. Otherwise, every member of the club will have to sign.
- Go to the monthly meetings of the hunt club occasionally to establish rapport. At the **annual meeting** (preferably in summer), inform hunters about any major land management practices such as a clearcut that would affect their hunting.
- Reduce or eliminate all known and potential **hazards** to hunters on your property, and keep accurate records of doing so in case someone gets hurt and files a libel suit against you. Describe in writing and map any hazard you cannot reduce. You also might want to ban ATVs and portable climbing tree stands, avoid single-strand gates or mark them clearly, and require all hunters to have passed an approved hunter education course, with proof.
- Obtain **lease payment** when the lease begins.
- Decide if any **permanent structure**, such as a shed or cabin the lessee wants to build on your property, is an asset to you, and if they are yours when the lease ends.
- Restrict use of **4-wheel drive vehicles** to existing roads.
- Have hunters **notify** you of their **presence.**

So, what actually goes into the actual lease?
1. Name and address of hunter, hunting group, or hunting club.

2. Duration of the lease.
3. Amount, method, and time of payment. Penalty for late payment.
4. Species to be hunted, and other activities allowed on your property.
5. Property description and boundaries, with map. Point out potential hazards. Make a tour.
6. Rules to prevent accidents and to protect property.
7. Duration of lease, and termination if you die, sell your property, or if anyone violates laws or the lease agreement.
8. Number of hunters and their guests allowed on your property at any one time for safety and enjoyment (e.g., 1 hunter per 25 acres for deer).
9. Restriction about alcohol, caliber of rifle, or types of equipment such as ATVs, deer stands, etc.
10. Requiring all hunters to have passed an approved hunter education course, with signature.
11. Hunters' responsibilities such as following a wildlife biologist's harvest recommendations, reporting harvest records, obeying game laws, evicting trespassers, closing gates, repairing broken fences, posting property, and dumping trash.
12. Your responsibilities, such as habitat maintenance or improvement (e.g., planting food plots), cleaning game, providing lodging, maintaining roads.
13. Your rights, such as hunting by family and friends, continuation of your land management for farming, forestry, etc.
14. Subleasing clause, i.e., allowing the hunter or hunting club to sublease to a third party—not a good idea.
15. Indemnity clause, which will protect you from liability if someone is injured on your land. But it will not relieve you of liability if you were negligent by not eliminating a hazard. You should include in the lease agreement the requirements for liability insurance, to protect yourself. The hunter or the hunting club should pay for liability insurance, with you listed on the policy, which you should determine cannot be canceled. You need a copy of the policy and a receipt of purchase.
16. Arbitration, to settle disputes between you and the hunter or hunting club. You and the hunter or hunting club should agree, in advance, to a neutral arbiter who could be a lawyer or someone else.

Finally, have the whole thing reviewed by a lawyer before it is signed. Anything not right should be corrected before you sign.

If you do not screen your potential hunters properly, you could end up with an unmanageable group with little regard for your rights or property. That could mean illegal hunting, overharvest, trash dumping, fire, damage to trees, fences, and roads, etc.

You can locate hunters by talking to friends, local hunters, local conservation groups, and by advertising in local newspapers and specialty magazines. Also list yourself with your local Chamber of Commerce. Another good way to advertise is with your computer, if you have one, by developing a home page website on the World Wide Web. Then talk to the hunter(s) or group representative who contacts you. Use a pre-developed list of questions, and ask some tough ones. Then, make a decision.

Leasing your land for hunting income can be a mutually beneficial experience, and another way to make your wildlife interests and investment pay.

White-tailed deer

# CHAPTER 12

# WHERE TO GET MORE HELP

**Conservation Directory**

It has everything!  A lot of information is available from a variety of sources encompassing some 500 pages. For starters, see your library about looking at the *Conservation Directory* (their copy or an inter-library loan) for addresses and phone numbers of private, state, provincial, federal, and international conservation organizations, agencies, and universities in the U.S. and Canada. Look up the ones listed for your state or province. It is updated yearly by the National Wildlife Federation, 8925 Leesburg Pike, Vienna, VA 22184, where you can order your own copy.

The Table of Contents contains the following:

U.S. Congress, Committees, and Subcommittees
U.S. Federal and International Government Agencies
State and Provincial Government Agencies
Non-Governmental Non-Profit Organizations
Non-Governmental For-Profit Organizations
Educational Institutions

Federally Protected Areas
Bureau of Land Management Districts
National Estuarine Research Reserves
National Forests
National Grasslands
National Marine Sanctuaries
National Parks
National Seashores
National Wildlife Refuges
National Wildlife Refuges Regional Directors

Indices
Organization Name Index
Keyword Index
Staff Name Index
Geographic Index

### Maps

Get your (1) aerial maps (air photos) from your state or provincial wildlife or forestry agency; (2) county plat maps, showing property ownership and boundaries, from your county, city, or university extension office; (3) topographic map from your city or county office, your library or your local sports shop or engineering office; (4) soil survey map (for best uses including wildlife) from your county office of the U.S. Natural Resource Conservation Service; and (5) wetland inventory map (if you have any) from your state or provincial wildlife agency. Also check with the local zoning office in your area to see how your land and surrounding land are zoned for certain land uses.

### Technical Assistance, Advice, and Labor

Talk to your local wildlife manager about where and how to get your soil and water tested, and recommendations for improvement.

You also might want to contact your local wildlife manager to find out what local private organizations (e.g., youth clubs, conservation clubs) would be willing to provide you with volunteer labor.

You also can get advice from private consultants, such as wildlife consultants and landscape consultants.

The university extension office in your principle state university has advice and pamphlets on various wildlife topics. Also check with your county Land Conservation Department (LCD) or the like, for technical help on various soil and water situations. The U.S. Natural Resource Conservation Service (NRCS), formerly the Soil Conservation Service (SCS), provides technical assistance too, so be sure to contact their office in your county.

For information on things like backyard wildlife and butterfly gardening, contact organizations like the National Wildlife Federation (8925 Leesburg Pike, Vienna, VA 22184), the Canadian Wildlife Federation (2740 Queensview Dr., Ottawa, ON K2B 1A2), the National Wildflower Research Center (4801 LaCrosse Av., Austin, TX 78739), the National Gardening Association (180 Flynn Av., Burlington, VT 05401), and the National Institute for Urban Wildlife (10921 Trotting Ridge Way, Columbia, MO 21044), among others.

### Cost Sharing

Use the technical assistance from the U.S. Natural Resource Conservation Service (NRCS) to help you with the cost-sharing programs from the Farm Services Agency (FSA), formerly the Agricultural Stabilization and Conservation Service (ASCS). That agency administers most of the federal cost-sharing programs. Both of those agencies are in the U.S. Department of Agriculture (along with the U.S. Forest Service), with offices in every state, and usually side by side. Your state conservation agency, Land Conservation Departments, and private conservation organizations also administer cost-sharing programs. Ask some questions of your local wildlife manager, county

# WHERE TO GET MORE HELP

agent, or other natural resource professional, and educate yourself on this subject.

Most federal cost-share programs require some kind of conservation plan before you get financial assistance from them. That is where the NRCS comes in. The NRCS can help you develop a conservation plan based on detailed soil surveys, wetland inventory maps, and site visits. They have the expertise, including their own wildlife biologists. Your plan can include wildlife habitat, wetland restoration or development, erosion control, and land use and productivity.

The amount of cost-share you receive can vary yearly by program, but is generally 50 to 75 percent of your total cost, and the sky is **not** the limit, i.e., be reasonable, and so will the FSA. The thing is, though, you do not get your money until **after** you complete the project. In any case, it is a good deal; you get the wildlife benefits and someone else pays half or more of the cost for doing it. Not bad.

Again, the cost-share programs vary, but have the following in common:

1. You have to apply to be considered, so be sure to apply **before** you do any work toward habitat improvement.
2. You can get technical assistance from wildlifers, foresters, other natural resource professionals, or experienced members of conservation organizations to help you design and implement cost-share practices.
3. You have to do the work for habitat development yourself, or hire it done. And in the agreement, you are responsible for maintaining and protecting the habitat work for a certain number of years, to protect the investment of the cost-sharing agency (i.e., the taxpayer) or conservation organization which footed half or most of the bill.
4. Contrary to popular belief, you do not have to allow public access to your property as a condition of cost-sharing, at least in most cases. The intent of cost-sharing is to provide additional wildlife habitat, not public access.

Be sure to check with your **state** or **provincial** conservation (wildlife) agency to determine what cost-sharing or other assistance might be available to you for improving wildlife habitat on your property. Wisconsin, for example, has a (1) Stewardship Incentive Program which provides cost-share to landowner/tenants for various forestry practices including wildlife management, (2) Managed Forest Law which provides property tax relief if you follow a prescribed forest management plan which can include wildlife habitat enhancement, (3) Priority Watershed Program which provides cost-share and technical help for wetland restoration, stream bank improvement, and planting permanent cover if your land lies within a state designated "priority watershed," (4) The Wisconsin Forest Landowner Grant Program which provides cost-share for management plan preparation, tree planting, timber stand improvement, wildlife habitat, soil and water protection, fisheries enhancement, fencing, buffer establishment, species protection, and historic and aesthetic enhancement, and (5) Glacial Habitat Restoration

Area which provides financial and technical help to restore wetlands and grasslands in certain counties. With 50 states and 10 provinces, no attempt will be made to list all the programs.

But here, for the most part, is what the feds have for the states. These are the main ones, mostly administered by the FSA, with an office in your county seat.

## Non-Farm Private Lands

**The Wildlife Habitat Incentive Program (WHIP)** provides cost-share mostly for upland wildlife habitat improvement, but some for wetland habitat.

## Farmland and Rangeland

**The Environmental Quality Incentives Program (EQIP)** provides cost-share and technical help for practices that enhance soil and water quality including stream bank improvement and other plantings for wildlife.

**The Conservation Reserve Program (CRP)** pays you rent for taking your highly erodible land out (from water erosion or wind erosion) of production for at least 10 years. The program has been highly beneficial to grassland wildlife, although trees and shrubs may be planted.

**The Conservation Farm Options (CFO)** provides cost-share to producers of wheat, feed grains, cotton, and rice who have land enrolled in the Agricultural Market Transition Act program. It includes conservation of soil and water; wetland restoration, protection, and creation; wildlife habitat development and protection; and similar conservation measures. You receive an annual payment, but must forgo other payments under the Environmental Quality Incentives Program, the Conservation Reserve Program, and the Wetlands Reserve Program in exchange for one consolidated payment.

**The Farmland Protection Program (FPP)** provides cost-share to help farmers with existing farmland protection programs to buy conservation easements of land threatened with conversion to non-agricultural uses, so that working farms can exist near cities.

**The Grassland Reserve Program (GRP)** provides cast-share and technical assistance for restoring or maintaining historically natural grassland or shrub land. To enroll, you must have at least 100 contiguous acres west or 50 acres east of the 90th Meridian and no longer produce row crops, fruit trees, vineyards, or any agricultural commodity requiring breaking the soil surface. You can hay and mow your land before the end of the nesting season, graze it, and build fire breaks and fences. You will receive fair market regular payments for a 30-year easement and do not have to forego other programs of federal assistance.

**The U.S. Bureau of Land Management** in the U.S. Department of Interior provides cost-share and technical assistance for rangeland

(including grassland) restoration.

## Forests and Woodlands

**The Forestry Incentives Program (FIP)** provides cost-share on private non-industrial forestland for tree planting, timber stand improvement, and related practices, some of which can be designed to improve habitat for wildlife and enhance water quality.

## Wetlands and Waterways

**The Wetlands Reserve Program (WRP)** provides up to 100 percent cost-share to restore and protect drained wetlands in exchange for retiring marginal agricultural land.

**The Partners for Fish and Wildlife Program (PFW)** often has contractors and project managers available, and will help you restore your wetland.

**The U.S. Fish and Wildlife Service** in the U.S. Department of Interior, which administers the above 2 programs, provides cost-share programs and technical assistance for wetland restoration.

## Non-governmental Organizations (NGOs)

Various non-governmental organizations (listed in the *Conservation Directory*) offer assistance to private landowners, e.g., Ducks Unlimited, Trout Unlimited, Pheasants Forever, the various state waterfowl associations, etc.

## Native Nurseries and Landscape Consultants

If you intend to plant things, always choose a seed and stock source near your property or area to improve success. Native species survive the best because they are adapted to your soil and climate, and they provide the best habitat; so avoid exotics (alien plants) if you can. Many plant nurseries also provide landscaping and consultation services. Your state or provincial wildlife agency probably has a list of plant nurseries in your area, so check for that list. Even the Yellow Pages in your phone book might be helpful. The U.S. Army Corps of Engineers keeps an updated list of wetland consultants.

## Publications and Internet

Check with your state or provincial wildlife agency and the university extension office at your principal state university for a list of publications that interest you. Look in the *Conservation Directory* (see beginning of chapter) for private organizations that mention publications of interest to you.

The following books are the best and most comprehensive, but will offer more information than you want:

Bookhout, T. A., editor. 1994. *Research and Management Techniques for Wildlife and Habitats*. The Wildlife Society, Bethesda, MD. 740pp.

Payne, N. F. 1998. *Wildlife Habitat Management of Wetlands*. Krieger Publ. Co., Malabar, FL. 549pp. (145 figures, 71 tables, over 700 references)

Payne, N. F., and F. C. Bryant. 1998. *Wildlife Habitat Management of Forestlands, Rangelands, and Farmlands*. Krieger Publ. Co., Malabar, FL. 840pp. (196 figures, 173 tables, over 1,500 references)

Try the Internet. Use some imagination with your key words. Try **Books,** then **Urban Wildlife** or **Backyard Wildlife** or **Deer,** etc. Try amazon.com or barnesandnoble.com. (See Chapter 9.) Try some of these Worldwide Web (www) addresses:

Association of State Wetland Managers: aswm.org
Bill's Wildlife Links: wildlifer.com/wildlifesites
Biodiversity Project: biodiversityproject.org
Bird Conservation Partners: partnersinflight.org
Canadian Wildlife Federation: cwf-fcf.org
Canadian Wildlife Service: cws-scf.ec.gc.ca
Ducks Unlimited: ducks.org
Environmental Protection Agency: epa.gov/owow/wetlands
Green Acres: epa.gov/greenacres
Horticultural Science Department, University of Minnesota:
	hort.agri.umn.edu/h5015/rrr.htm
Isaak Walton League of America: iwla.org/sos/wetland.html
National Audubon Society: audubon.org
National Wildlife Federation: nwf.org/habitats
Natural Resources Conservation Service: nrcs.usda.gov
Nature Conservancy, The: tnc.org
Northern Prairie Wildlife Research Center: npwrc.usgs.gov
Prairie Enthusiasts: prairie.pressenter.com
Society for Ecological Restoration: ser.org
Society of Wetland Scientists: sws.org
U.S. Army Corps of Engineers: usace.army.mil
U.S. Bureau of Land Management: blm.gov
U.S. Fish and Wildlife Service: fws.gov
U.S. Forest Service: fs.fed.us
U.S. Geological Survey: usgs.gov
Wild Ones Natural Landscapers: for-wild.org
Wildlife Habitat Council: wildlifehc.org
Wildlife Management Institute: wildlifemgt.org
Wisconsin Woodland Owners Association: wisconsinwoodlands.org

And do not forget your field guides, mentioned in Chapter 2. Have some fun with those. They are small enough to pack in the field. Most of them are in the Peterson field guide series; the titles begin with *A Field Guide to the*

Birds *(eastern)*
*Western Birds*
*Mammals*
*Reptiles and Amphibians (eastern)*

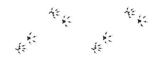
# WHERE TO GET MORE HELP

    *Western Reptiles and Amphibians*
    *Animal Tracks*
    *Trees and Shrubs*
    *Eastern Trees*
    *Western Trees*
    *Rocky Mt. Wildflowers*
    *Wildflowers (eastern)*
    *Pacific States Wildflowers*
    *Southwestern and Texas Wildflowers*

Other good ones are:
    *A Guide to Field Identification of Birds of North America*
    *Stokes Field Guide to Birds: Eastern Region*
    *Stokes Field Guide to Birds: Western Region*
    *Stokes Wildflower Book - East of the Rockies*
    *Stokes Wildflower Book - From the Rockies West*
    *The Birder's Handbook: A Field Guide to the Natural History of North American Birds*
    *Newcomb's Wildflower Guide (northeastern)*
    *Grasses: an Identification Guide (northeastern)*
    *Wetland Plants and Plant Communities of Minnesota and Wisconsin*
    *A Great Lakes Wetland Flora*
    *Wetland Plants of Ontario*

The National Audubon Society also publishes a series of field guides to plants and animals (e.g., *The Audubon Society Field Guide to North American Wildflowers: Eastern Region, The Audubon Society Field Guide to North American Birds: Western Region*). An oldie but a goodie is: *American Wildlife & Plants: A Guide to Wildlife Food Habits* (1951).

You also might appreciate C. Henderson's books available from Minnesota Bookstore, 117 University Ave., St. Paul, MN 55155:
    *Landscaping for Wildlife*
    *Lakescaping for Wildlife and Water Quality*
    *Woodworking for Wildlife*

For backyard or urban wildlife, various books exist such as:
    *The New Gardening for Wildlife: A Guide for Nature Lovers* (by B. Merilees, Whitecap Books, Toronto, 2000)
    *Urban Wildlife Habitats: a Landscape Perspective* (by L. W. Adams, University of Minnesota Press, Minneapolis, 1994)
    *The Wildlife Gardener* (by J. V. Dennis, Alfred A. Knopf, New York, 1985)
    *The Naturalist's Garden* (by R. S. Ernst, The Globe Pequot Press, Old Saybrook, CN, 1987)

*The Wildlife Garden: Planning Backyard Habitats* (by C. Seidenberg, University Press of Mississippi, Jackson, 1995)

*Backyard Battle Plan: The Ultimate Guide to Controlling Wildlife Damage in Your Garden* (by C. Rutledge, Viking Penguin, New York, 1998)

*The National Wildlife Federation's Guide to Gardening for Wildlife: How to Create a Beautiful Backyard Habitat for Birds, Butterflies, and Other Wildlife* (by C. Tufts, P. Loewer, and H. P. Loewer, National Wildlife Federation, Bethesda, MD, 1995)

*The Backyard Naturalist* (by C. Tufts, National Wildlife Federation, Bethesda, MD, 1988)

*The Audubon Guide to Attracting Birds* (by S. W. Kress, Charles Scribners Sons, New York, 1985)

*The Bird Feeder Book: an Easy Guide to Attracting, Identifying, and Understanding Your Feeder Birds* (by D. Stokes and L. Stokes, Little, Brown and Co., Boston, 1987)

*Songbirds in Your Garden* (by J. K. Terres, Thomas Y. Crowell Co., New York, 1968)

*Integrating Man and Nature in the Metropolitan Environment* (by W. Adams and D. L. Leedy, National Institute for Urban Wildlife, Columbia, MD, 1987)

In addition, the National Wildlife Federation also will send you a backyard wildlife kit for your area, to get you started.

Armed with information from sources like these, you will be prepared to advance upon your land to improve it for wildlife.

Common loon

# APPENDIX

**Appendix I. Ratings of some tree species for values to wildlife and as firewood. (Carey and Gill 1980)**

| Tree | Value to Wildlife | | | | Value as firewood | Remarks |
|---|---|---|---|---|---|---|
| | All wildlife | Songbirds | Upland gamebirds | Fur and game mammals | | |
| Oaks | Excellent | Excellent | Excellent | Excellent | Excellent | Retain a variety of species. |
| Black cherry | Excellent | Excellent | Good | Good | Good | May have high timber value when mature. |
| Apples | Excellent | Good | Good | Good | Excellent | Rare; especially attractive to grouse. |
| Pines | Excellent | Excellent | Fair | Good | Fair | Good as kindling. |
| Flowering dogwood | Excellent | Excellent | Good | Fair | Excellent | High aesthetic qualities. |
| Maples | Good | Good | Fair | Excellent | Excellent | High aesthetic qualities in fall. |
| American beech | Good | Fair | Fair | Excellent | Excellent | Aesthetic in fall; important to squirrels. |
| Alders | Good | Good | Good | Fair | Good | Locally important to songbirds and game birds. |
| Aspens | Good | Fair | Good | Excellent | Fair | Especially attractive to grouse. |
| Birches | Good | Fair | Good | Good | Excellent | Important to northern wildlife. |
| Spruces | Good | Good | Fair | Good | Fair | Good as kindling; important to northern wildlife. |
| Hackberry | Fair | Good | Fair | Fair | Excellent | Important winter food for songbirds. |
| Hickories | Fair | Fair | Fair | Good | Excellent | Especially attractive to squirrels. |
| Ashes | Fair | Fair | Fair | Fair | Excellent | Supplies mast in fall. |
| American basswood | Fair | Fair | Fair | Fair | Fair | Good as kindling. |
| Black walnut | Fair | Fair | Fair | Fair | Excellent | May have high timber value when mature. |
| Black tupelo | Fair | Fair | Fair | Fair | Fair | Locally important to songbirds and game birds. |
| Eastern cottonwood | Fair | Fair | Fair | Fair | Fair | Good as kindling. |
| Elms | Fair | Fair | Fair | Good | Fair | High water content when green; hard to split; cut if diseased. |
| Balsam fir | Fair | Fair | Fair | Fair | Fair | Good cover for snowshoe hares. |
| Eastern hemlock | Fair | Fair | Fair | Fair | Fair | Attractive to northern wildlife. |
| Black locust | Fair | Fair | Fair | Fair | Excellent | Low wildlife; high firewood; nitrogen fixer. |
| Magnolias | Fair | Fair | Fair | Fair | Good | Low wildlife; good firewood. |
| Eastern red cedar | Fair | Good | Fair | Fair | Fair | Good as kindling; attractive to songbirds. |
| Sassafras | Fair | Fair | Fair | Fair | Good | Berries eaten by insectivorous birds. |
| Sweetgum | Fair | Fair | Fair | Fair | Fair | High water content when green; high aesthetic value. |
| Sycamore | Fair | Fair | Fair | Fair | Fair | Aesthetic; high water content when green; hard to split. |
| Yellow poplar | Fair | Fair | Fair | Fair | Fair | Good as kindling; aesthetic. |
| Willows | Fair | Fair | Fair | Fair | Fair | Attractive to northern wildlife. |

Note: Fur and game mammals = rabbits, squirrels, foxes, skunks, etc.

## Appendix II. Example 1 of sample timber sale contract with wildlife considerations. (DeStefano et al. 1994)

## TIMBER SALE CONTRACT

This Contract is entered into by and between _____ of _____ (Seller),

and _____ of _____ (Purchaser).

    The Seller hereby authorizes the Purchaser to enter upon the following described lands (the Premises) for purposes of cutting and removing timber marked or otherwise designated by the Seller.

    Those Premises are further described on the map(s) or diagram(s) attached to and made a part of this Contract.

## CONTRACT PERIOD AND TERMINATION

1. The Purchaser shall cut all timber or forest products described in paragraph 6 and complete all other performance described herein with reasonable diligence so performance is completed no later than _____. The period of this contract begins when both parties sign it, the Purchaser providing the owner with all required bonds and certificates of insurance.

2. The Seller or Agent shall notify the Purchaser in the event of a breach of any condition of the Contract, at which time all operations shall cease immediately, and continued occupancy on the Premises shall be a trespass. Upon notification, operations may not be resumed nor may timber be cut or removed without written authorization from the Seller.

3a. The Purchaser has deposited cash, a surety bond, a certified check, or other form acceptable to the Seller in the amount of $_____ as a performance bond, to assure proper performance and to be held until the completion of all conditions of the Contract to the satisfaction of the Seller.

b. Upon breach of any condition of this Contract, the performance bond shall be applied to actual damages incurred by the Seller.

c. If timber or other forest products not specifically described in this Contract or designated by the Seller for cutting are cut, damaged, or removed by the Purchaser, the Seller may pursue any remedies for the unlawful use of the Seller's property and the cutting, damage, or removal of property without consent, including the seeking of criminal or civil charges for theft, timber theft, or criminal damage to property in addition to its Contract remedies for breach.

d. The Seller's damages upon the Purchaser's failure to perform this Contract include, but are not limited to (1) the Purchaser's bid value of timber not cut and removed under this Contract; (2) double the mill value, as determined by the Seller, for timber cut, removed, or damaged without authorization under or in violation of this Contract; (3) all costs of sale area cleanup, restoration, or completion of performance not completed by the Purchaser; (4) all costs of resale of timber not cut and removed as required under this Contract.

e. Additional damage provisions are hereby listed:

4. No forest products may be removed from the Premises until the products are paid for by the Purchaser or guarantees for payment satisfactory to the Seller are provided.

5. Title to any forest products cut under this Contract shall remain with the Seller until payment is received.

## PRODUCTS TO BE REMOVED

6. The Purchaser shall cut, remove, and pay for the following timber or forest products during the period of this contract:

## PAYMENTS

7a. LUMP SUM SALE:

(a) The Purchaser agrees to pay Seller $_____ under the following schedule:

**Appendix II. (continued)**

(b) The Seller is not obligated to return the payment in part a, or any portion of it in the event the Purchaser fails to remove all timber or forest products authorized for removal.

b. SCALE PRODUCTS SALE: (As an alternative to a lump sum payment, the payment may be designated by price per cord or MBF per species with an estimate of forest products available.) Payment to the Seller shall be made based upon the following and as further described herein:

| SPECIES | PRODUCTS | ESTIMATED VOLUME | PRICE PER UNIT *MBF | CORD | TOTAL ESTIMATED VALUE |
|---|---|---|---|---|---|
| | | | | | |

**TOTAL**
    \* Board feet (BF) in thousands (M).

8. Log and tree volumes shall be determined by the Scribner Decimal C system.

9. Cored means a standard measure of piled wood 4' x 4' x 96" to 100". Cord products of other dimensions shall be converted to standard cords.

## UTILIZATION
10. Maximum stump height shall not exceed stump diameter, and for stumps of diameter less than 10 inches it shall not exceed 10 inches.

11. Timber or forest growth, whether mature or not, may not be damaged through careless operations or unnecessary equipment use.

12. The Purchaser agrees to complete all operations as described herein without waste or nuisance on the premises.

13. Additional equipment and operation requirements:

## NOTICE OF INTENT TO CUT AND COMPLIANCE WITH LAWS
14. The _____ shall make and file a written declaration to the county clerk of his or her intention to cut forest products pursuant to section 26.03, Wis. Stats., and comply with all other notice requirements and laws and ordinances with respect to work under this Contract.

## SLASH AND DEBRIS DISPOSAL
15. Slash falling in any lake or stream, in a right-of-way, or on land of an adjoining landowner shall be immediately removed from the waters, right-of-way, or adjoining land. Tops from felled trees may not be left hanging in standing trees. All trees shall be completely felled and not left leaning or hanging in other trees.

16. Other slash disposal requirements:

17. The Purchaser shall remove, to the satisfaction of the Seller, all solid waste, trash, and debris generated by the Purchaser.

## ROADS, CAMPS, SURVEY CORNERS
18. Location, construction, and use of logging roads, mill sites, and camp sites is subject to advance approval by the Seller. All such areas or facilities used or constructed by the Purchaser must be operated, maintained, and restored before terminating the Contract in a manner satisfactory to the Seller. Purchaser shall repair damage to existing roads.

19. Logging roads that intersect town, county, or state roads or highways must have the intersections approved by the proper authorities before construction and cleared of all unsightly debris at the time of construction.

20. The Purchaser agrees to pay for the cost of repair or replacement of property or any land survey monuments or accessories which are removed or destroyed or made inaccessible.

21. Other restoration requirements (i.e., seeding, gravel, rutting, culvert removal, etc.):

22. Erosion control requirements:

**Appendix II. (continued)**

## LIABILITY

23. The Purchaser agrees to protect and indemnify the Seller and the Seller's employees and agents from and against all causes of action, claims, demands, suits, liability, or expense by reason of loss or damage to any property or bodily injury to any person, including death, as a direct or indirect result of timbering operations under this contract or in connection with any action or omission of the Purchaser, who shall defend the Seller in any cause of action or claim. In addition, the Purchaser agrees to furnish the Seller with a certificate of insurance of current coverage under the Worker's Compensation Law, Chapter 102, Stats., and public liability insurance for the period of logging operations on the Seller's property in the amount of:

a. Personal injury: $300,000 single limit liability or $100,000 bodily injury per person and $300,000 per occurrence.

b. Property damage: $100,000

## GENERAL

24. The Purchaser is an independent contractor for all purposes including Worker's Compensation and is not an employee or agent of the Seller. The Seller agrees that the undersigned Purchaser, except as otherwise specifically provided herein, shall have the sole control of the method, hours worked, time, and manner of any timber cutting to be performed hereunder. The Seller reserves the right only to inspect the job site for the sole purpose of insuring that the cutting is progressing in compliance with the cutting practices established under this Contract. The Seller takes no responsibility for supervising or directing the performance of any of the harvesting to be performed by the undersigned Purchaser or of its employees. The Seller further agrees that it will exercise no control over the selection and dismissal of the Purchaser's employees.

25. The Seller agrees to initially designate the timber to be sold and might make inspections for the purposes of ascertaining whether the timber has been cut and the Contract has been complied with. All work shall be performed in a workman-like manner. Work shall be performed in accordance with the requirements of the Contract. The Seller has clear and unencumbered title to the stumpage subject to this Contract.

26. The Purchaser agrees to take reasonable precautions to prevent the starting and spreading of fires. The Purchaser is responsible for damage and forest fire suppression costs, including that provided in ss. 26.14 and 26.21, Wisconsin Stats., caused by the Purchaser's operation under this contract.

27. This Contract or work under it may not be assigned or subcontracted in part or in whole without prior written approval from the Seller and may be changed or amended only in writing. The Purchaser agrees to notify the surety, if any, of any such change or amendment,.

28. This Contract, together with specifications in the request for bids as well as reference to parts and attachments, shall constitute the entire agreement, and any previous communications or agreements pertaining to this Contract are hereby superseded. Any amendments to this Contract shall be in writing signed by both parties.

Seller _____   Date _____

Purchaser _____   Date _____

_____   Date _____

### Appendix III. Example 2 of sample timber sale contract with wildlife considerations. (Hassinger et al. 1981)

I, Mark Hamilton of Masten, Pennsylvania, (Purchaser) agree to purchase from Woodrow Meristem of Pomfret Center, Pennsylvania, (Seller) the trees described below.

I. Location of Sale: The 42-acre woodland is in Derry Township, Tioga County, Pennsylvania, at the intersection of PA Route 804 and Legislative Route 7221, as shown on the attached map.

II. Trees to be Cut: Cut all designated trees and/or trees marked with yellow paint. Reserve all hemlock, hickory, dogwood, serviceberry, and black gum. Additional trees of special wildlife value to be left marked with blue paint. Also not to be cut are any trees within 100 feet of Brougher Run except those marked with yellow paint by Seller.

III. Conditions of Sale:

A. The Purchaser agrees to the following:
   (1) To pay the Seller the sum of $16,350 for the above designated or marked trees, and to make payment in advance of cutting.
   (2) To waive all claim to the above described trees unless they are cut and removed on or before 1 calendar year from the date on this contract. In the event Purchaser is unable to complete the sale in the time allowed, due to circumstances beyond his control, the Seller and Purchaser may agree on an extension of time for this contract.
   (3) To construct a log-loading site about $1/2$ acre in size in the southeast portion of the tract at a location agreed upon by the Seller and Purchaser.
   (4) To do all in his power to prevent and suppress forest fires on, or threatening, the sale area.
   (5) To avoid unnecessary injury to all trees not designated to be cut.
   (6) To repair damages caused by logging to ditches, fences, bridges, roads, trails, or other improvements damaged beyond ordinary wear and tear.
   (7) Not to assign this Agreement in whole or in part to anyone else without the written consent of the Seller.
   (8) To remove all tops and slash from felled trees within 25 feet of the adjoining highway. No slash will be left across or on the public road, cleared field, or Brougher Run. Tops may be left on skid trails to prevent erosion.
   (9) To leave standing all marked property boundary trees.
   (10) To take precautions to prevent soil erosion and other conditions detrimental to the property resulting from logging operation. Should such conditions occur, Purchaser will correct them. He also will remove all oil cans, paper, and other trash resulting from the operation.
   (11) To furnish to Seller 20 pounds of perennial ryegrass seed and 2 pounds of timothy seed which Seller will apply to the log-loading site and roads upon completion of this timber sale.
   (12) To maintain public liability and workman's compensation insurance policies for the duration of this contract.

B. The Seller agrees to the following:
   (1) To guarantee title to the forest products covered by this Agreement, and to defend it against all claims at his expense.
   (2) To present a map (attached) to the Purchaser with correctly located property boundary lines. The Seller will indemnify the Purchaser for all trespass claims originating as a result of errors in the boundary line location made by the Seller.
   (3) To allow the Purchaser to make necessary logging-road improvements such as bridges and gates which shall be removed or left in place as agreed upon by the Seller and the Purchaser. Trees designated for cutting may be used to construct such improvements.
   (4) To grant freedom-of-entry and right-of-way to the Purchaser and his employees on and across the area covered by this Agreement, and also other privileges usually extended to purchasers of timber which are not specifically covered, provided they do not conflict with specific provisions of this Agreement.

C. In case of dispute over the terms of this Agreement, we agree to accept the decision of an Arbitration Board of 3 selected persons as final. Each of the contracting parties will select 1 person, and the 2 selected will select a third to form this Board.

Signed this _____ day of _____, 20_____

Witness:

_____          (Signed) _____

                                                                          Purchaser

_____          _____

                                                                          Seller

**Appendix IV. Wildlife values, characteristics, and limitations of some shrubs, trees, and vines in Colorado and similar places. (Rutherford and Snyder 1983)**

| Value classification | Species | Primary wildlife species value | Priority use locations | Planting form | Plant characteristics | Limitations | Comments |
|---|---|---|---|---|---|---|---|
| Shrubs recommended for priority use in wildlife plantings. | Wild plum | All plains upland game | Rangeland, farmlands, and riparian zones. Prefers sandy soils. | Thickets | Excellent growth form and root-sprouting perpetuation. Excellent height, closed canopy yet open growth form near ground, fruits consumed by numerous wildlife. | Subject to winter browsing by rabbits and rodents. | Choke cherry can be substituted in better moisture sites. |
| | Squawbush sumac (quailbush or skunkbush) | Quail, cottontails, prairie grouse | Dry rangelands and farmlands. | Scattered or thickets, shelterbelt edges | Long-lived, drought-tolerant, and high survival rate. Dense spreading growth form. | 3- to 6-ft. height. Limited spreading and root sprouting. | Not highly susceptible to browsing. Limited food value to lesser prairie chickens and others. |
| | Willow | Bobwhite, cottontails, pheasants, deer | Riparian and wet sites. | Thickets or small clumps | Attains good height, but rather open canopy. Rapid growth and spreading characteristics. | Requires wet sites. | Slips can be cut and stuck in mud to start new thickets easily and economically. |
| Shrub species, which need further evaluation. | Buffalo-berry | Deer, doves, bobwhite, pheasants, sharp-tailed grouse | Riparian or with supplemental water. | Thickets or small clumps | Moderately tall, spreading growth form highly suited for deer, doves, cottontails. | Apparently needs some supplemen-tal water as in riparian zones. | Beautiful specimens can develop. |
| | Elderberry | Mourning doves, quail, grouse, pheasants, deer | Sandy ranges or riparian zones. | Thickets or small clumps | Moderately tall and shabby with overhanging growth form. | Uncertain. | Should be tested further. |
| | Fragrant sumac | Scaled quail, bobwhite | Sandy ranges. | Thickets or small clumps | Short to medium height. | Possible winter hardiness. | Needs testing in some areas. |
| | Bristly locust | Scaled quail, bobwhite, mourning doves | Sandy ranges. | Thickets or small clumps | Reportedly forms thickets similar to wild plum, adapted to poor soils. | Unknown | Recommended by some seed suppliers. |
| | Fourwing saltbush | Scaled quail, cottontails | Shortgrass ranges. | Scattered to thickets. | Excellent low growth form and extremely drought-tolerant for use in marginal areas. | | Difficult to transplant. |
| Shrubs for supplement to taller species and for direct seeding. | Buckbrush or snowberry, currant, wild rose, fourwing saltbush, rabbitbrush | Quail, cottontails | Varied riparian to dry rangeland. | Scattered to thickets. | Generally short (2-4 ft.) growth form for supplemental shrub protection. | Generally not tall enough for protection during winter snows. | Suggested for supplemental direct seeding in riparian and rangeland locations. |
| Trees for use in wildlife plantings. | Rocky Mountain juniper | Mourning doves, deer, pheasants, non-game birds | Better farmlands. | Clump plantings, snow barriers, shelterbelts | Long-lived, fair survival, retains dense, low cover for wildlife. | Sometimes difficult to establish. Slow-growing. Needs supplemental water. | Subject to destruction by wildfires. |
| Other trees for potential consideration. | Osage-orange | Mourning doves, pheasants, non-game birds. | Farmlands, preferably under irrigation. | Clump plantings, shelterbelts | Hardy, long-lived, spreading growth form similar to mulberry. | Adapted to more eastern farmlands. | Use in farmlands (preferably irrigated). |
| | Box elder | Same as above. | Same as above. | Same as above. | Short-lived, fast-growing, substitute for elms. | Needs better soil and moisture conditions. | Same as above. |
| | Golden willow | Deer | Wet areas. | Visual barriers in hunting areas. | Fast-growing, medium to tall. | Needs wet sites. | Not of major importance. |
| Woody vines recommended for use as wildlife plantings. | Frost grape and Virginia creeper | Bobwhite, cottontails | Riparian zones. | Scattered next to shrubs. | Form a canopy of protection over shrubs or low-growing vegetation. | Needs riparian or supplemental moisture. | Shrub-vine combination provides excellent cover. |
| Woody vines for potential consideration. | Trumpet vine and vining honeysuckle | Same as above. | Same as above. | Same as above. | Same as above. | Same as above. | Needs evaluation in various sites and moisture situations. |

**Appendix V. Characteristics of some shrub and tree species for use in hedgerows for wildlife in plains areas of Colorado and similar places.** (Rutherford and Snyder 1983)

| Species | General height (ft.) | Root sprouting | Growth form | Tolerances | | | Soil preference | Suggested planting pattern | |
| | | | | Cold | Drought | Alkaline | | In rows (ft.) | Between rows (ft.) |
|---|---|---|---|---|---|---|---|---|---|
| Wild plum | 6.5-10 | E | Thicket | G | F | G | Sandy | 12-18 | 12-16 |
| Squawbush sumac | 3-5 | P | Low, spreading | G | E | E | Loam | 12-18 | 12-16 |
| Honeysuckle | 6.5-10 | Some | Erect, spreading | G | G | G | Sandy | 6-8 | 12-16 |
| Willow | 6.5-10 | G | Thicket | G | P | E | Sandy | 3-6 | 16-24 |
| Buffalo-berry | 12 | Some | Tall, spreading | G | F | G | Sandy loam | 6-16 | 16-24 |
| Elderberry | 12-19.5 | ? | Tall, spreading | G | G | G | Sandy | 6-16 | 16-24 |

Note: G = good; P = poor; F = fair; E = excellent.

**Appendix VI. Wildlife food (F), cover (C), and nesting (N) values of selected woody plants.** (Wenger 1984)

### MODERATE WILDLIFE VALUE

| | |
|---|---|
| American mountain ash | F |
| Black tupelo | N |
| Cockspur hawthorn | F, C, N |
| Common prickly ash | F, C |
| Dotted hawthorn | F |
| Downy hawthorn | F, C, N |
| Eastern cottonwood | F, N |
| Eastern hemlock | C |
| Eastern larch | N |
| Engelmann spruce | F, C, N |
| Frosted hawthorn | F |
| Glossy hawthorn | F, C, N |
| Mockernut hickory | F |
| Pecan | F |
| Pignut hickory | F |
| Prairie crabapple | F |
| Red mulberry | F |
| Shagbark hickory | F |
| Smooth sumac | F |
| Staghorn sumac | F |
| Washington hawthorn | F |

### HIGH WILDLIFE VALUE

| | |
|---|---|
| Allegheny serviceberry | F |
| American beech | F |
| Balsam fir | C, N |
| Bigtooth aspen | F, N |
| Black oak | F |
| Black willow | C, N |
| Blackhaw | F, C |
| Common persimmon | F |
| Devil's walking-stick | F, C |
| Douglas-fir | F, C, N |
| Flameleaf sumac | F |
| Hazel alder | C, N |
| Nannyberry | F, C |
| Post oak | F |
| Quaking aspen | F, N |
| Shadblow serviceberry | F |
| White fir | C, N |

### VERY HIGH WILDLIFE VALUE

| | |
|---|---|
| Alternate-leaf dogwood | F, C, N |
| Black cherry | F |
| Black maple | F |
| Blackjack oak | F |
| Box elder | F |
| Bur oak | F |
| Chestnut oak | F |
| Chinkapin oak | F |
| Common choke cherry | F |
| Common hackberry | F |
| Eastern red cedar | F |
| Eastern white pine | F, C, N |
| Flowering dogwood | F, C, N |
| Gray birch | F |
| Jack pine | C, N |
| Mountain maple | F |
| Northern red oak | F, N |
| Paper birch | F |
| Pin cherry | F |
| Pin oak | F |
| Pitch pine | C, N |
| Ponderosa pine | C, N |
| Red maple | F |
| River birch | F |
| Scarlet oak | F, N |
| Shingle oak | F, N |
| Striped maple | F |
| Sugar maple | F, C, N |
| Swamp white oak | F, N |
| Sweet birch | F |
| White oak | F, N |
| Yellow birch | F |

**Appendix VII. Food and cover plants useful to attract wildlife to residential and other areas.
(Wenger 1984)**

| Large trees | Small trees | Large shrubs | Low shrubs and vines | Forbs and grasses |
|---|---|---|---|---|
| | | **Southeast** | | |
| Mountain ash | Cherry | Dogwood | Bayberry | Lespedeza |
| Beech | Crabapple | Elderberry | Blackberry | Panic grass |
| Hackberry | Dogwood | Sumac | Spicebush | Sunflower |
| Live oak | Hawthorn | High-bush blueberry | Virginia creeper | Bristlegrass |
| Loblolly pine | Holly | Arrowwood | Greenbrier | Ragweed |
| Pecan | Palmetto | | Mapleleaf viburnum | Knotweed |
| Slash pine | Persimmon | | | Pokeweed |
| Blackgum | Red cedar | | | |
| Red maple | Serviceberry | | | |
| Box elder | Mulberry | | | |
| | | **Southwest** | | |
| Live oak | Crabapple | Manzanita | Blackberry | Filaree |
| Pin oak | Sweet acacia | Catclaw acacia | Juniper | Sunflower |
| Pinyon pine | Mesquite | Cholla (cactus) | Prickly pear | Turkeymullein |
| Box elder | Desert ironwood | | Virginia creeper | Bristlegrass |
| Saguaro (cactus) | Mulberry | | Sagebrush | Ragweed |
| | | | | Knotweed |
| | | **Northeast** | | |
| Beech | Cherry | Autumn olive | Blackberry | Panicgrass |
| Birch | Crabapple | Dogwood | Spicebush | Sunflower |
| Colorado spruce | Dogwood | Elderberry | Snowberry | Timothy |
| Hemlock | Hawthorn | Sumac | Coralberry | Bristlegrass |
| Sugar maple | Red cedar | Winterberry | Virginia creeper | Ragweed |
| White oak | Serviceberry | High-bush blueberry | Greenbrier | Knotweed |
| White pine | Mulberry | High-bush cranberry | Mapleleaf viburnum | Pokeweed |
| Blackgum | | | Bittersweet | |
| Red maple | | | | |
| Box elder | | | | |
| | | **Northwest** | | |
| California black oak | Dogwood | Elderberry | Blackberry | Filaree |
| Colorado spruce | Hawthorn | Golden current | Oregon grape | Sunflower |
| Douglas-fir | Serviceberry | High-bush cranberry | Snowberry | Tarweed |
| Lodgepole pine | Mountain ash | | Coralberry | Timothy |
| Ponderosa pine | Thornapple | | Gooseberry | Turkeymullein |
| Box elder | Squaw apple | | Buckthorn | Bristlegrass |
| | | | Sagebrush | Ragweed |
| | | | | Knotweed |

## Appendix VIII. Some woody plants recommended for planting to attract wildlife[a] to backyard and elsewhere. (National Wildlife Federation 1984)

| Woody plants[b] | Northeast/North Central | Southeast | Rockies/Great Basin | Northwest | Southwest |
|---|---|---|---|---|---|
| | | | Region* | | |
| Low shrubs | Beach plum—MG<br>Blueberry—SGMB<br>Coralberry—SH<br>Huckleberry—SGMB<br>New Jersey tea—BM | Beautyberry—SGM<br>Blackberry—SGM<br>Blueberry—BSG<br>Saw palmetto—BMS<br>Smooth sumac—MSG | Mormon tea—MG<br>Prairie sagebrush—GM<br>Rabbitbrush—MB<br>Smooth sumac—SGM | Evergreen huckleberry—MSG<br>Mahala mat—BMG<br>Manzanita—SGM<br>Rabbitbrush—MB<br>Salal—SGH | Beloperone—BH<br>Buffaloberry—SGM<br>Redberry buckthorn—SGBM<br>Skunkbush—SM<br>Trumpet bush—H |
| Tall shrubs | Arrowwood viburnum—SGM<br>Bayberry—SGM<br>Pfitzer juniper—SG<br>Red-osier dogwood—SGMB<br>Spicebush—SGB<br>Winterberry—SGMB | Hercules club—BSM<br>Red buckeye—H<br>Southern blackhaw—GMB<br>Wax myrtle—S<br>Yaupon—SB | Choke cherry—SGMB<br>Golden currant—SGMB<br>Mountain mahogany—MB<br>Sand cherry—SGMHB<br>Serviceberry—SGMB | Blue elderberry—SGM<br>Cascara buckthorn—SG<br>Osoberry—SGM<br>Red currant—SGMHB<br>Serviceberry—SG<br>Tall Oregon-grape—SM | Bitterbrush—MB<br>Creosote bush—M<br>Desert-willow—H<br>Serviceberry—SG<br>Shrub live oak—GMS<br>Sugar sumac—SGM |
| Small trees | Flowering dogwood—MGB<br>Nannyberry—SGMB<br>Sassafras—SBGM<br>Serviceberry—SGM<br>Staghorn sumac—SGM | American holly—SB<br>Cabbage palmetto—BM<br>Dahoon—SBG<br>Flowering dogwood—SMGB<br>Persimmon—MGS<br>Serviceberry—SGM | Limber pine—MSG<br>Rocky Mountain clump maple—MGS<br>Rocky Mountain juniper—SGMB<br>Utah juniper—SGMB<br>Western red birch—GMSB | Hawthorne—SGM<br>Madrone—SGB<br>Mountain ash—SGM<br>Pacific dogwood—MSGB<br>Vine maple—SGM | Choke cherry—SGMB<br>Hackberry—SGB<br>Ironwood—MG<br>Madrone—SGB<br>Paloverde—MH<br>Velvet mesquite—MB |
| Large trees (deciduous) | American beech—MGS<br>Blackgum—SGM<br>Northern red oak—MGSB<br>Shagbark hickory—MBGS<br>Sugar maple—SGM<br>White oak—MGSB | Bald cypress—G<br>Hackberry—BSGM<br>Pecan—MBG<br>Tulip poplar—HBSM<br>Willow oak—MGS | Emory oak—MSB<br>Fremont cottonwood—MGSB<br>Quaking aspen—GSMB | Bigleaf maple—MGS<br>Oregon white oak—MSG<br>Red alder—SGMB | Arizona sycamore—B<br>Bigtooth maple—MGS<br>Gambel oak—MGSB<br>New Mexico locust—BM |
| Large trees (evergreens) | Eastern hemlock—SGM<br>Eastern red cedar—SBG<br>Red pine—SGM<br>White cedar—GSM<br>White pine—MS<br>White spruce—GSM | Carolina hemlock—SMG<br>Eastern red cedar—SBGM<br>Live oak—MGSB<br>Loblolly pine—MS<br>Longleaf pine—SM | Douglas-fir—MSGB<br>Lodgepole pine—MSB<br>Pinyon pine—MSG<br>Ponderosa pine—MSB<br>Subalpine fir—MSB<br>White fir—MSB | Douglas-fir—GMS<br>Western hemlock—SGM<br>Western red cedar—SMB<br>Western white pine—SM<br>White fir—GMSB | Blue spruce—MSG<br>Emory oak—MSGB<br>Pinyon pine—MSG<br>Ponderosa pine—MSB<br>Rocky Mountain juniper—SGBM |

* Residents of the Great Plains can choose plants from the lists for the regions most similar in climate.

[a] B = butterfly adult or caterpillar, H = hummingbird, S = songbird, G = game bird, M = mammal.

[b] All plants furnish shelter and reproductive cover for a variety of insects, birds, and perhaps some mammals; some are especially attractive as food. Low shrubs are 0.5 to 8 ft, tall shrubs are 6 to 15 ft, small trees are 12 to 50 ft, and large trees are 50 to 200 ft.

# MORE WILDLIFE ON YOUR LAND

---

## Appendix IX. Sample hunting lease agreement, example 1. (Yarrow 1998)

---

*This hunting lease agreement is for educational purposes only. It is important to check with your attorney before writing and signing a binding legal agreement. This lease may be more or less inclusive than the parties desire. If the lessor wants to provide other services or rights, such as guides, cleaning game, or allowing the lessee to improve the habitat, those provisions should be included.*

### HUNTING LEASE AGREEMENT

**STATE OF:**

**COUNTY OF:**

**TRACT:**

This Lease Agreement (the "Lease") entered into as of the day of _____, by and between _____ _____ hereinafter referred to as Lessor, and _____ a/an (state whether an individual, a partnership, corporation, or unincorporated association) hereinafter referred to as Lessee.

The Lessor agrees to lease the Hunting Rights, as defined below, on \_\_\_\_\_ acres more or less, to Lessee for $ _____ ($_____/Acre), for a term beginning on _____, (the "Commencement Date") and ending on _____ (the "Expiration Date") on the following described property (the "Land").

See Attached Description

The Hunting Rights shall consist of the exclusive right and privilege of propagating, protecting, hunting, shooting, and taking game and waterfowl on the Land together with the right of Lessee to enter upon, across, and over the Land for such purposes and none other.
This Hunting Lease Agreement shall be subject to the following terms and conditions:

### PAYMENT
1. The Lessee shall pay to the Lessor _____, the amount of one (1) year's Rent in full, on or before _____ by check payable to Lessor.

### COMPLIANCE WITH LAW
2. Lessee agrees for itself, its licensees and invitees to comply with all laws and regulations of the United States and of the state and local governments wherein the Land lies relating to the game or which are otherwise applicable to Lessee's use of the Land. Any violation of this paragraph shall give Lessor the right to cancel this Lease immediately.

### POSTING
3. Lessee shall have the right to post the Land for hunting to prevent trespassing by any parties other than Lessor, its Agents, Contractors, Employees, Licensees, Invitees, or Assigns provided that Lessee has obtained the Lessor's prior written approval of every sign designed to be so used. Every such sign shall bear only the name of the Lessee. Lessor reserves the right to prosecute any trespass regarding said Land but has no obligation to do so.

### LESSOR'S USE OF ITS PREMISE
4. Lessor reserves the right in itself, its Agents, Contractors, Employees, Licensees, Assigns, Invitees, or Designees to enter upon any or all of the Land at any time for any purpose of cruising, marking, cutting, or removing trees or conducting any other acts relating thereto; no such use by Lessor shall constitute a violation of this Lease. This right reserved by Lessor shall be deemed to include any clearing, site preparation, controlled burning and planting or other forestry work or silvicultural practices reasonably necessary to produce trees and timber on the Land. Lessee shall not interfere with Lessor's rights as set forth herein.

### GATES/BARRIERS
5. Lessor grants to Lessee the right to install gates or other barriers (properly marked for safety) subject to the written permission of Lessor and the terms and conditions relating thereto as set forth elsewhere in this Lease, on private roads on the Land. Lessee agrees to provide Lessor with keys to all locks before installation and at all times requested by Lessor during the term of this lease.

### ROAD OR FENCE DAMAGE
6. Lessee agrees to maintain and surrender at the termination of this Lease all private roads on the lands in at least as good a condition as they were when leased. Lessee agrees to repair any fences or other structures damaged by itself, its Licensees, or Invitees.

### ASSIGNMENT
7. Lessee may not assign this Lease or sublease the hunting rights the subject of this Lease without prior written permission of Lessor. Any assignment or sublease in violation of this provision will void this Lease and subject Lessee to damages.

### FIRE PREVENTION
8. Lessee shall not set, cause, or allow any fire to be or remain on the Land. Lessee covenants and agrees to use every precaution to protect the timber, trees, land, and forest products on the Land from fire or other damage. To that end, Lessee will make every effort to put out any fire that may occur on the Land. Should any fire be started or allowed to escape onto or burn upon the Land by Lessee or anyone who derives his/her/its right to be on the Land for Lessee, Lessor shall have the right immediately to cancel this Lease without notice; any payments heretofore paid shall be retained by Lessor as a deposit against actual damages, refundable to the extent such damages as finally determined by Lessor are less than said deposit. In addition, Lessor shall be entitled to recover from Lessee any damages which Lessor sustains as the result of such fire. Lessee shall immediately notify the appropriate state agency and Lessor of any fire that Lessee becomes aware of on Lessor's lands or within the vicinity thereof.

### INDEMNIFICATION AND INSURANCE
9. Lessee shall indemnify, defend, and hold harmless Lessor, its directors, officers, employees, and agents from any and all loss, damage, personal injury (including death at any time arising therefrom) and other claims arising directly or indirectly from or out of any occurrence in, upon, or at the said Lands or any part thereof relating to the use of said Land by Lessee, Lessee's invitees, or any other person operating by, for, or under Lessee pursuant to this Lease. Lessee further agrees to secure and maintain a $1,000,000 public liability insurance policy in connection with the use of the Land with Lessor named as insured and with such insurance companies as shall be agreeable to Lessor. This indemnity shall survive the termination, cancellation, or expiration of this Lease.

### RULES AND REGULATIONS
10. Lessor's rules and regulations attached hereto as Exhibit "A" are incorporated herein by reference and made an integral part hereof. Lessee agrees that any violation of said rules and regulations is a material breach of this Lease and shall entitle Lessor to cancel this Lease at its option effective upon notice by Lessor to Lessee of such cancellation. Lessor reserves the right from time to time to amend, supplement, or terminate any

**Appendix IX. (continued)**

such rules and regulations applicable to this Lease. In the event of any such amendment, supplement, or termination, Lessor shall give Lessee reasonable written notice before any such rules and regulations shall become effective.

### MATERIAL TO BE SUBMITTED TO LESSOR
11. If this Lease is executed by or on behalf of a hunting club, Lessee shall provide Lessor, before its execution, a membership list including all directors, officers, and/or shareholders, their names and addresses, and a copy of Lessee's Charter, Partnership Agreement, and Bylaws, if any. During the term of this lease, Lessee shall notify Lessor of any material change in the information previously provided by Lessee to Lessor under this paragraph 11.

### LESSEE'S LIABILITY RE: TREES, TIMBER, ETC.
12. Lessee covenants and agrees to assume responsibility and to pay for any trees, timber, or other forest products that might be cut, used, damaged, or removed from the Land by Lessee or in connection with Lessee's use of the Land or any damages caused thereupon.

### NO WARRANTY
13. This Lease is made and accepted without any representations or warranties of any kind on the part of the Lessor as to the title to the Land or its suitability for any purposes, and expressly subject to any and all existing easements, mortgages, reservations, liens, rights-of-way, contracts, leases (whether grazing, farming, oil, gas, or minerals) or other encumbrances or on the ground affecting the Land or to any such property rights that may hereafter be granted from time to time by Lessor.

### LESSEE'S RESPONSIBILITY
14. Lessee assumes responsibility for the condition of the Land; Lessor shall not be liable or responsible for any damages or injuries caused by any vices or defects therein to the Lessee or to any occupant or to anyone in or on the Land who derives his or their right to be thereon from the Lessee.

### USE OF ROADS
15. Lessee shall have the right to use any connecting road(s) of Lessor solely for ingress, egress, or regress to the Land. But such use will be at Lessee's own risks and Lessor shall not be liable for any latent or patent defects in any such road nor will it be liable for any damages or injuries sustained by Lessee arising out of or resulting from the use of any of the Lessor's roads. Lessee acknowledges its obligation of maintenance and repair for connecting roads in accord with its obligation of maintenance and repair under paragraph 6.

### SURRENDER AT END OF TERM
16. Lessee agrees to surrender the Land at the end of the term of this Lease according to the terms hereof. No renewal of this Lease will occur by implication or by holding over.

### MERGER CLAUSE
17. This Lease contains the entire understanding and agreement between the parties, all prior agreements between the parties, whether written or oral, being merged herein and to be of no further force and effect. This Lease may not be changed, amended, or modified except by a writing properly executed by both parties hereto.

### CANCELLATION
18. Anything in the Lease to the contrary notwithstanding, it is expressly understood and agreed that Lessor and Lessee each reserve the right to cancel this Lease, with or without cause, at any time during the Term hereof after first giving the other party thirty (30) days prior written notice thereof. In the event of cancellation by Lessee, all rentals paid and unearned shall be retained by the Lessor as compensation for Lessor's overhead expenses in making the Land available for lease, and shall not be refunded to Lessee.

### APPLICABLE LAW
19. This Lease shall be construed under the laws of the State first noted above.


IN WITNESS WHEREOF, the parties have caused this Agreement to be properly executed as of the day and year first written above.


LESSEE: _____ DATE _____


LESSOR: _____ DATE _____


WITNESS: _____ DATE _____


The forgoing document was subscribed, sworn to, and acknowledged before me this day of _____, 20_____,


by _____ and _____.


My commission expires: _____ Notary Public _____

---

### Appendix X. Sample hunting lease agreement, example 2. (Yarrow 1998)

---

*This hunting lease agreement is for educational purposes only. It is important to check with your attorney before writing and signing a binding legal agreement. This lease may be more or less inclusive than the parties desire. If the lessor wants to provide other services or rights, such as guides, cleaning game, or allowing the lessee to improve the habitat, they should be included.*

### HUNTING LEASE AGREEMENT

_____, owner of _____ farm (legal description of the land, list county and state) herein referred to as "Landowner," for good and sufficient consideration, as hereinafter set forth, leases hunting rights on those portions of the _____ farm, hereinafter described, to _____ and others so executing this agreement and hereinafter referred to as "Lessees," on the following terms and conditions:

1. The tract of land, hereinafter referred to as "lease" upon which hunting rights are granted, is the _____ farm described herein consisting of about _____ acres.

*(description of land with aerial photograph if available)*

Lessees understand the location and boundaries of said tract and agree that no hunting rights are granted hereunder on any tract other than the tract herein designated and that no hunting or discharging of firearms shall be done by Lessees while traveling to or from the lease.

2. This agreement and the rights and duties granted and incurred hereunder shall be for a term beginning with the opening of _____ season in 20_____, and the closing of _____ season in 20_____, as set for _____ County, (state), under regulations enforced by the (state wildlife agency) unless terminated pursuant to provisions of this agreement hereinafter set forth. Either the Landowner or Lessee may cancel this agreement by giving written notice of its intent to do so thirty (30) days before the date that rental for the second or third year of the term here provided is due. In that event, Lessee shall be relieved of the obligation to pay further rental under the terms and shall deliver possession of the premises.

3. Lessee will pay to Landowner at _____ county, (state), $_____ in cash, one-half to be paid on or before June 1, 20____, the balance to be paid on or before October 1, 20____. Failure to pay the second installment shall thereupon cancel the lease; the amount already paid shall be forfeited as liquidated damage for the breach of agreement. A $_____ deposit will be required to insure that lease premises are left in a clean and orderly condition. Farm personnel will inspect the premises within 30 days after the lease expires. If clean-up is necessary, the farm will do it, and the $_____ deposit will be forfeited by the Lessees. If the premises are determined by farm personnel to be clean and orderly, the $_____ deposit will be returned to the Lessees within 60 days after expiration of the lease.

4. Lessees shall not assign this lease or sublet the leased premises without the written consent of _____.

5. Lessees shall at all times abide by and obey all state and federal hunting laws and regulations. Lessee shall be responsible for the conduct of Lessee's guests or members in connection with the hunting laws, and shall be responsible for any violation of the hunting laws or regulations by said Lessee, its guests, or members. Any violation of the hunting laws or regulations of any governmental authority shall result in immediate cancellation of this lease by the Landowner upon written notice to Lessees. In the event of the cancellation of said lease due to violation of game laws by Lessees, its guests, or members, no prorata of the rent previously paid shall be made; it will be forfeited as liquidated damages, and Lessees shall, upon receipt of such notice, immediately vacate and surrender to the Landowner possession of the leased premises. During the period when Lessees have access to the leased premises, Lessees shall continually protect them against trespassers and squatters, and to the best of Lessee's ability have such persons apprehended and prosecuted.

6. This lease agreement is expressly made subject to the "General Conditions of Lease," attached hereto as Exhibit "A."

7. If Lessees default in the performance of any of the covenants or conditions hereof, including the "General Conditions of Lease" attached as Exhibit "A," then such breach shall cause an immediate termination of this lease and a forfeiture to Landowner of all money prepaid. The Lessee shall have no further rights under the term of this lease agreement. If a lawsuit arises out of or in connection with this lease agreement and the rights of the parties thereof, the prevailing party may recover not only actual damages and costs but also reasonable attorneys' fees expended in the matter.

8. Landowner shall not be liable for any injuries, deaths, or property damage sustained by (1) any Lessees hereto, (2) any employees of Lessees, (3) any business invitees of Lessees, (4) any guest of Lessees, (5) any person who comes to the leased premises with the express or implied permission of Lessees on the _____ farm with permission of the Lessee hereunder except for such injury, death, or property damage as may be sustained directly as a result of Landowner's sole negligence. Lessee jointly and severally agrees to indemnify Landowner, his agents, or his employees against any claim asserted against Landowner or any of Landowner's agents or employees as a result of any personal injury, death, or property damage arising through: (1) the negligence of a Lessee or any persons on the farm with the permission of a Lessee, or (2) the concurrent negligence of a Landowner or his agents or employees on the _____ farm with the permission of the Lessee.

All minors permitted by Lessee to hunt, fish, or swim on the leased premises shall be under the direct supervision of one of their parents (or guardian). When children are present on the leased premises, the parents (or guardians) shall be fully responsible for their acts and safety and agree to hold Landowner harmless therefore, regardless of the nature of the cause of damage, whether property or personal injury, to themselves or others.

9. The leased premises are taken by Lessee in an "as is" condition, and no representation of any kind is made by _____ regarding the suitability of such premises for the purpose for which they have been leased.

10. This lease may not be terminated or repudiated by Lessee except by written notice signed and acknowledged in duplicate before a Notary Public by Lessee, and such termination or repudiation shall not be effective until Lessee has mailed one executed copy of it to Landowner by registered mail and filed the other executed copy for record in the office of the County Clerk, _____ County, (state). This lease shall be binding upon the distributes, heirs, next of kin, successors, executors, administrators, and personal representatives of each of the undersigned. In signing the foregoing lease, each of the undersigned hereby acknowledges and represents:
      (a) That he has read the foregoing lease, understands it, and signs it voluntarily; and
      (b) That he is over 21 years of age and of sound mind.

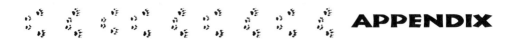 

**Appendix X. (continued)**

In witness whereof, the parties have signed this the _____ day of _____ 20_____.

LESSEES: _____ DATE: _____

LANDOWNER: _____ DATE: _____

WITNESS: _____ DATE: _____

STATE OF: _____ COUNTY OF _____

The foregoing document was subscribed, sworn to, and acknowledged before me this day of _____, 20____, by _____ and

_____.

My commission expires: _____ Notary Public _____

---

## Appendix XI. Sample annual hunting lease agreement, example 3.
## (May be used for Season Lease) (Wilkins 1988)

State of _____ County of _____

Subject to the terms and conditions set forth in this document, _____ (hereinafter called LESSOR)

does hereby grant to _____ (hereinafter called LESSEE)

the right to access and hunt only the following game species:

*(List species.)*

which may be found upon and harvested from the following property(s):

*(Describe property. Refer to an attached map.)*

The hunting land comprises _____ acres, more or less.

1.  The term of this lease shall run from (date)_____ to (date)_____.

2.  The LESSEE hereby agrees to:

   a.  Pay the LESSOR the sum of ($) _____ per acre

      totaling ($) _____ on or before (date) _____.

   b.  Allow LESSOR to hold in deposit the sum of ($) _____
      refundable at the termination of this lease if the lease agreement has been adhered to and no damages have been placed upon the LESSOR
      as a result of the actions of the LESSEE.

   c.  Abide by hunting regulations prescribed by LESSOR.

   d.  Abide by all state and federal hunting regulations.

   e.  Harvest game species only in accordance with HARVEST PLAN prescribed by LESSOR.

   f.  Be personally responsible for the actions and activities of all persons hunting under this lease and to act as a representative in matters
      regarding all activities carried out under this lease.

   g.  Maintain proper safety procedures regarding firearms, particularly by seeing that all firearms are unloaded while in vehicles and in vicinity
      of all buildings.

   h.  Maintain proper vigilance aimed at preventing fires or damage by other means to the leased area.

   i.  See that vehicles are driven only on established roads and see that all gates are left as originally found.

   j.  Maintain a no hunting or shooting zone within 200 yards of any occupied building and around all other designated areas.

   k.  Keep records of all game harvested and supply these records to the LESSOR.

   l.  Remove all structures placed or constructed by LESSEE from the lease area at termination of this lease unless prearranged with LESSOR.

**Appendix XI.  (continued)**

    m. Limit number of hunters so as not to exceed _____ with number on lease property at any one time

        not to exceed _____.

    n. Provide the LESSOR with a current certificate of insurance covering the LESSOR, LESSEE, and all guests of the LESSOR against damages and liabilities.  Coverage shall be in at least the amount of $500,000.00.

    o. Abide by all written rules and regulations supplied at the onset of this agreement.

3. The LESSOR hereby agrees:
    a. That only the LESSEE and his GUESTS shall have hunting rights on the leased area during the term of this lease except those reserved as follows:

        _____

        _____

    b. That quotas of game species offered the LESSEE be reasonable and equitable, commensurate with the management goals established for the leased area.
        *(Note: If quotas are established, they should be attached and referred to in the lease document.)*

    c. To establish a game harvest plan and hunting harvest quotas, after consultation with LESSEE, and advise LESSEE of the quotas for leased area, or portions thereof.
        *(Note:  If a game harvest plan is established, it should be attached and referred to in the lease document.)*

4. Agricultural and/or forestry practices are necessary on the premises and take precedence over the rights given in this agreement. Hunting shall not interfere with any such practices.

5. It is mutually agreed that failure to abide by the terms and stipulations above by any person present on the leased area under this lease will constitute cause for the forfeiture of all hunting rights, deposits, and fees.

6. LESSEE shall not assign or otherwise convey any rights granted by this agreement to other persons without the expressed written consent of the LESSOR.

7. The addresses of the parties hereto for the communication of notices are, unless altered by written notice, as follows:

    For the LESSOR: _____

    For the LESSEE: _____

8. This agreement will be renewed automatically on an annual basis unless written notice is delivered on or before

    (date) _____.

9. In case any one or more of the provisions contained in this lease shall for any reason be held to be invalid, illegal, or unenforceable in any respect, all other provisions and this agreement shall be construed as if such invalid, illegal, or unenforceable provision has never been contained herein.

10. This agreement shall be construed under and in accordance with the laws of the State of _____.

11. LESSEE RECOGNIZES THE INHERENT DANGERS ASSOCIATED WITH HUNTING, BOTH NATURAL AND HUMAN CREATED.  LESSEE RECOGNIZES THAT ACCIDENTS INVOLVING FIREARMS, AMMUNITION, FALLING TREES, HIDDEN GROUND OPENINGS, POISONOUS PLANTS, AND VARIOUS OTHER DANGERS MIGHT FORCIBLY OCCUR ON THE PREMISES AFOREMENTIONED.  LESSEE ACKNOWLEDGES HIS RECOGNITION OF THESE DANGERS AND THE POSSIBLE EXISTENCE OF DANGEROUS PHYSICAL CONDITIONS UPON THE PREMISES SUCH AS BUT NOT LIMITED TO THOSE DESCRIBED ON THE ENCLOSED MAP.  WITH THE AFOREMENTIONED RECOGNITIONS IN MIND, LESSEE AGREES TO INDEMNIFY AND HOLD HARMLESS LANDOWNER AND ALL OF HIS/HER FAMILY, SERVANTS, EMPLOYEES, AND AGENTS FROM ALL CLAIMS, SUITS, LOSSES, PERSONAL INJURIES, DEATHS, PROPERTY LIABILITY, AND ALL OTHER LIABILITY RESULTING DIRECTLY OR INDIRECTLY FROM OR ON ACCOUNT OF HUNTING ACTIVITIES ENGAGED IN BY LESSEE OR LESSEE'S GUESTS ON THE PREMISES HERETOFORE MENTIONED.  LESSEE WILL REIMBURSE LANDOWNER FOR ALL EXPENSES AND SUITS INCLUDING BUT NOT LIMITED TO, JUDGMENTS, ATTORNEY'S FEES, AND COURT COSTS.

*(Note: This liability release must be on the same page as the signatures.  It is the landowner's responsibility to ensure that each lessee has read and understood its meaning.)*

Executed in duplicate on this _____ day of _____, 20_____.

| | |
|---|---|
| _____ Lessor | _____ Lessee |
| _____ Lessor | _____ Lessee |
| _____ Lessor | _____ Lessee |
| _____ Lessor | _____ Lessee |
| _____ Lessor | _____ Lessee |

_(Note: If the hunting group is not incorporated, all hunters should sign the lease agreement.)_

---

## Appendix XII. Exhibit "A," General conditions of lease (examples of optional clauses). (Yarrow 1998)

_____ LANDOWNER, LEASE TO _____ LESSEE

These general conditions of lease are applicable to the lease agreement between _____, hereinafter referred to as LANDOWNER, and _____, LESSEE. Lessee and all persons authorized to Lessee to hunt upon the leased premises shall he hereinafter collectively referred to as "Hunters."

1. It will be the responsibility of the Lessee to furnish each hunter or guest with a copy of these general conditions of lease.

2. Lessees understand and agree that the leased premises are not leased for agricultural, grazing, or timber purposes.

3. Lessee acknowledges that Landowner owns the property herein leased, mainly for agricultural purposes and growing timber. Lessee shall in no manner interfere or obstruct Landowner's farming, livestock, or forestry operations.

4. Landowner reserves the right to deny access to the leased premises to any person or persons for any of the following reasons: drunkenness, carelessness with firearms, trespassing on property of adjoining landowners, acts which could reasonably be expected to strain relationships with adjoining landowners, any other activities which to the ordinary person would be considered objectionable, offensive, or cause embarrassment to Landowner or be detrimental to Landowner's interest. Failure of Lessee to expel or deny access to the premises to any person or persons after being notified to do so by Landowner might result in the termination of this lease at discretion of Landowner.

5. No hunter shall be allowed to:
   (a) shoot a firearm from a vehicle;
   (b) erect a deer stand within 150 yards of the boundary of the leased premises;
   (c) permanently affix a deer stand in trees:
   (d) abuse existing roads by use of vehicles during wet or damp conditions;
   (e) fire rifles or other firearms in the direction of any house, barn, other improvements, or across any haul road located on the leased premises;
   (f) build or allow fires on the leased premises, except in those areas specifically designated by Landowner in writing, and shall be kept fully liable for such fires; and
   (g) leave open a gate found closed or close a gate found open.

6. Hunters shall at all times maintain a high standard of conduct acceptable to _____.

---

## Appendix XIII. Sample of short-term agreement. (May also serve as the access permit for short-term agreements) (Wilkins 1988)

State of _____ County of _____

Subject to the terms and conditions set forth in this document, _____

(hereinafter called LANDOWNER) does hereby grant to _____
(hereinafter called PERMITEE) the right to access and hunt only the following game species.

_(List species)_

**Appendix XIII.** (continued)

which might be found upon and harvested from the following property(s).

*(Describe property; refer to an attached map)*

1. The term of this permit shall run from (date) _____ to (date) _____

2. The PERMITEE hereby agrees to:
   a. Pay LANDOWNER in advance a fee of $ _____ .

   b. Abide by all state and federal hunting regulations.

   c. See that vehicles are driven only on established roads and see that all gates are left as originally found.

   d. Maintain a no hunting or shooting zone within 200 yards of any occupied building and around all other designated areas.

   e. Keep records of all game harvested and supply these records to the LANDOWNER.

   f. Remove all structures placed or constructed by PERMITEE from the property at termination of this lease unless prearranged with LANDOWNER.

   g. Abide by all written rules and regulations supplied at the onset of this agreement.

3. LANDOWNER will authorize no more than _____ people to hunt on this tract during the period of this permit.

4. This agreement shall be construed under and in accordance with the laws of the State of _____ .

I, the undersigned PERMITEE, do hereby assume all risks associated with hunting (and/or any other intended activity) and do hereby release _____ and all their properties and their agents of any and all negligence.

Executed in duplicate on this _____ day of _____ 20_____ .

_____      _____
              LANDOWNER                                PERMITEE

---

## Appendix XIV. Sample of hunting access permit.
## (May be used for courtesy hunting permit when written permission is required.)
## (Wilkins 1988)

---

### HUNTING PERMIT

Date: _____

To whom it may concern: The bearer of this permit, _____
has permission to hunt on the following property:

_____
*(Name of farm or ranch)*

located at _____ during the period_____

He/she agrees to obey the current State and Federal hunting regulations and to repair or pay for any property damages which they might cause. He/she has been shown the property boundaries and agrees not to hunt on adjacent properties without written permission.

Landowner: _____

Permitee: _____

# BIBLIOGRAPHY

## CREDITS FOR FIGURES, TABLES, AND APPENDIXES
(Copyright permission where needed has been obtained).

Ambrose, R. E., C. R. Hinkle, and C. R. Wenzel. 1983. Practices for protecting and enhancing fish and wildlife on coal surface-mined land in the south-central U.S. U.S. Fish and Wildlife Service FWS/OBS-83/11.

Anderson, M. A. 1989. Opportunities for habitat enhancement in commercial forestry practice. Pages 129-146 in G. P. Buckley, editor. Biological habitat reconstruction. Belhaven Press, New York.

Armleder, H. M., R. J. Dawson, and R. N. Thomson. 1986. Handbook for timber and mule deer management co-ordination on winter range on the Caribou Forest region. Land Management Handbook 13, British Columbia Ministry of Forestry, Victoria.

Atlantic Waterfowl Council. 1972. Techniques handbook of waterfowl habitat development and management. 2nd edition. Atlantic Waterfowl Council, Bethany Beach, DE.

Bailey, J. A. 1984. Principles of wildlife management. Wiley, New York.

Carey, A. B., and J. D. Gill. 1980. Firewood and wildlife. U.S. Forest Service Research Note NE 299.

Cole, C. A., T. L. Serfass, M. C. Brittingham, and R. P. Brooks. 1996. Managing your restored wetland. Cooperative Extension, College of Agricultural Sciences, Pennsylvania State University, University Park.

Connecticut Department of Environmental Protection. 1989. Guidelines for enhancing Connecticut's wildlife habitat through forestry operations. Connecticut Department of Environmental Protection Wildlife Bureau Publication TA-H-9.

Connors, M. A. Undated. Community wildlife involvement program field manual. Ontario Ministry of Natural Resources, Toronto.

DeStefano, S., S. R. Craven, R. L. Ruff, D. F. Covell, and J. F. Kubisiak. 1994. A landowner's guide to woodland wildlife management, with emphasis on ruffed grouse. University of Wisconsin Extension, Madison.

Elderkin, R. L., and J. Morris. 1989. Design for a durable and inexpensive guzzler. Wildlife Society Bulletin 17:192-194.

Eng, R. L., J. D. Jones, and F. M. Gjersling. 1979. Construction and management of stockponds for waterfowl. U.S. Bureau of Land Management Technical Note 327.

Evans, K. E., and R. R. Kerbs. 1977. Avian use of livestock watering ponds in western South Dakota. U.S. Forest Service General Technical Report RM-35.

Giles, R. H., Jr. 1978. Wildlife management. W.H. Freeman, San Francisco.

Guthery, F. S., R. W. Whiteside, T. T. Taylor, and T. Shupe. 1984. How to manage pheasants in the southern high plains of Texas. Management Note 3, Texas Tech University, Lubbock.

Gutiérrez, R. J., D. J. Decker, R. A. Howard Jr., and J. P. Lassoie. 1979. Managing small woodlands for wildlife. Information Bulletin 157, College of Agriculture and Life Sciences, Cornell University, Ithaca, NY.

Harris, L. D. 1984. The fragmented forest: island biogeography theory and the preservation of biotic diversity. University of Chicago Press, Chicago.

Hassinger, J., C. E. Schwartz, and R. G. Wingard. 1981. Timber sales and wildlife. Pennsylvania Game Commission, Harrisburg.

Henderson, C. L. 1987. Landscaping for wildlife. Minnesota Department of Natural Resources, St. Paul.

Henderson, C. L. 1992. Woodworking for wildlife: homes for birds and mammals. Minnesota Department of Natural Resources, St. Paul.

Henderson, F. R., editor. 1984. Guidelines for increasing wildlife on farms and ranches. Cooperative Extension Service, Kansas State University, Manhattan.

Herkert, J. R., R. E. Szafoni, V. M. Kleen, and J. E. Schwegman. 1993. Habitat establishment, enhancement, and management for forest and grassland birds in Illinois. Natural Heritage Technical Publication 1. Illinois Department of Conservation, Springfield.

Herricks, E. E., A. J. Krzysik, R. E. Szafoni, and D. J. Tazik. 1982. Best current practices for fish and wildlife on surface-mined lands in the eastern interior coal region. U.S. Fish and Wildlife Service FWS/OBS-80/68.

Hogg, D. 1990. Moose management: the forest habitat. Pages 30-33 in M. Buss and R. Truman, editors. The moose in Ontario: Book 1—moose biology, ecology and management. Ontario Ministry of Natural Resources, Toronto.

Hunter, M. L., Jr. 1990. Wildlife, forests, and forestry: principles of managing forests for biological diversity. Prentice-Hall, Englewood Cliffs, NJ.

Johnson, T., and R. A. Jacobs. 1986. Gallinaceous guzzlers. Section 5.4.1, U.S. Army Corps of Engineers wildlife resources management manual. U.S. Army Engineer Waterways Experiment Station Technical Report EL-86-8.

Jones, J. D. 1975. Waterfowl nesting island development. U.S. Bureau of Land Management Technical Note 260.

Judd, M., P. D. Schwartz, and T. L. Peterson. 1998. Wildlife and your land. Wisconsin Department of Natural Resources, Madison.

Kalmbach, E. R., and W. L. McAtee. 1969. Homes for birds. U.S. Fish and Wildlife Service Conservation Bulletin 14.

Karsky, R. 1988. Fences. U.S. Bureau of Land Management and U.S. Forest Service Technical and Development Program 2400-Range, 8824 2803.

Klessig, L., and M. Kroenke. 1999. Country acres: a guide to buying and managing rural property. Cooperative Extension, College of Natural Resources, University of Wisconsin, Stevens Point.

Kosciuk, J. R., and E. P. Peloquin. 1986. Elevated quail roosts. Section 5.1.5, U.S. Army Corps of Engineers wildlife resources management manual. U.S. Army Engineer Waterways Experiment Station Technical Report EL-86-18.

Lokemoen, J. T., and T. A. Messmer. 1994. Locating, constructing, and managing islands for nesting waterfowl. Utah State University Cooperative Extension Service, Logan.

Mapston, R. D., and R. S. ZoBell. 1972. Antelope passes: their value and use. U.S. Bureau of Land Management Technical Note D-360.

Maser, C., R. G. Anderson, K. Cromack Jr., J. T. Williams, and R. E. Martin. 1979. Dead and down woody material. Pages 78-95 in J. W. Thomas, technical editor. Wildlife habitats in managed forests: the Blue Mountains of Oregon and Washington. U.S. Forest Service Agricultural Handbook 553.

Melton, B. L., R. L. Hoover, R. L. Moore, and D. J. Pfankuch. 1987. Aquatic and riparian wildlife. Pages 260-301 in R. L. Hoover and D. L. Wills, editors. Managing forested lands for wildlife. Colorado Division of Wildlife and U.S. Forest Service, Denver.

Messmer, T. A., M. A. Johnson, and F. B. Lee. 1986. Homemade nest sites for giant Canada geese. North Dakota State University Cooperative Extension Service, Fargo.

Meyer, M. I. 1987. Planting grasslands for wildlife habitat. U.S. Fish and Wildlife Service Northern Prairie Wildlife Research Center, Jamestown, ND.

Mitchell, W. A. 1988. Songbird nest boxes. Section 5.1.8, U.S. Army Corps of Engineers wildlife resources management manual. U.S. Army Engineer Waterways Experiment Station Technical Report EL-88-19.

Mosby, H. S. 1955. Live trapping objectionable animals. Virginia Polytechnic Institute Agricultural Extension Service Circular 667.

National Wildlife Federation. 1984. Wildlife planting guide. National Wildlife Federation, Washington.

Nixon, C. M., and L. P. Hansen. 1987. Managing forests to maintain populations of gray and fox squirrels. Illinois Department of Conservation Technical Bulletin 5.

Ohlsson, K. E., A. E. Robb Jr., C. E. Guindon Jr., D. E. Samuel, and R. L. Smith. 1982. Best current practices for fish and wildlife on surface-mined land in the northern Appalachian coal region. U.S. Fish and Wildlife Service FWS/OBS-81/45.

Payne, N. F., and F. Copes. 1988. Wildlife and fisheries habitat improvement handbook. U.S. Forest Service, Washington.

Payne, N. F. 1998. Wildlife habitat management of wetlands. Krieger Publishing, Malabar, FL.

Payne, N. F., and F. C. Bryant. 1998. Wildlife habitat management of forestlands, rangelands, and farmlands. Krieger Publishing, Malabar, FL.

Perkins, W. C. Undated. Kentucky tree planting manual. Kentucky Department of Natural Resources and Environmental Protection, Frankfort.

PFRA Tree Nursery. Undated. Planting trees for wildlife habitat. PFRA Tree Nursery, Indian Head, Saskatchewan.

Poston, H. J., and R. K. Schmidt. 1981. Wildlife habitat: a handbook for Canada's prairies and parklands. Canadian Wildlife Service, Edmonton, Alberta.

Powers, J. E. 1979. Planning for an optimal mix of agricultural and wildlife land use. Journal of Wildlife Management 43:493-502.

Ridlehuber, K. T., and J. W. Teaford. 1986. Wood duck nest boxes. Section 5.1.2, U.S. Army Corps of Engineers wildlife resources management manual. U.S. Army Engineer Waterways Experiment Station Technical Report EL-86-12.

Roach, B. A., and S. F. Gingrich. 1968. Even-aged silviculture for upland central hardwoods. U.S. Forest Service Agricultural Handbook 355.

Royar, K. 1995. Snowshoe hare. Pages 44-47 in A landowner's guide: wildlife habitat management for Vermont woodlands. Vermont Departments of Fish & Wildlife and Forests, Parks & Recreation, Montpelier.

Rutherford, W. H., and W. D. Snyder. 1983. Guidelines for habitat modification to benefit wildlife. Colorado Division of Wildlife, Denver.

Rutske, L. H. 1969. A Minnesota guide to forest game habitat improvement. Minnesota Department of Conservation Technical Bulletin 10.

Schulz, J. W. 1984. Manipulation of habitat for ruffed grouse on the Wakopa Wildlife Management Area, North Dakota. Pages 109-124 in W. L. Robinson, editor. Ruffed grouse management: state of the art in the early 1980s. 45th Midwest Fish and Wildlife Conference, St. Louis.

Shaw, S. P. 1977. Timber cutting to enhance wildlife food supplies. Transactions of the Northeast Fish and Wildlife Conference 34:113-118.

Steele, J. L., Jr., and C. O. Martin. 1986. Half-cuts. Section 5.3.2, U.S. Army Corps of Engineers wildlife resources management manual. U.S. Army Engineer Waterways Experiment Station Technical Report EL-86-14.

Stoecker, R. E. 1982. Creating small islands for wildlife and visual enhancement. Pages 48-50 in W. D. Svedarsky and R. D. Crawford, editors. Wildlife values of gravel pits. University of Minnesota Agriculture Experiment Station Miscellaneous Publication 17.

Taber, R. D., and I. M. Cowan. 1969. Capturing and marking wild animals. Pages 277-317 in R. H. Giles Jr., editor. Wildlife management techniques. 3rd edition. The Wildlife Society, Washington.

U.S. Army Corps of Engineers. 1979. Design memorandum for wildlife habitat development, Supplement 1, Lower Snake River project. U.S. Army Engineer District, Walla Walla, WA.

U.S. Fish and Wildlife Service. 1976. Nest boxes for wood ducks. U.S. Fish and Wildlife Service Wildlife Leaflet 510.

U.S. Forest Service. 1983. Slickrock water development. Number 83.9. Intermountain Region, Odgen, UT.

U.S. Natural Resources Conservation Service. 1998. Riparian forest buffer. U.S. Department of Agriculture, Washington.

Wenger, K. F. 1984. Forestry handbook. Wiley, New York.

Wilkins, N. 1988. Developing hunting enterprises on private lands. Agricultural Extension Service, University of Tennessee Institute of Agriculture, Knoxville.

Wilson, L. D., and D. Hannans. 1977. Guidelines and recommendations for design and modification of livestock watering developments to facilitate safe use by wildlife. U.S. Bureau of Land Management Technical Note 305.

Yarrow, G. K. 1998. Developing a hunting lease: considerations, options, and realities. Pages 86-99 in J. S. Kays, G. R. Goff, P. J. Smallidge, W. N. Grafton, and J. A. Parkhurst, editors. Natural resources income opportunities on private lands conference. University of Maryland Cooperative Extension Service, College Park.

Yoakum, J., W. P. Dasmann, H. R. Sanderson, C. M. Nixon, H. S. Crawford. 1980. Habitat improvement techniques. Pages 329-403 in S. D. Schemnitz, editor. Wildlife management techniques manual. 4th edition. The Wildlife Society, Washington.

Zeleny, L. 1976. The bluebird: how you can help its fight for survival. Indiana University Press, Bloomington.

Osprey

# INDEX

# INDEX

# INDEX

Dig a large enough pond in your backyard, add a cup of salt, and you too could be the proud owner of a whale like this humpback of Notre Dame Bay, Newfoundland.

Raccoon

For book orders, please contact

KRIEGER PUBLISHING COMPANY
1725 Krieger Drive
Malabar, FL 32950
1-321-724-9542
info@krieger-publishing.com